Advance Praise for
A Killer by Design

"As the FBI Behavioral Science Unit (BSU) grew and evolved in the late 1970s, Ann Burgess led the way for the unit's training, research, and operational work to reach out to mental health professionals beyond the typical investigative/prosecutive perspective. She helped the BSU to add this new perspective and insight to its understanding of the behavior of both offenders and victims. Ann's new book, *A Killer by Design*, tells the behind-the-scenes story of her long-term work with the BSU from her unique perspective. I highly recommend this book."

—Kenneth V. Lanning, twenty-year member of the FBI BSU and author of *Love, Bombs, and Molesters: An FBI Agent's Journey*

"Countless investigators and detectives around the world do work every single day that is based on the research and discoveries of Dr. Ann Burgess—me included. But here, for the first time, we are able to experience the fascinating—and often heart-wrenching—stories behind these facts, figures, and procedures alongside Ann as she worked the cases that would serve as the foundation of criminal profiling. This is a riveting book and will become a staple on the shelves of both experts and armchair detectives."

—Sarah Cailean, criminal behaviorist

"With her keen insight, decades of groundbreaking research in a male-dominated field, and relentless commitment to the victims of the worst imaginable crimes, Dr. Burgess has been a bona fide trailblazer in the forensic arena. This poignant, gripping, and long-overdue account will soon prove a classic of the true crime genre."

—**Michael H. Stone, MD, and Gary Brucato, PhD, authors of** *The New Evil: Understanding the Emergence of Modern Violent Crime*

"One of my jobs at the BSU was to get the data that Dr. Burgess was analyzing in Boston to my police fellowship program. I'd compare what the police fellows said on cases with what Dr. Burgess said. The foundational profiling tools we brought into the mix—which helped develop a well-defined, disciplined, and logical approach to the field of criminal profiling—stood the test of time. In *A Killer by Design*, readers get a behind-the-scenes look of what it was like to be at the forefront of such important work, and it's a must-read for anyone who wants to know what criminal profiling is *really* like, outside of movies and TV shows."

—**Judson M. Ray, MS, EdM, FBI profiler (retired)**

A **Killer** by Design

A Killer by Design

MURDERERS, MINDHUNTERS, AND MY QUEST TO DECIPHER THE CRIMINAL MIND

Ann Wolbert Burgess

AND STEVEN MATTHEW CONSTANTINE

New York

Hachette Books

Hachette Book Group

1290 Avenue of the Americas

New York, NY 10104

HachetteBooks.com

Twitter.com/HachetteBooks

Instagram.com/HachetteBooks

First Edition: December 2021

Published by Hachette Books, an imprint of Perseus Books, LLC, a subsidiary of Hachette Book Group, Inc. The Hachette Books name and logo is a trademark of the Hachette Book Group.

The Hachette Speakers Bureau provides a wide range of authors for speaking events.

To find out more, go to www.hachettespeakersbureau.com or call (866) 376-6591.

The publisher is not responsible for websites (or their content) that are not owned by the publisher.

Print book interior design by Jeff Stiefel.

Library of Congress Cataloging-in-Publication Data

Names: Burgess, Ann Wolbert, author. | Constantine, Steven Matthew, author.

Title: A killer by design: murderers, mindhunters, and my quest to decipher the criminal mind / by Ann Wolbert Burgess & Steven Matthew Constantine.

Description: First edition. | New York: Hachette Books, 2021. | Includes bibliographical references and index.

Identifiers: LCCN 2021011086 | ISBN 9780306924866 (hardcover) | ISBN 9780306924880 (ebook)

Subjects: LCSH: Burgess, Ann Wolbert. | FBI Academy. Behavioral Science Unit—Officials and employees—Biography. | FBI Academy. Behavioral Science Unit—History. | Psychiatric nurses—United States—Biography. | Forensic nursing—United States—History. | Criminal behavior, Prediction of—United States—History. | Serial murder investigation—United States—History. | Serial murderers—United States—Psychology.

Classification: LCC HV7911.B853 B87 2021 | DDC 364.3092 [B]—dc23

LC record available at https://lccn.loc.gov/2021011086

ISBNs: 9780306924866 (hardcover), 9780306924880 (ebook)

Printed in the United States of America

LSC-C

Printing 1, 2021

In Memory of
Robert Kenneth Ressler
Robert Roy Hazelwood
Lynda Lytle Holmstrom

CONTENTS

Contents

AUTHOR'S NOTE

To the reader:

TW: violence, murder, kidnapping, sexual assault, domestic abuse (including children and animals), sexism/misogyny, racism, mental health.

Please note that this book is an account of my work interacting with law enforcement officials, victims of disturbing crimes, and violent criminals. The conversations in this book come from transcriptions and recordings of true events as they actually happened. However, in instances when records were unavailable, I've conveyed conversations based on contextual documentation and the best of my memory.

Some of the content is graphic in nature, but it has not been sensationalized or embellished. I have made a point of remaining faithful to the reality of events as they occurred—so as not to undermine the true nature of the crimes or the trauma they inflicted. It is my sincerest hope that this book reminds us to never forget the victims, and helps honor and memorialize those whose narratives appear within its pages.

INTRODUCTION

It Starts with a Test

One by one, I examined the photos sprawled out on the table in front of me. They were divided into three sets, each a standard forensic collection of overviews, midranges, and close-ups. In the first set, labeled "Danny 9.21," the setting of the overviews painted an almost idyllic scene in the quiet Nebraska countryside. But the landscape was only for context. The real focus of the pictures was the small body hidden within them, partially covered by tall grass growing along an unpaved road. The midrange photos were even more unsettling. These depicted the lifeless male victim—a child or young teenager—bent backward in an unnatural slump. His wrists and ankles were bound with rope, and he was naked except for a pair of navy-blue underwear. Close-ups focused on the boy's mutilated body: his sternum torn apart in a chaos of stab wounds, a deep laceration across the back of his neck, his hair matted in tangles of dirt and dried blood. There were flies everywhere.

As I placed these photos back on the table and picked up the next pile, "Christopher 12.5," I was overcome by a sense of déjà vu. These pictures, taken just yesterday, showed the continuation of a pattern. They depicted a second male victim, indistinguishable in age and appearance from the first, whose body had been found in the same remote stretch of Nebraskan countryside as that of "Danny 9.21." The similarities were striking. In this set, however, fall had changed to winter, and by closely inspecting the midrange images I could see a thin layer of snow coating the boy's pale skin—just enough to cover his wounds and the features of his face so he looked something like a mannequin. Close-ups revealed puddles of frozen blood outlining the victim's head and abdomen. The two photos from the autopsy— brightly lit and sharply focused on the small body draped across the examination table—were even more chilling. The first showed a deep incision where a knife had been pressed into the back of the victim's neck and then wrenched, counterclockwise, for several inches, from the right ear to just beneath the chin. The second focused on seven lacerations along the victim's belly and chest. It was hard to tell whether these cuts were random or were intended to convey some sort of meaning.

I took a sharp breath to collect my thoughts on that December morning. It was the early 1980s, and I was standing alongside five agents in a large underground conference room known as "the bomb shelter" in the heart of the FBI Academy in Quantico, Virginia. There were no pictures on the walls, no phones, no distractions. The only window was a small square of wire-reinforced glass that looked out on empty offices and an empty hall. This was an area of Quantico that few people knew about. It belonged to the FBI's Behavioral Science Unit (BSU), and our isolation was a daily reminder of the controversial nature of our work. We hunted serial killers. Our job was to study them, learn how they thought, and find ways to catch them as quickly as possible. We did this through a novel technique called "criminal profiling"—a technique that, at the time, our colleagues throughout the Bureau regarded with varying degrees of skepticism or disdain. But criticism didn't matter, only results. And we were determined to prove just how effective our approach could truly be.

Criminal profiling was the reason we had all gathered that winter morning. Special Agent Robert Ressler was working an urgent case out of Nebraska, and the previous night, he'd faxed each of us on the small team within the BSU a briefing and arranged for the room to be set up and ready to go by the time we arrived before the sun came up. We were waiting for Ressler himself to appear. And as we waited, we kept busy with the various documents that stretched across the massive table in front of us. There were case files, autopsy reports, witness testimonies, sketch artist depictions, suspect lists, and the collection of forensic photos I held in my hands. The whole array was equal parts horrifying and impressive.

At least, for me it was. Because, despite being part of the BSU for several months, and despite the lead role I'd taken in developing the core methodologies of criminal profiling, the agents kept me at arm's distance. They didn't know what to make of me. I'd been brought on as an expert in victimology and violent sexual crimes—something I knew the agents respected me for—but I was still considered an outsider, a wildcard, a break-glass-in-case-of-emergency type of resource. I may have been an expert, but I wasn't an agent. And that's why the morning's session was so important. It was the first active case I'd been asked to attend. It was a test, a test to see if I could handle working alongside the agents as a member of their inner circle. For me, the session had already begun.

There were other factors at play, too. Not only was this my first active case as part of the team, but I also had to contend with the fact that I was the lone woman in the BSU, and one of only a very small handful within the male-dominated halls of Quantico. I could feel the intense scrutiny I was under. And I'd be lying if I said I wasn't frustrated by the burden of my position from time to time. All I wanted was a chance to prove myself. I'd seen behind the curtain of one of the most closed-off agencies in the world, and I was ready to make my mark.

It's simple, really. From the moment you walk through the doors of the FBI, the Bureau drills you to see if you'll crack. You might be recruited on the basis of your skills, talents, and strengths, but you're measured on the basis of your faults. That's just how the culture works. It's hard and reductive, in a way—this technique of assessing people based off their likelihood to fail—but it's effective. And for the ones who last, for the ones who persist through a wave of trial by overwhelming pressure, they are initiated. They become necessary. They're given a role and they're expected to excel. That was how it had worked for the five agents standing beside me that morning, and that's all I wanted for myself.

So, tuning out the thrum of speculation and suspense that hummed around me, I collected my thoughts and refocused on the individual sets of photos. I knew that each set held unseen details and hidden clues that could make or break the case. The answers were there. I just needed to find them.

"Hey, Ann. How you holding up?"

The voice startled me. I put down the photos, all except for one, and turned to see who'd asked the question. Agent John Douglas was waiting for a response.

"Good," I said. "But whoever this guy is, he's starting to get more confident. Look at these lacerations." I handed Douglas the picture of the second victim's chest. "The cuts aren't frantic anymore. He's becoming more deliberate."

Douglas nodded.

I knew he wasn't interested in the picture or what I'd found. He was checking to see if I could stomach the case in all its graphic detail. I'd seen him do this before. Like the Bureau at large, Douglas and the other agents were constantly probing their colleagues for weakness—and they weren't subtle about it at all. In fact, one of Douglas's favorite tests involved a human skull that he kept prominently displayed on his desk. If someone came into his office and couldn't look directly at the skull, they failed. The only way to pass was to acknowledge it and move on, as if the skull didn't bother you.

I'd passed the skull test, and I'd passed a whole range of other tests, too. In fact, by the time Douglas and I were standing in the bomb shelter that morning, I'd proven myself enough times to have received a formal letter of recognition from the FBI's acting director, James D. McKenzie, officially welcoming me to the BSU. But despite the Bureau's unprecedented step of bringing me—an outsider and a woman—fully onboard, the agents themselves still weren't completely convinced. They needed proof that I could handle seeing violence in its rawest form.

Passing this final test meant that I'd be able to join Douglas and Ressler on the secret project they'd been working on, informally, since earlier that year. They had a compelling idea that challenged investigative norms. For decades, law enforcement had dismissed certain crimes as acts of pure insanity beyond rational comprehension. But Douglas and Ressler thought differently. They believed that, by interviewing incarcerated killers to learn what motivated their behaviors, they might uncover insights about criminal behavior that could help investigators flip the script and use offenders' own psychology against them. The Bureau saw enough potential in the concept to green-light Douglas and Ressler's off-the-books interviews with incarcerated serial killers into an official FBI study on the psychology of criminal minds. But neither Douglas nor Ressler had much background in psychology. They needed help formalizing their approach and organizing their method of data collection so that they could make sense of their findings. That's where I came in.

As an established psychiatric professional with a doctorate in hand, I understood both the psychology of disturbed individuals and the steps needed to develop this type of messy, nonnumerical research into a standardized study. I'd also been working with sexual assault and trauma victims for years, which meant I had direct experience handling the types of unspeakable violence we were sure to see in the days ahead. But, most importantly, I knew just what was at stake here, and I understood what a profound effect this work could have on society as a whole. It could save countless victims from being forced to bear the same horrific trauma as my former patients. It could break new ground in understanding criminal psychology. It could revolutionize the fight against crime like nothing the world had ever seen before. My job was to make sure that it did.

CHAPTER 1

When the FBI Calls

I cut my teeth learning about the violent side of human nature as a doctoral student studying psychiatric nursing. I was fascinated by the human mind, how it worked, and how its instabilities could lead to the most extreme forms of behavior. But as was typical in the 1970s—an era in which overt sexism was woven into the culture—men in charge often dismissed my interest in understanding what motivated these abnormal behaviors as "a phase," "a novelty," or, worst of all, "cute." In those days, women who pursued a career in nursing were expected to conform to the "handmaiden" stereotype—doll-like figures in stark-white dresses, tall stockings, and pristinely starched caps. Our value was measured by how well we could carry out a physician's orders, not by what we could contribute ourselves. But that wasn't going to work for me. I wanted to make a difference. And I wanted to make it on my *own* terms, regardless of the archaic expectations that had long been imposed on my gender.

Of course, I wasn't the type to make things easy on myself. In addition to the cultural hurdles I faced, I also had to contend with the reality that psychiatric nursing was a largely unknown concept at the time. In fact, the specialty itself had only become a required part of professional nursing education in 1955—a response to the end of World War II and the growing need for qualified professionals to care for returning service members with psychiatric needs. Couple that with the fact that nursing had reached the highest possible degree level only a few years prior to my graduation, and it all added up to me being one of a very small number of known experts in an even lesser-known field. I was in uncharted territory.

My first opportunity to help patients with psychiatric needs came via graduate work at Spring Grove State Hospital in Maryland. It was a large institution, but its psychiatric units were overcrowded and underfunded, so I was given the freedom to work with "whichever patients you can help the most." Initially, I was drawn to the female patients suffering from mental illness. I realized almost immediately that the vast majority of these women hadn't been born with mental illness, nor had they developed it at a young age. The common thread tying most of these women together was that they were victims of sexual assault. These women had been attacked, stigmatized, and then forced to manage the trauma of their experiences on their own, silently, or face the likely consequence of being blamed for instigating their own vicious assault. It was an impossible burden. It took a continuous toll. And once they could no longer bear it, they ended up in a hospital ward.

One patient in particular stood out to me. Her name was Maria, she was in her early twenties, and her husband had cruelly divorced her immediately after discovering that she'd been raped. When I first met Maria, she spent her days rubbing her hands together and mumbling as she paced back and forth across the hospital's long wooden halls—wide-plank pine floors that were faded and somewhat bluish from the small impact of countless steps. I paced alongside her in support, hoping that she'd eventually open up to me. This went on for several weeks, until one day, after racing after her as she shuffled faster and faster up and down the hall, I leaned closer to hear what Maria was mumbling. She looked straight at me, and with all the chaos of a hissing teakettle, sputtered, "Stop following me, you goddamn red-headed bitch."

I *did* stop—right in my tracks. Something about Maria's words clicked. Up until that moment, it hadn't even crossed my mind that two people could interpret an event so differently, each with their own starkly opposed realities playing out inside their heads. In my mind, I'd been comforting Maria and offering her companionship. But to Maria, my proximity and relentless insistence had seemed almost predator-like. I realized that this dynamic, to a much larger degree, was also a core element in violent interactions. I'd been so focused on the victim's experience that I hadn't considered the fact that there was a whole other person involved in these attacks, one that I'd simply dismissed as cruel or domineering or sick. I realized that if I wanted to fully understand the nature of a crime, I'd have to see both the victim and the perpetrator as two halves of the same story. I needed to learn *why* offenders behaved as they did and what was going on in their minds as they carried out such unspeakable acts of violence.

That experience with Maria marked a turning point in my career. In the weeks that followed, I switched from working with female patients suffering from mental illness to concentrating on the male patients in the psychiatric unit's forensic ward—where individuals with court-related matters were placed until their cases could be heard. Many had committed serious offenses such as sexual assault or rape, and, for that reason, not even the doctors paid them much attention—and certainly no one talked to them about their crimes. But that made these men all the more compelling to me. I wanted to know how they thought about their crimes and their victims and to see what I could learn from them. To be clear, my interest wasn't in reforming these men. I simply saw them as an opportunity in the nascent field of criminal psychology to gain insights from perpetrators that might prove useful to helping victims later on. I had nothing to lose. So, I began meeting with them using an interview-based approach that focused on their early childhood and adolescent history and that facilitated a complete retelling of their crimes in their own words.

My interest and my interview approach seemed to surprise the men I spoke with. They'd been treated like pariahs from the moment they'd been admitted to the ward. And yet, as they slowly opened up—sometimes cautiously, sometimes amusedly, sometimes aggressively as they relived each and every moment of their crimes—they exposed a deeper behavioral commonality, too. They all had the same habit of staring at me with great attention to see how I'd respond to the explicit details of their violence. They wanted to see if I'd squirm. It appeared to be a strange yet near universal obsession with control. And although they'd each been characterized as having some sort of underlying mental illness—schizophrenia, psychotic depression, or one of myriad other common diagnoses that were catchalls for conditions poorly understood at the time—I could tell that something else was going on. Something worth pursuing.

I was intrigued. It felt like I was on the brink of grasping a vitally important insight that could help explain the dynamics between victims and offenders. This was exactly the type of difference-making work I'd been looking for. My colleagues, on the other hand, weren't the least bit interested. They preferred to dismiss sexual violence as indecent, a fringe part of society, or a "women's issue" that shouldn't be discussed—as if men weren't even involved.

That stance, however, was thoroughly out of touch with the facts. Forcible rape was one of the four major violent crimes perpetrated in the United States. It was a large-scale problem—with 37,990 cases reported in 1970 alone—that was compounded by a lack of treatment options available for victims who struggled with the psychological aftermath.

"You're missing the point," I said, whenever my colleagues waved me off. "This is an opportunity to understand a unique type of human behavior that's never been studied before. It's unmapped research. It's a chance to do something that's equally important as it is good."

They all answered the same way: "Let it go. It's not worth the damage it could do to your career. Don't you want tenure in the future?"

I couldn't believe it. These professionals—many of them friends and mentors I worked with daily and looked up to as leaders in the psychiatric field—were complicit in perpetuating the exact stigma I wanted to expose. They either didn't get it or they didn't want to get it. Either way, they were making the problem worse.

———————

That realization was defining for me. When it became clear that my colleagues at the hospital would never understand the importance of taking a closer look at this type of behavior, I quit my job to start a new career in academics. I knew how important it was to help patients one at a time, but I wanted to effect change on a systemic level. I wanted to break down barriers that kept victims from getting the treatments and supports they deserved. Academia was that next step. It allowed me to continue my research aimed at more fully understanding the psychology of offenders in crimes of rape, sexual assault, and sexual violence. And it created an opportunity to change the larger cultural perception that served to enable the proliferation of these types of crime, which were still stubbornly entrenched in an outdated blame-the-victim mentality.

Whereas my female patients at Spring Grove State Hospital had taught me the importance of seeing victim and perpetrator as two halves of the same story, my male patients, I'd come to realize, had shown me how far-reaching the element of control really was. Control—or, rather, a lack of feeling in control—was the reason why so few women came forward to report or talk about their trauma. And it was the reason why the psychoanalytic view of sexual violence—the prevailing theory that rape happened because of the clothing women wore or because they fantasized about being raped—had gone unchallenged for decades, despite making no sense at all. Control caused stigma, and stigma kept the whole problem strictly buttoned up. After all, no one ever asked what the victims thought.

That's what motivated Lynda Lytle Holmstrom and me to launch an interdisciplinary research project that focused on the victim response to rape. Lynda was a sociologist colleague of mine whom I'd met shortly after taking a psychiatric nursing faculty position at Boston College. The goal of our research was to better understand the emotional and traumatic effects of sexual violence, which often far outlasted the physical effects of the act itself. We hoped our research would not only help clinicians recognize and understand the signs of rape trauma but also lead to more widespread services for victims. Our method worked like this: over the course of a year, every time a victim of rape was admitted to the Boston City Hospital Emergency Room, the triage nurse immediately called me and Lynda, and we were allowed to interview the victim right away. Our approach was strikingly different from how typical research was done at the time. Rather than enlisting a large group of investigators to indifferently analyze subjects in a clinical manner—as if victims were simple data points to be observed—Lynda and I met patients on their terms, often in the privacy of their own hospital cubicles in the emergency room. We treated them as individuals. They shared their stories, and, in turn, we provided them with crisis intervention counseling; this was at a point in history when few victims were receiving this type of specialized care. The exchange was nonmonetary: we neither paid victims nor were we paid for our services. But the insights both sides gained were invaluable. Our approach helped us better connect with victims, and it gave a name—for the first time—to the concept of *rape trauma syndrome*: the psychological trauma victims experience after an attack. Most importantly, it worked. In all, we interviewed 146 individuals from the ages of three to seventy-three and collected twenty-nine hundred pages of notes to be cataloged, analyzed, and interpreted. We gave these victims a voice.

In 1973, we published our findings in the *American Journal of Nursing* as "The Rape Victim in the Emergency Ward." And in 1974, we followed up with a second major paper in the *American Journal of Psychiatry* titled "Rape Trauma Syndrome," which expanded our reach beyond nursing to a psychiatric audience. One of the biggest takeaways from our study was that sexual violence was more about power and control than the act of sex itself. This novel understanding of the victim's experience had a dramatic ripple effect. It helped to systemically validate victim trauma by bringing new awareness, and a demand for change, to how law enforcement interacted with victims, how healthcare institutions responded to victims' needs, and how the legal system processed rape cases. But the ripples from this study extended much further than I could have ever anticipated. They took on a power and momentum all their own, upending not only the systemic perception of sexual violence but also the course of my career.

That study put me square in the sights of the FBI.

Independent of our research, the FBI had already noticed a sharp increase in violent sexual crimes in the late 1970s. Part of the Bureau's mission was to understand and confront new trends in violence. This meant that, as reports overwhelmed local law enforcement offices, the epidemic of sexual violence became the Bureau's problem to solve. Initially, the Bureau responded with their standard approach: they assigned agents in the Training Division of the FBI Academy the task of educating law enforcement departments across the country on how to better understand and respond to these types of crimes. And they assumed that this trend, like all trends, would eventually pass. But there was a problem. No one at the Academy knew anything about sexual violence. None of the agents had the background or expertise to speak about issues of sexual assault, rape, sexual homicide, or victimology. They simply couldn't engage with the issue or educate other officers of the law.

Despite this lack of knowledge, the Bureau's expectation was clear. They sent an updated directive to the entire training division making it crystal clear that sexual violence was now a mandated part of all educational work. A new BSU agent named Roy Hazelwood received this directive and made a point of mentioning the topic of the new teaching assignment while conducting a hostage negotiation education session with the Los Angeles Police Department in 1978, but then, admitting he knew very little about rape victimology, he quickly moved on to other topics. He'd done this sort of skipping over before without any comment or effect. But this time was different. At the end of the training, a female officer—who was also a nurse and who worked weekends in the emergency ward at the local hospital—approached Hazelwood to tell him about an article she'd read that explained the physical and psychological nature of sexual violence. She thought its findings might be useful for the types of cases he'd mentioned. Hazelwood was interested. He saw this as an opportunity to gain insights into a problem no one in the FBI seemed to understand. He asked the officer for the particulars, and the following week, she mailed him a copy of the article I'd co-published.

Around that same time, in the fall of 1978, I was focused on teaching classes and developing a new research project. It was mid-September, the semester had just started, and I was working on a new grant to understand heart attack victims and their psychosocial risks of returning to work. There was a knock on my office door, and my assistant leaned in and informed me that I had a phone call.

"Can you take a message?" I asked, without looking up. "I'm very busy."

She stayed there for a moment, I could feel her staring at me, before finally whispering, "I think you need to take this. It's the FBI."

Well, that certainly got my attention. I nodded and asked her to leave, then slowly picked up the phone. "Hello?"

The voice on the other end responded in a clipped, staccato style. "Hello. This is Supervisory Special Agent Roy Hazelwood. Is this Professor Ann Burgess?"

"Yes," I replied.

"The same Ann Burgess who wrote an article titled 'The Rape Victim in the Emergency Ward'?"

"That's right."

"Good," he said. "I hope I'm not interrupting anything. I've been wanting to speak with you about the specific nature of your work."

Hazelwood's tone quickly changed after that. His crisp formality gave way to something more soft-spoken and precise. He was friendly but still careful with his words, speaking in long, slow sentences that seemed to dance around whatever point he was intending to make. Initially, I had no idea what had inspired him to look up my number. It took a few minutes for him to explain how he came across my article, and a few minutes more to get to the reason behind his call.

"You see, even at an institution with as many resources as the FBI, we sometimes—on rare occasions, anyway—look for outside expertise to offer new perspectives. And this trend in violence that you mention in your article has been difficult for us to wrap our head around." He paused. "I suppose that's because so few individuals come forward to talk about their experience. The thing is, I suspect we've been looking at this whole problem backwards. We wind up with statistics that help measure the scope of a problem. Whereas you, you managed to drill down into the human element of what's going on, and I'm interested to know how you did that. I'd like you to come down to Quantico to give a lecture on your research. I think that would go a long way in helping our agents learn something valuable about victimology and violent sexual offenders."

I hesitated. Up to that point, I'd been speaking primarily to nursing groups and rape crisis staff about my research. Female groups were receptive to the topic. They connected to my work. And they connected to me. They understood why, as an undergrad, I'd raced across Boston Common after my hospital shift, eager to make it back to the Tri Delta sorority house before dark. But more importantly, they understood the fear I experienced one night when a group of teenage boys rushed out of an alley and started harassing me, grabbing my nursing cape and holding my arm until I finally managed to pull free. I wasn't sure if an audience of men would react the same way. I wavered a moment, but curiosity got the best of me.

"All right, Agent Hazelwood," I said. "Fax me the details. I'd like to see how the FBI trains agents to think about sexual crimes."

───────────

The audience for my first lecture at the FBI Academy consisted of a group of forty or so male agents, who, for the most part, looked exactly like their pop culture portrayals on TV: rugged athletes with fresh crew cuts dressed in near-identical crisp blue shirts. They even seemed to act the part, settling into their seats five minutes early, with notebooks and pens in hand.

Optimistic, I began with a question. "What do you all know about victimology in cases of rape?"

Several agents looked down, and some quietly smirked. But no one responded.

My brief illusion of high-minded G-men abruptly crumbled.

"Because, traditionally, it's been defined by sex," I said. "But the truth is, that's not how it works. Rape is an act of power and control. Victims know this, and it's the reason so many don't come forward. They feel helpless, overwhelmed, and ashamed. They're violated in the most absolute sense of the word. And in the rare cases when victims do come forward and ask for your help, it's because of a tiny belief that you can help get back what was taken and corrupted and made ugly in their absence of control. That's what you should know about rape. Because in that moment when a victim comes forward, how you respond is the most important thing in the world."

I looked up from my notes and noticed they were all sitting straight up in their seats. I had their attention now.

"All right," I said. "Let's look at a few cases."

I dimmed the overhead lights and turned on a projector, then clicked through a series of photographs showing blood-stained underwear, bedrooms upturned by violence, and close-ups of women's faces covered in bruises and marks of abuse. Some agents took notes, but most just stared at the severity of the crimes. None of them smirked after that.

That first lecture went well enough, and I was soon brought back to lead classes on a regular basis. It was surreal. With the exception of the Bureau's female clerks and secretaries—a group that tended to avoid contact with me beyond inquisitive stares—I was often the only woman in the building. And given my area of expertise, I can only imagine the rumors circulating about me as the FBI's new expert in sexual violence. But Hazelwood went out of his way to make sure I didn't have any issues. He took the time to explain the nuances of the Bureau's culture and to ask for my opinion about cases and research he was working on. He also made a habit of introducing me to other agents. These conversations tended to be brief, professional, and aloof—as most of my interactions with the agents were—but there were notable exceptions.

One such exception happened early on, just after newly appointed Assistant Director Ken Joseph announced that all Academy instructors—including the Behavioral Science Unit's "mindhunters," as they were called in reference to their interest in learning how serial killers thought—were to undertake original research. This directive marked a noticeable shift in the Bureau's traditional way of thinking. It spoke to a changing of the guard. Leadership from the Hoover era had begun to step down or retire or otherwise move on, and with them went the belief that, as Joseph's predecessor, Assistant Director John McDermott, once described it, "the FBI's job was to catch criminals, get them to court, and incarcerate them. Research was the job of a sociologist." Times were changing. Hazelwood understood this and saw it as an opportunity to schedule a meeting between me and two of his colleagues: Robert Ressler and John Douglas.

"They want to know more about your study," Hazelwood said, ushering me into an elevator that carried us several floors belowground. "They were impressed with the scope of your work, because . . . well," he paused. "I probably shouldn't discuss it, but they've got a side project you might be interested in. I think you'll get along just fine."

Hazelwood was right. I connected with Ressler and Douglas right away. Partly because of my comfort in talking about violence, and partly because I showed a genuine interest in their work when few others had. But it also had a lot to do with Ressler's belief that learning from outside perspectives was important.

Douglas, on the other hand, was initially more standoffish, but he opened up once Ressler began explaining the backstory of their not-quite-by-the-books study.

"We're calling it the criminal personality study," Douglas said. "It was Bob's idea to visit prisons and interview serial killers when we traveled for the Academy. We'd been seeing all these cases of crimes with no apparent motive, and it seemed like the best way to get answers was to interview convicted killers themselves. Turns out that was the easy part. Our badges got us into the prisons, no problem. We were able to get recordings with everyone from Edmund Kemper to Sirhan Sirhan to Richard Speck."

"Right," Ressler interjected. "But the hard part is figuring out what the recordings actually *mean*. They're just interviews at this point. That's why Hazelwood's descriptions of your work stood out to us. There might be some overlap between the techniques you used and what we're trying to figure out. What do you think?"

Interest piqued, I agreed and listened to the tapes right then and there.

What I heard was like eavesdropping on the rawest fringes of humanity. One by one, I hit play and listened closely until each cassette whirred to a stop. I took notes and listened again. The conversations showed the killers' arrogance and were fascinating and haunting. The interviews were also poorly structured and had zero footing in any conventional school of research. They showed no uniformity between sessions, no apparent planning, and no eye toward future analysis. The only goal seemed to be to keep the killers talking. Still, I was impressed. Ressler and Douglas really were engaged in a type of behavioral investigation that had never been done before. I told them so at our next meeting.

"I think you have something here," I said. "This could lead to a whole new way of understanding criminal behavior. As far as I know, no one's ever tried to figure out why serial killers kill. The implications are profound."

"I knew it." Douglas smiled, turning to Ressler.

"Hold on a second." Ressler paid no attention to Douglas. Instead, he carefully focused on me. "What is it you think we have here, exactly? Because to my ears, this is just a bunch of sickos fantasizing about their crimes and not offering much else. What am I missing?"

"There's a lot missing at this point: background information, upbringing, history of violence," I admitted. "But all of that can be fixed by formalizing your approach and coming up with the right methodology. You need a script of questions to establish a baseline so you can measure one interview against the next. You have to treat this like real research with a real goal of data collection and analysis. That's the only way you'll figure out what makes killers tick. And you need to publish your findings so that others can make sense of them too."

"Like, a book?" Douglas asked.

"I was thinking a journal article that could help validate the findings," I said. "But maybe a book."

Without even looking at Ressler, Douglas asked if I'd help them.

———◆———

Thanks to the nature of their work, the agents already had access to an incredible catalog of the exact types of criminal cases this project needed: serial killers who incorporated acts of rape or sexual violence into their crimes. It was all at our fingertips. The challenge was to come up with a rigorous and comprehensive approach that could stand up to the intense scrutiny we were sure to face from the FBI. In fact, Ressler had already been called into Director William

Webster's office for a lunch meeting, where, without notice, he'd been asked to explain the nature of the criminal personality study as the other attendees ate. He did so, but the result was a stern warning from the director himself that there'd be no tolerance for any "shoebox research." Ressler wasn't worried about that. But he was mad as hell about paying $7.61 for a sandwich he never got a chance to eat.

For my part, I understood what was at stake. My work on the rape study, and the skepticism I'd faced from my colleagues in academia, had prepared me for whatever forms of bureaucratic oversight and scrutiny lay ahead. I knew that our project would be seen as a challenge to the status quo. It would be mocked, stonewalled, and expected to fail. As far as most people were concerned, killers were plain sick. That was it. There were no subtitles to figure out, no lessons to be learned, and any effort spent on the topic would be seen as effort wasted. But none of that mattered to me. I knew that psychological truths were never quite so simple. More importantly, I knew that good research would always bring the truth to light. I trusted the process.

My biggest concern was how broad and overarching the criminal personality study was at that point. It needed to be broken up into distinctly focused parts—at least three—to make it a more manageable study. First, we'd analyze the interviews conducted with convicted offenders, which would help us understand crimes that had no apparent motive. Then, we'd analyze the serial killer cases—thirty-six in total—to see what information about the perpetrators' upbringing and personality could be matched to the patterns and behaviors of their crimes. And finally, we'd create the foundation for constructing the criminal profile itself. Each part was clearly connected to the others. But as a research process, to make any methodological sense the whole undertaking needed to be organized as individual phases that could build off of each other.

I also couldn't help wondering how long it would take for Douglas and Ressler to fully trust me. Even after asking for my help, they still kept their guard up when I was around—they were careful in how they spoke about victims and hesitant to share a case's violent details. But whether they did this as a way of protecting their own interests or attempting to protect me, I wasn't yet sure.

So, I stayed the course and focused purely on what I could control. Because interviews would be the study's main data collection tool— the backbone of the project—it made sense to design a methodology around the interviewing approach. The goal was to learn as much as possible about the nature of serial killers while focusing on three main points: why the subjects killed, how they thought about their violence, and how their violence evolved. I began by developing a data instrument that was made up of five separate sections on fifty-seven color-coded pages that included 488 items per individual criminal and that would address everything from offender demographics to victim characteristics, assailant motives, victim selection, assault tactics, assault characteristics, and myriad other forensic details. This process was inspired by a colleague of mine, psychologist Nick Groth, who used a similar tool to learn about the motivations of incarcerated rapists at Somers Correctional Facility in Connecticut. What was different, though, was that my tool wouldn't be used by academics. It would be used by FBI agents in close quarters with some of the most notorious killers ever known. I needed to refine Nick's idea into something more adaptive and intuitive to fit the reality of the task ahead.

The resulting data collection tool was deftly simple. It looked like a questionnaire, and it read like a questionnaire, but its true function was to subtly guide the conversation while keeping the agent in control. And control, of course, was the crucial element. It was what would allow us to get specific types of information—not just whatever information the offender decided to offer. It was the key that would unlock a serial killer's mind so we could understand how that mind worked and what made it different. That was what we were after. So I made sure to design the interview questions in such a way that the focus stayed heavily on the subject's retelling of the crime, as well as their history of violence and their earliest memories of fantasy and violent thoughts.

We also looked at documentation from official crime reports, forensic photography, medical examiners' reports, psychological evaluations, and information on the victims. This step was crucial. It gave us a reference to draw from in order to determine how the criminal's view aligned with evidence from the case itself, and to confront the criminal if their interview was inconsistent or otherwise strayed from the facts. In the end, we developed an academic approach to organizing both qualitative and quantitative information that we could then use to explore the psychological composition of violent criminals. In other words, it's how we'd crack the code of who these killers were. It's how we'd use their own minds against them.

News of the BSU's innovative research into criminal behaviors spread through Quantico like wildfire. Everyone seemed to have an opinion. Some groups within the FBI rooted against us, dismissing our work as the stuff of armchair detectives or—at best—an unreliable approach that could never compete with the work of agents in the field. But others acknowledged the practical applications of our analysis and were interested in seeing proof of its results. This made our job a little easier. If we could provide evidence-based examples that demonstrated a clear value of our work, we could tilt the Bureau's perception in our favor. That's where the profiling phase, the third part of the criminal personality study, came into play. Profiling would bridge the gap between research and real-world results. Profiling would empower agents to solve complex cases faster than ever thought possible. Profiling would be the study's payoff.

After designing a methodology for the first two phases of the criminal personality study, data collection and analysis, we turned our attention to the third phase. We decided the best way to move profiling forward was to develop a step-by-step approach that was manual-like in its thoroughness and clarity. We were already collecting the relevant data through our research, we just needed to refine it—to shape our understanding of criminal psychology into a blueprint for defining what motivated and differentiated a serial killer on the basis of their victims, methods, and crime scenes. And we knew that the technique needed to be easy to understand but powerful as a tool. We called it the criminal profile-generating process, and it worked by following five distinct stages:

Profiling inputs: This first stage focuses on data collection. Data includes crime scene analysis (physical evidence, pattern of evidence, body positions, weapons), victimology (background, habits, family structure, last seen, age, occupation), forensic information (cause of death, wounds, pre/postmortem sexual acts and wounds, autopsy report, laboratory reports), preliminary police report (background information, police observation, time of crime, who reported crime, neighborhood socioeconomic status, crime rate), and photos (aerial, crime scene, victim).

Decision process models: Stage two looks at homicide type and style, primary intent, victim risk, offender risk, escalation, time for crime, and location factors.

Crime assessment: Stage three zeroes in on the reconstruction of the crime, crime classification, organized/disorganized/mixed, victim selection, control of victim, sequence of crime, staging, motivation, and crime scene dynamics.

Criminal profile: Stage four is the construction of the composite profile of the offender. This process defines physical characteristics, habits, pre-offense behavior leading to crime, and post-offense behavior of the perpetrator and offers recommendations for investigators who are looking to narrow down a pool of suspects.

Investigation and apprehension: The last stage involves working with local law enforcement to track down and then capture the offender.

It was Douglas who came up with the final piece of the puzzle. He reasoned that the best way to demonstrate the effectiveness of this profiling process was to ask local law enforcement to send in reports from their most challenging unsolved murder cases so that our team could work on them. He stressed that the BSU should always be available to help local police with difficult investigations. "That's the whole point of doing this," he said. "We can focus the search on the most likely suspects and offer proactive techniques to draw the real criminals out."

The number of responses that poured in from police stations across the country was telling. The BSU received dozens of cases in the first few months alone. And as reports kept coming in, the team had to implement a rule stating that the FBI wouldn't get involved until local law enforcement had spent at least three months trying to solve a case on their own. Still, there were plenty of cases to choose from. Now it was time to get to work.

The eight-member profiling team each began working through cases as diligently as possible, gathering three to six available BSU agents to work each one. Multiple cases were going on at any given time. What made it tricky, though, was that profiling was just one part of our research, and research was just a small part of the overall job at that point. Research had to be squeezed in between lectures, road school, case assignments, and whatever else the Bureau threw our way. The other challenge was that Douglas and Ressler enacted a strict rule stating that no one could start profiling until local investigators had sent in all their investigative information. It was hard to wait, given the urgency of these serial cases and the likelihood of follow-up attacks. But it made methodological sense and maintained the integrity of our work—besides, one sharp look from Douglas or Ressler was more than enough warning to keep anyone from straying from the process.

Despite all the hurdles, despite the weekends spent at the office—and endless stretches of long days and sleepless nights—when we did come together for profiling, the sessions clicked. For each investigation, a lead agent was assigned and given all the details of a case in advance. This agent would then present the case to the rest of the group as clearly and concisely as possible. Their job was to stick to the facts. They gave the basic who, what, and when of each case, supplemented by any available police reports or autopsy information. Then they opened it up to questions so they could clarify any investigative details.

The real profiling started after that. That's when the team picked at the threads of the case: the clues left behind at the crime scene, the characteristics of the victim, and the nuances of the attack. From there, we could see the case through an offender's eyes and begin to describe who this person was in the clearest details. We could zero in on their unique behaviors and characteristics to figure out who the "unsub"—the unknown or unidentified subject—was and where they were going next. To put it simply: profiling was how we thought our way into an offender's head.

These meetings were intense—graphic in their descriptions, and passionate in their debates. There was an element of theater in the rapid back-and-forth exchanges, but meetings always ended with a comprehensive profile that the lead agent could send back to the original law enforcement agency that had asked for our help.

Of these early cases, one particularly gruesome report came in from Nebraska. It caught the eye of BSU unit chief Roger Depue, who immediately called Ressler and told him to catch the first available flight to Omaha. A serial killer had just taken a second child victim. Local investigators had no leads. But from the crime scene photos and autopsy reports they sent in, one thing was clear: the killer was gaining confidence. If he wasn't stopped soon, there'd be a third victim, then a fourth, and more and more after that. The clock was ticking. We had to move fast.

CHAPTER 2

The Bomb Shelter

"At some point, all serial killers make a mistake. You just never know what that mistake's going to be."

Ressler said this after the first Nebraska boy went missing. It wasn't the first time I'd heard him say it. In fact, I'd heard all the agents say it at one point or another. It was like an aphorism they used, a truism that made the most difficult cases easier to bear. And it worked, I guess—this collegial shorthand for optimism and support. It was comforting. But in my mind, it also felt like an excuse. It felt like a tacit admission of our own lack of control in cases of life and death, which bothered me. And at the same time, taking back our control from these offenders was what motivated my work, because I knew that profiling could give us a leg up. If we developed profiling to the fullest potential I knew it had, we could turn the tables. We wouldn't have to wait anymore for serial killers to slip up. We could track them down before they even got the chance.

I was thinking about this that December morning when Ressler asked me to attend the team's briefing on the case in Nebraska.

The request initially caught me off guard. Although I'd worked on the studies and the methodologies to develop the BSU's profiling techniques, I wasn't an agent and I'd never been down to the bomb shelter to work on an active case. But none of that mattered to him.

"Listen," he said, "don't start worrying about the rules now. I need all the help I can get on this one. I need to figure it out before there's another attack."

He was right, of course. This was an opportunity for me to help victims. And if anyone saw my involvement in the case as a violation of standard protocol, well, I'd deal with the consequences later. More important things were at stake.

Ressler's urgency carried over to the profiling session the next morning. As soon as he walked into the bomb shelter, he turned off a row of overhead fluorescent lights, went straight for the projector, and immediately turned his attention to me and the rest of the team.

"All right," he began. "Let's be smart. This asshole's going after kids. I don't want anyone else getting hurt."

He dove straight into the specifics of the case, clarifying certain details using photos and witness testimony. He was careful to limit his presentation to the facts. This was a deliberate and incredibly important part of the process. Whenever we started to develop a new profile, the lead agent was expected to remain as neutral as possible and not to reveal any personal opinions or bias that might affect how the team categorized the unsub at the center of the case.

This unsub was a vicious killer of children. He'd murdered two known victims at this point, but likely there were more.

On a Sunday morning in mid-September 1983, thirteen-year-old Danny E. quietly got out of bed and dressed for his daily newspaper route across the small town of Bellevue, Nebraska. It was still dark as he felt his way down the hall, crept past his parents' bedroom, and stepped outside, where the buzz of katydids filled the air. He unlocked his bike—careful not to rattle the noisy chain—and walked it to the end of his driveway. A car's headlights flashed in the distance. It was five fifteen. The sun was just below the horizon as he peddled barefoot to the local convenience store, picked up his assignment of papers, and folded his stack on the floor by the window. Then he set out on his regular route.

A couple hours later, just after seven a.m., Danny's father woke up to a phone call from the boy's supervisor.

"I'm getting complaints about missing deliveries," the supervisor grumbled. "Can you put Danny on the phone?"

"What do you mean?" Danny's father asked. "Hey, Danny?" He knocked on Danny's door and waited a moment before yelling again. "Danny!"

Still no response. Danny wasn't there. Neither was his bike. Getting worried, Danny's father jumped in his car to retrace the delivery route. He started at the convenience store, talked with the clerk, then drove past one, two, three houses before finding his son's bicycle leaning against a fence. Danny, however, was nowhere to be found. All but three newspapers were still neatly tucked within the cloth delivery bag on the bike. At that point, Danny's father called the police.

Local investigators immediately organized a missing person's search. They combed the area and performed a systematic building-by-building inspection. They examined every inch of Danny's bike, but found no signs of a struggle. They checked with extended family, including an aunt and uncle who were traveling out of state, but no one knew where Danny was. A witness reported seeing an unfamiliar car parked near where the bicycle was found earlier that morning and described an individual getting out of the car and looking down the street. But there were no specific details—no clues that made the information viable. Danny had all but disappeared into thin air.

Two and a half days later, after investigators expanded the borders of their search, the body of a young boy was found partially hidden in some high grass along an unpaved country road. His ankles and wrists had been tied behind his back. His mouth was taped shut. And his body had been treated savagely: a bad laceration on the shoulder, some contusions to the face, a gash on his leg, cuts on his neck that penetrated all the way down to the spinal column, and multiple stab wounds on his chest that tore open the insides of his body. He was naked except for his navy-blue underwear. The rest of his clothes were never found.

The medical examiner's report attributed Danny's death to loss of blood from the numerous stab wounds that ravaged his body. The wounds to the leg and back were considered to have occurred post-mortem and seemed to suggest symbolism or intentional patterns in their crisscross-like shape, but this wasn't entirely clear. It could have just been cutting for cutting's sake, which seemed to make sense because there was also a slice of flesh missing from the victim's shoulder. There was no evidence of sexual assault and very little evidence left by the offender. The report did note, however, that the rope used to tie up the victim was unusual, distinctive. It had blue fibers on the inside, a feature that only became visible when the ropes were cut from the boy's ankles and wrists.

At the request of the special agent in charge (SAC) of the Omaha FBI office, Ressler was asked to write a preliminary profile of the unsub. Ressler agreed, but only after flying out to Nebraska to speak with investigators in person first. His findings struck him as eerily similar to two previous cases known to the FBI, both of which were unsolved and both of which involved young boys of a similar age. The first was from a year earlier, in nearby Des Moines, where another newspaper delivery boy had vanished on a Sunday morning while out on his morning route. The boy had never been found. The second case had occurred in Florida and involved a young boy who disappeared while shopping with his mother in an outdoor mall. Several days later, the boy's head was found floating in a canal. Investigators spoke to several witnesses who claimed to see a man luring the boy away from the mall and into a car with an out-of-state license plate. At the time, it wasn't enough to make an arrest. And the investigation fizzled out soon afterward, with the FBI forced to watch from the sidelines as a result of lack-of-jurisdiction policies and other red tape.

After speaking with the investigators in Nebraska, visiting the crime scene, and evaluating the case files, Ressler determined that Danny had likely been targeted by a serial killer. He framed his preliminary profile of the unsub with this in mind, describing the killer as a male in his late teens to early twenties who likely knew Danny and who saw murder as an act of dominance and control. The absence of sexual violence suggested the offender wasn't interested in sex, at least not in any traditional sense. He might even be asexual. There wasn't a lot of information to go off of at the time, so this first profile was somewhat thin and drew heavily on the victim's age, the lack of crime in the area, and the typology of known serial killers with similar victims that we'd already come to understand from our work on the serial killer study. Ressler shared this analysis with the joint task force—a team of local and state police, military authorities, and agents from the Omaha FBI office. None of the agencies involved had experienced a child murder as brutal as this before. But they knew that a coordinated effort of shared resources and expertise was their best chance to figure it out.

"Unfortunately, not much came out of that first profile." Ressler flipped the overhead lights back on. "It was too generic of a description: white male, teenager, worked in the area, probably attached himself to some sort of club or social group to try to fit in. There just wasn't enough information to work with. Certain things happened: hypnosis, forensic work, polygraphs for witnesses, sketch drawings based on someone that may or may not have been in the vicinity when the abduction happened. But, basically, they came up empty. So that's case one. That's Danny. Any questions?"

"Yeah." Hazelwood was the first to speak up. "That slice of flesh from the victim's shoulder. Was it eventually found or did it stay missing?"

"Missing," Ressler answered.

"And how big was it?"

"Probably about the size of a silver dollar." Ressler thought for a moment. "Just one clean cut, like if you sliced off the end of a ham or something."

"Hey, Bob," Douglas chimed in. "Was the side of the road just the disposal site or was it the murder site as well?"

"It was pretty well determined that the road was just the disposal site," Ressler said. "In fact, there were pebble indentations all over the body, but no pebbles in the field where the body was found. The victim was either killed in a gravel area, or the body was left laying on gravel somewhere before it was transported to the field."

An idea started to form in my head. The pictures showed the body by a dirt road, but not really concealed. It looked like a dump and run. And that can lead to slipups. "Did they check for tire tracks? Were there any useful forensics? To me, the disposal looks anxious, rushed."

"The tracks weren't clear enough for impressions," Ressler replied. "No shoe prints either. We think the unsub just pulled over and dumped the body. It wasn't positioned or anything. Just dropped."

Agent Ken Lanning raised his hand. Ressler nodded in his direction.

"You talked about ropes with colored fibers," Lanning said. "How did that pan out? Did the victim have any rope marks on his extremities?"

"Good question. When they looked at the victim's arms and legs after cutting off the ropes, there were no deep marks or other indications he'd been tied for any substantial period of time. Even the grass in the field left more of an indentation than the ropes did. The rope was sent to our lab but didn't match any known samples."

Lanning tried to ask a follow-up, but Douglas interjected. "How would you classify the victim? Passive? Aggressive? Assertive?"

"He was kind of a typical Midwestern macho kid," Ressler said. "Pretty normal. Searches of his room showed no drugs or connections to the type of person who might be capable of doing something like this."

"How about the weapon?" I asked. "Any indication about the type of knife?"

"The wounds were three to three and a half inches deep," Ressler said. "Best guess is this was some type of hunting knife. No unusual serrations or double blades or anything like that. Something that would've been easy to get in a store."

Lanning raised his hand, but Ressler ignored him to press on with his own train of thought—as the youngest agent on the team, Lanning often got kid-brother-type treatment.

"Look," Ressler continued, "you're all asking good questions, but no one's focusing on the bike. That's what stands out for me. I mean, you'd expect the bike to be tossed to the ground instead of leaning purposefully against the fence. So, what—did the guy know the kid? Did he have a gun? There's something personal here. There's something important about the aspect of control. You can see it in the aggressiveness of the attack and the way the kid was tied up. But there's no sexual assault. So, what happened during those twenty-four hours between the abduction and when he was killed?"

"Watch yourself, Bob," Douglas said. "You're leading a little bit, getting into the profiling here. We don't know if it was personal or not."

Ressler paused. The buzz of fluorescent lights swelled overhead.

"Yeah, you're right," he admitted. "Let's get to the second homicide. Let's talk about what happened Friday of last week."

Ressler loaded a new carousel of slides in the projector, turned off the row of overhead lights, and flipped on the projector's switch.

"You'll notice how similar the victims look, how similar the dump sites are, and how similar the wounds appear to be. There's a lot that links these cases. This second one's just more severe than the first."

Christopher W., the son of an officer at Offutt Air Force Base, was abducted at approximately seven thirty a.m. on Friday, December 2. Christopher, a wisp of a kid, tall and lanky, was somewhat new to the area and still hadn't made any friends. But he was known around town because of his father's rank and because they lived in a GI-packed neighborhood within a mile of the base. That's where a witness saw him talking to a white male: on the outskirts of the Offutt Air Force Base, just south of Omaha and right next to Bellevue, Nebraska. The witness wasn't close enough to make out any details beyond the suspect's race (white), age ("fairly young"), and how cold the two of them looked, with thick puffs of breath hanging between them as they spoke. Christopher jumped into the back seat of the unsub's car without any signs of struggle, fight, or argument. The boy may have looked worried, but he seemed to enter the car by choice.

"I just figured he was getting a ride to school," the witness said.

That was the last time Christopher was seen alive. His body was found three days later in a location similar to where the previous victim had been found. It was the same type of rural, wide-open space—just a field, bordered by woods, in the middle of nowhere.

Investigators were lucky to even find him. That particular weekend had brought bad storms across the state, and hunters happened to find the victim's body before it was covered in snow. The men had driven to the outskirts of town to shoot grouse. After parking their car on the side of the road, they noticed two sets of footprints leading away from the road but only one set coming back out. They followed the tracks for about 150 yards before stumbling across the body, and immediately called local authorities.

The task force connected this case to the previous case right away. Like the first victim, this child was naked except for his underwear. He also had similar deep slashes along his chest and stomach, and his neck was cut from the top of the spine to under the chin, possibly in an attempt at decapitation. Again, there was no evidence of sexual activity. He was thirteen, weighed approximately 125 pounds, and was by all accounts a pretty straitlaced kid.

However similar the victims and their disposal sites seemed to be, three differences between the two cases were notable. First, the most recent victim was found with his clothes placed in an organized pile just a few feet away from the body, whereas the first victim's clothes were never found. Second, there were no ropes involved in the more recent attack. And third, the preliminary report from the lab showed that the most recent body had endured more postmortem cutting than the previous victim had.

"That's about it." Ressler turned the lights back on. "Details are still coming in and there's still another witness to interview. But that's all the task force knows right now. Local police are working with the area's newspapers and TV stations to ask for the public's help. There's a hotline the public can call with tips, license plate numbers, or descriptions of suspicious persons. And there's a notice to the public to report anyone talking to kids or anyone lurking around. Questions?"

"You said the clothes were folded," Douglas said. "Can you show us that slide again?"

Ressler clicked the projector in reverse a few times. "Here. It's kind of hard to see. But these are more deliberately placed than just being thrown on top of each other. It's not that they're neat, exactly, but it's deliberate. Kind of like how you'd fold a coat over itself rather than just chucking it around. It's worth noticing the order of the stacked clothes here."

Ressler paused, giving us all a moment to write in our notebooks. Then Lanning spoke up.

"I'm just wondering if there's any indication of organ removal."

"No." Ressler shook his head. "The wounds are just slashing. It looks like there'd be some sort of pattern, but apparently it's just cutting for cutting's sake."

"I don't know about that," Lanning pushed back. "It looks too similar to the last victim. I'd call it ritualistic at this point. It's anger."

"Okay, wait a minute. Let me backtrack a second," Ressler said. "We had our own guys take a look at the forensics on the first victim. Still nothing on the slashing, but they came up with a different interpretation for the piece of flesh missing from the kid's arm. They found a dental imprint. It was only a partial, but the takeaway was that the wound could be covering for a biting fetish."

"What about victimology?" I asked. "I think it's important to consider the victims' characteristics in all this and what might connect them to the offender, but none of the photos give us a clean look of the victims' faces. Is age the key factor or are they similar looking, too?"

"They did look very similar," Ressler said. "And in terms of victimology, there's a lot there. This guy chose easy victims. He picked on young males, not females—that's significant. You look at the type of guy who chooses boys, basically, as his victims, and I think that's key to his personality. This guy's a coward. And yeah, yeah, I know. I'm being biased." He shrugged and glanced quickly at Douglas, confessing to the slipup before anyone could complain. "So, let's just do it. Let's get into a little profiling here."

This last part was the real reason for the meeting. Every single person in the room that morning had already familiarized themselves with the case—we'd studied the briefings. And although Ressler's presentation was thorough and insightful and added new context through its photos and slides, it was still mostly a review. Its true purpose was simply pretext for an elite group of profilers to collaborate on narrowing down the search to the smallest possible suspect pool. That's how the process worked. Each agent brought unique insights and perspective that helped define who the suspect was. It was both art and science. And although some people within the Bureau found fault in it for that reason, I saw this as an advantage. It also meant the process needed to be as rigorous as possible. Each piece of evidence, each carefully considered detail, was tested, given context, and refined to form a clearer view of the suspect as a comprehensive individual. The end result established a whole that was greater than the sum of its parts. Profiling couldn't name the exact person responsible for a crime, but it could use all available evidence to create a deep and nuanced portrait of the suspect—complete with their age, race, physical stature, job, education, hobbies, and almost any other detail imaginable.

For the Nebraska case, we used every piece of evidence at our disposal to come up with the most comprehensive description possible. We started with Ressler's original profile, which already deduced that the killer likely worked a job that put him in close proximity to young males, possibly as a soccer coach or scoutmaster. And because of the killer's crude use of a knife to cut away evidence of bite marks on his victims, Ressler believed the unsub read police and detective magazines that discussed forensic science. We also agreed that the killer was obsessed with control and would be intently watching the news coverage of his crimes to see how he was being portrayed by the media. To this, we added basic demographics that our ongoing research on serial killers had made fairly obvious. He was white, given that serial killers tended to kill within their race; he was young, since younger victims were a sign of sexual immaturity; and his excessive degree of violence spoke to deep feelings of anger and inadequacy in the world.

But it was always the smallest, subtlest details that could make or break a profile. That needed to be our focus. We described the unsub as follows:

He's a white male in his late teens or early twenties. He owns a well-maintained car, something presentable enough that his victims feel comfortable getting inside. He's able to project confidence and an ease of conversation with his preferred victims because of his similarity in age. But that confidence is only surface level, as is evident from the preplanned nature of the attacks—the killer was prepared with ropes and bindings to control his victims—compared to the rushed manner of disposing of their bodies, which shows lack of experience and urgency.

The use of ropes also suggests a sexual nature to the crimes, which is in line with the absence of outright evidence for sexual assault before or after death. There's an element of bondage in the ropes that's consistent with sexual control. And the lack of follow-through is evidence of sexual immaturity, limited experience, and paranoia. The aggressive knife wounds show the killer's frustrations and anger at not being able to convert the attack into a sexual experience. This suggests that the killer is driven to live out a sexual fantasy, which is likely rooted in his own sexual trauma as a child.

The killer's habit of morning abductions points to a blue-collar shift worker, something along the lines of a semiskilled mechanic who works at night. This again points to average intelligence, with likely some high school education but nothing more. He's not married, not comfortable around women, not sexually experienced. He's emotionally stunted and impulsive. He's local to the area. He has a fixation on young boys and is likely involved in an activity that allows him to associate with these kids, such as a little league team or similar interest. He lives alone in an apartment. He reads detective magazines as a form of pornography. He'll have a juvenile record that shows previous sex offenses with young boys. He's a loner and wants to get out of town but can't because of limited employment potential. He's gaining confidence and will likely expose himself through high-risk behavior.

We also noted that the killer would likely strike again sooner rather than later. The local police wouldn't want to hear it—they were already overwhelmed by the ugliness of the case as it currently stood—but we needed to keep them grounded in the reality of what was most likely to happen. Besides, the unsub had shown signs of progressing in his technique from the first victim to the second. And with the holidays coming up and schools closing for winter vacation, kids would be outside the safety of their classrooms and more vulnerable to attacks. The opportunity would be too tempting to resist.

Over the weeks that followed, investigators identified numerous suspects to bring in for interrogation. This included a person of interest known to force young boys into his car to engage in pedophilia. But although this led to an arrest and conviction, it was unconnected to the Danny E. and Christopher W. cases. December passed with no further incidents. So did the start of January.

The case finally broke on the morning of January 11. School had started again, and a female teacher at a church day care center noticed a suspicious car lingering around the parking lot. The teacher began writing down the license plate number, but the male driver backed up, parked his car, and threatened to kill her if she didn't give him the piece of paper. The teacher managed to push past him and run inside to call the hotline number she'd seen on the news. The man fled.

Local police and special agents from the Omaha FBI office were quick to respond. They traced the car to a nearby garage and found that it was the rental of an airman stationed at Offutt Air Force Base. The airman's own car was currently at the garage for repairs. Agents looked through the car's windows and saw rope similar to the rope found on the first victim. They contacted officers from the Air Force Office of Special Investigations (OSI) to gain immediate access to the residence of the car's owner, a radar technician named John Joseph Joubert IV. This authorized search and seizure uncovered more matching rope, a large hunting knife, and several dozen heavily read detective magazines, one of which had a dog-eared page to a story about killing a newsboy. The findings—along with twenty-one-year-old Joubert's physical appearance as a young white male with a weak build—checked all the boxes of the profile perfectly.

As it turned out, Joubert was a low-level worker who performed basic daily maintenance on Air Force equipment during overnight shifts. He had also been in the Boy Scouts for years and was an assistant scoutmaster of a troop on the air base.

During Joubert's interrogation, he initially denied killing the boys, but he wavered when confronted with the evidence. When investigators told him that the rope in his car matched the rope found on the first victim, Joubert explained that he was an assistant scoutmaster and that the head scoutmaster had given him the rope as a gift. He then said he wanted to speak with the scoutmaster. That presented us with a strategic opportunity. It played into an interrogative technique of easing a suspect's fears by bringing in someone who's already gained their trust. This meeting was arranged, and after a lengthy conversation between the two, Joubert took the scoutmaster's advice and confessed to the murders of Danny E. and Christopher W. He said he killed the boys soon after picking them up. He also admitted that he'd never had a consenting sexual relationship and was sexually turned on by young boys. What's more, he got off on reading detective magazines about dominance, power, and control.

Joubert's confession further matched the FBI profile. He was emotionally stunted, sexually ambivalent, and impulsive, just like we predicted. This became most clear in his list-like retelling of how he killed Danny:

> I'd set my alarm clock to get up [at five thirty] in the morning to go out and do it. I got in my car, went to a Quick Shop, and saw a kid there. He was delivering papers. I drove past him in the parking lot. As I drove past him, it popped into my head to pick up the kid and put him in the trunk and take him some place. I walked up behind him, put my hand over his mouth, and said, "Don't make a sound." I then put the tape over his mouth, bound his hands behind his back. I thought, I can't do it here.... I drove to a dirt road and parked. I then took him out of the trunk and told him to take off his shirt and pants. I remember putting my hands on his throat. He got his hands loose and tried to stop me. I told him, "Don't worry," and then pulled out a knife, which was a fishing fillet knife. It was inexpensive. The tape came from the hospital. I had cut my finger with an exacto [X-Acto] knife while working on my models and was given tape at the hospital.

Joubert then described stabbing Danny once in the chest and listening to his screams before slowly stabbing him over and over again, becoming more and more sexually aroused with each thrust of the knife.

There was no hint of emotion throughout Joubert's confession until he brought up the large laceration on Danny's left thigh. "It was to cover up a bite mark," he explained. "It was important that I killed the boys by the manual. It had to be done right." He then stressed that he didn't feel anything when he actually killed Danny—he was simply acting out a well-rehearsed fantasy. "I know it sounds ridiculously cold," Joubert added, describing how he then went to "McDonald's with blood all over my hands, went to the men's washroom, and washed my hands. I then ordered breakfast and ate it. Afterwards I went home, fell into bed, and slept soundly for one or two hours."

Joubert had many of the same characteristics as others within the serial killer study I was working on at the time. He fit a discernable pattern that was becoming clearer and clearer with each case I reviewed. In some ways, researching Joubert's background actually helped verify what I'd suspected from the start: serial killers developed according to a certain logic. That they became a serial killer wasn't totally random or chaotic but rather based more on a twisted design, a blend of the murderer's upbringing, personality, and psychology—all of which combined and caused them to respond to certain triggering situations in horrifically violent ways. Joubert was a textbook example.

Joubert's parents divorced when he was young, and his mother uprooted the family to Maine, where she struggled to make money. Frustrated and angry, Joubert began lashing out. He committed his first series of violent acts over a four-month period when he was just thirteen years old. It started when he stabbed a six-year-old girl with a pencil or screwdriver as she rode past him on her bike. Several weeks later, he used a knife to stab a twenty-seven-year-old woman as she walked past him on the street. And two months after that, he used an X-Acto knife to slash the throat of a nine-year-old boy—the boy survived but needed a dozen stitches to close the two-inch wound. These attacks served as a preliminary test for Joubert as he developed his murderous fantasies.

Joubert said he'd been suffering from violent fantasies for as long as he could remember. The earliest one he could recall was from when he was six. In it, he snuck up behind his babysitter, strangled her, and then gobbled her up until she was all gone. Joubert said he replayed this fantasy in his head over and over, repeating it and improving it throughout his childhood and up to his first murder. He couldn't remember when his fantasies switched from women to young boys. But he did know that fantasy seemed more authentic than reality. Reality had been a series of letdowns and limitations. Fantasy allowed him to indulge his imagination.

Following his arrest, the psychiatrist in charge of evaluating Joubert observed: "He seems so separated from emotional experiences as to suggest some sort of chronic dissociative process. I suspect that he is dimly aware of this defect or lack in himself, and, in part, the homicides were an attempt to experience strong emotions."

Joubert seemed to agree with this assessment. He believed his fantasies were a way of forgetting the episodes of family violence he witnessed while he was young, including multiple incidents of domestic violence between his father and mother. From that point forward, Joubert began to have fantasies anytime he felt stress.

"I would think these thoughts, and that would relieve the tension," he said. "I have learned that it made me feel better, and as I grew up it became a habit."

He also volunteered insights about the age of his victims. "I was very unhappy from age eleven to thirteen, and I think selecting boys that age was like targeting myself."

Other details within the report stood out to me as well and I made sure to include them in our ongoing serial killer study at the FBI. First, as part of his psychiatric testing, Joubert demonstrated both a high IQ and an excellent memory. Second, his retelling of the events was so objective, so detached, and so clinical in manner that it seemed as if he was recalling a movie rather than his own horrific acts of violence. And third, both his thoughts and his actions were extremely well structured.

My takeaway was that Joubert was a bright, meticulous, and well-organized individual with little to no ability to empathize with others. At the same time, he had enough awareness of his differences that he felt deeply isolated because of them. This led Joubert to construct an intricate routine of fantasies in an attempt to bridge his emotional divide with the reality of the world around him. But it wasn't enough. He needed to cause others pain in order to feel any sort of real emotion. And in his pursuit of victims, in his methods of provoking suffering in others, he found a parasitic way of feeling the emotions he had long been denied.

The Joubert case marked a pivotal moment for Douglas, Ressler, and me. Up until then, our main focus had been on interviewing convicted serial killers and analyzing the data as part of our criminal personality study. But by applying the research side of our findings to the investigative technique of criminal profiling, we'd taken the critical next step. We'd demonstrated the untapped potential of real-time criminal profiling to help with even the most urgent investigations. We'd confirmed that profiling, though still in its infancy, could be a powerfully effective tool. And last, though no less important, we'd shown that profiling could be successful even within the complex framework of interagency collaboration—shared resources at the state, local, and federal levels. Profiling worked.

Right away, Ressler began including the Joubert case as part of his Academy assignments to stress how important interagency collaboration could be. And it was during one of these early lectures that a police officer from Portland, Maine, noted the similarities between the Nebraska case and an unresolved case from his jurisdiction. The officer asked to speak with Ressler after class, at which point he went on to explain that the Maine case had taken place while Joubert was still living nearby, three months prior to joining the Air Force. Ressler agreed that the similarities were too coincidental to ignore. He asked for copies of the investigative records and learned that, on August 22, 1982, eleven-year-old Richard "Ricky" Stetson was found murdered from a stab wound and strangulation. What stood out most, however, were the forensic photos of a human bite mark on the victim's leg, which the offender had seemingly attempted to cover up with a series of crisscross slashes. Ressler used this bite-mark analysis to prove that Joubert was responsible for the Stetson murder in Maine in addition to the two murders he committed in Nebraska.

The Joubert case was important on a larger scale, too. It was covered by the national media as the "Woodford Slasher" case, named after Woodford County, Nebraska, where the crimes had occurred. This was the first time the BSU had been in the spotlight like that. And our success earned a nod of approval from the FBI director William Webster himself, who wrote a letter of commendation about the profile's critical role in breaking the case wide open. The national media attention also played a role in the case getting published in the *Congressional Record*, tied to a note saying, "All parties involved deserve the highest commendation."

This public show of support was a huge step forward in validating the Behavioral Science Unit to the FBI at large. Traditionalists in the Bureau still saw profiling as far too academic to make any lasting impact on real-world crimes. But even our staunchest detractors couldn't deny our recent success. We'd proven that there was value in understanding the criminal mind. We were on the right track.

To finally be recognized on a national level was incredibly validating, but to be able to actually use criminal profiling in an active case to hunt down a killer was the most satisfying reward of all. It made all the other stuff—the doubts I'd had, the testing I'd endured, the endless chorus of criticism—seem small and unimportant. We'd used criminal profiling to save an untold number of potential child victims. But this was only the beginning. The 1980s would see a peak in the number of active serial killers, like nothing ever known before. Joubert represented only a glimpse of that violence. For us, the work had just begun.

CHAPTER 3

Profiling the Profilers

Early on, as I learned to navigate both my responsibilities in academia and my new work with the BSU, the frequent flights from Boston to DC were like traveling between two worlds. It was exciting. It felt like those trips were my transition from mild-mannered Professor Burgess to an intrepid agent in the fight against crime. And to take it all a step further, few people knew about my alternate identity. That was important to me because I had a young family that I wanted to keep separate from the deeply unsettling cases I reviewed at the BSU. But compartmentalizing wasn't always easy. I never knew when the agents might call—sometimes with a simple question, and sometimes with an urgent request to "get down here as soon as you can." I had to be ready for whatever came my way. Because, regardless of the day-to-day joys or challenges in my ordinary world, the stakes of those agent calls were often life and death. That was the simple reality of it. And I'd known what I was agreeing to from the start.

I made a habit of keeping a luggage bag packed and ready with basic supplies—a "go bag," as the agents called them—and found myself using it often. Whenever I got a call, I grabbed my things and caught the first flight down. In those days, the twin-engine propeller shuttle from Boston to DC required no reservations. There was no security either. I just picked up my ticket, walked aboard, and settled into my seat. If the plane was full, they promised to "roll another one out." They even provided a sandwich and drink. And when we landed, there was always a driver waiting to pick me up in a nondescript black car. I'd review case materials and notes on the long, long drive to the Academy—the landscape changing from federal buildings, to houses, to forests, and to what finally felt like the middle of nowhere.

This was the late 1970s, shortly after the Academy moved from DC to a Marine Corps base in Quantico, Virginia, forty miles south of the nation's capital. The new site consisted of 547 acres of converted farmland, rolling hills, and humid swamps. It was naturally secluded, with the Potomac River to the east and a stand of old-growth forest to the west. It was quiet. And as the Bureau grew in size, scope, and investigative specialties, Quantico became an increasingly significant asset based on its sheer size alone. In 1969, they started construction on a large-scale complex that would provide state-of-the-art facilities for new-agent training. And by the time I arrived, the FBI had morphed into two distinct branches in two separate locations: DC remained home to headquarters—called the Bureau—while Quantico became home to the Academy—a training division dedicated to classes, marksmanship, lab work, and other specialized research programs.

But Occam's razor cuts both ways. As much as law enforcement was advancing, crime was constantly evolving in sophistication and ingenuity as well. The Bureau knew this and recognized the importance of staying one step ahead. That's what Quantico offered. It expanded the way agents were educated through the use of forensic training, lab work, and staged crime scenes. It emphasized marksmanship and practical shooting techniques within realistic training grounds. And, perhaps most importantly, for the first time in FBI history the Bureau provided dedicated resources for understanding the psychology behind criminal behaviors. Over the past decade, there'd been an alarming surge in the number of unusual cases, such as kidnappings, rapes, and serial murders. The FBI wanted to know why. Thus, the BSU was born—and tasked with the job of figuring it out.

I experienced this modernization of the FBI firsthand during my earliest visits to the BSU as a guest lecturer. It was hard not to be impressed. The new facilities had theater-style auditoriums, twenty-four classrooms, two dormitories, a dining hall, a gym, a state-of-the-art library, and a large firing range. The whole complex was a hive of activity, buzzing not only with agents but also with visiting officers from the military and law enforcement from all over the country. In many ways, it had all the familiarity of a college campus. But here—just as within the Bureau at large—a tradition of discipline and loyalty reigned supreme.

Although my circumstances at the Academy were unique, the standard I was held to wasn't. After all, Quantico was hallowed ground. To enter meant passing a background check, obtaining the right paperwork, and identifying myself with the unmistakably large visitor's badge that kept me accounted for at all times. It also meant subjecting myself to the Bureau's relentless scrutiny and hierarchal methods of operation. This was something I learned right away, during one of my first lecture visits. I had arrived late at night, signed in, and was escorted to a special guestroom in the smaller of two dorms, where I quickly fell asleep. After what felt like mere minutes, I was suddenly jolted awake by a reveille-like barrage of guns blasting no more than a hundred yards away. It was six a.m. The firing range had just opened. But despite how startling it was to wake up that way, I knew I could never mention it to the agents. I needed to prove myself both flexible and fully composed in this new terrain. This was just another test to see how I'd cope with the unexpected elements of the job.

My initiation phase at the FBI Academy lasted about three years—starting with that first call from Hazelwood in 1978 and ending with the success of the Joubert case in the early eighties. That's how I transitioned from lecturing at the Academy to joining the more specialized team of agents in the BSU. At least, that's the official story of how I ended up there—few people knew about all the off-the-record work I'd been doing since almost the first moment I stepped foot in the door helping agents develop their side projects. Still, I was just excited to be part of the team. I joined Ressler as codirector of the criminal personality study, which we'd broken up into the serial killer study and the profiling process. And thanks to recent grant funding from the National Institute of Justice, I was responsible for overseeing the criminal personality study's budget and design, as well as the research direction of eight project staff at Boston City Hospital, where the study's data entry, statistical analysis, and interview and profiling sessions transcription took place.

It was Hazelwood who first greeted me after I got the news that I was in. He was anxious to share the excitement with the rest of the BSU down in their subterranean offices near the infamous bomb shelter. So he took me on a shortcut to the elevators, leading me through the building's fully stocked gunroom, where an instructor was holding a tutorial for agents-in-training as we passed. The group immediately stopped and stared at us.

"It's all right," Hazelwood said. "She's with us."

I smiled, pausing a moment to take it all in. That was the first time I'd felt as confident in my role in the Bureau as I was in the value of my work.

But the moment didn't last long. "Hey, Ann, what are you standing around for?" Hazelwood asked.

I hurried to join him in the elevator just as he pushed an unmarked button that took us down, down, down to the familiar subterranean floor. When the doors finally opened, Douglas was there to meet us with a joke.

"Congratulations, Ann. You're now an official member of the National Cellar for the Analysis of Violent Crimes," he said. "Below sixty feet of soil, we're ten times deeper than dead people down here."

The agents all laughed. I joined in as well, but it struck me as odd that the FBI tucked us out of sight and left us to our own devices. We were several stories belowground in a windowless space originally designed as a secure site for federal law enforcement officials to retreat to in the event of a national emergency. No one checked on us, and few people even knew we were there. It spoke volumes. Despite the Bureau's new interest in figuring out the meaning behind criminal behaviors, and despite our success on a few early profiling cases, the work itself was still too unproven to garner much in the way of resources or support. It was up to us to demonstrate the consistency and wider application of our work. We'd simply have to do it on our own.

This isolation, I quickly noticed, played a formative role in the very identity of the BSU. All of the agents had their own unique teaching assignments* and all of them were fully committed to developing their own specialized research projects as well. They worked hard. But at the same time, their lack of shared responsibilities brought out a fierce sense of independence among them. It also meant that they rarely all came together as a unit. The exception was when we received unprecedented cases that required multiple opinions from

---

* In addition to teaching full-time at the Academy, BSU agents were responsible for occasional two-week "road school" assignments. Road school was done in pairs and consisted of the two agents traveling to the assigned city on Sunday, teaching for the full workweek, and then moving on to a second city to teach for the second week.

specialized backgrounds, things like arson, bombings, or ritualistic violence. And yet, after tallying up a few early successes in this arena, we began to see more and more of these unprecedented cases sent our way. We were quickly gaining a reputation as the FBI's go-to source for the strangest cases that no one else could solve. This impacted the BSU's dynamics. It was a subtle change at first. But despite each agent maintaining their individual interests, our collective sense of purpose was bringing us closer as a team.

The other shared characteristic I noticed among the agents of the BSU was their distrust of authority. It wasn't that they were outright defiant or anything like that. It was more a habit of being elusive or misleading in situations when it played to their favor. This was most visible in how they treated their own unit chief, Roger Depue. Depue was a pioneering member of the BSU who served as an instructor and administrator after rising up the ranks to become unit chief in the late 1970s. He made his way by following orders and staying out of trouble. And although he was well liked and respected by the agents, he struggled to keep them in line. He called them stubborn, and he once described his job as similar to coaching a football team made up of only quarterbacks, adding that the agents "were all different with very strong ideas about what they wanted to do and how to do it."

Depue's assessment hit the nail on the head. The agents as I came to know them were a rare collection of personalities. For the Bureau, they were different in terms of not only their characters and interests but also their backgrounds—how they ended up at the FBI. Still, they were bound together by a common thread: They each had an innate understanding of criminal psychology. None of them was formally trained in studying human thoughts or behaviors—they just had a knack for it. It clicked. I saw it in the way they analyzed investigative materials, detected patterns of behavior, and were sought after by field teams to help quickly interpret crimes and their motives. These agents were good at their jobs, and their enthusiasm for their work extended beyond the day-to-day tasks. They all wanted to develop their unique skills into something more.

But there was a catch. Collectively, the BSU had enormous potential to reimagine how the FBI applied psychology to criminal violence. They just had to start seeing themselves as a team first. And to do that, the agents needed to recognize what each of them could offer to the group as a whole. I figured that, by learning about them as individuals and collaborating with them on their interests, I could help speed up the process. It didn't take long before I was involved in joint projects with each of the team's four "first-generation profilers," as they were known within the unit: Roy Hazelwood, Ken Lanning, John Douglas, and Robert Ressler.

Hazelwood was one of the longest-standing agents of the BSU. Originally from Idaho, he had a military background and had joined the FBI in 1971. He was Midwestern friendly in a way that stood out from the severity of other agents. He was funny, too, and enjoyed telling the story of how he ended up in the unit. It happened during the winter of 1978. Hazelwood had just completed the FBI's Management Aptitude Program, and his high marks in executive expertise made him a premier candidate for transfer to a field office of his own. But Hazelwood wanted to stay in Virginia, where he had a house and was raising a family. He decided to put in for the only available assignment stationed in Quantico at that time: the sex crimes instructor's slot at the BSU. He got the job, and when he started that January, he was taken down to the lower levels of the building to a converted mop closet in the darkest, most remote corner of the subterranean complex—his new office. He turned on the light and saw a pair of black lace panties nailed to the wall above his desk as a welcome gift.

Hazelwood stuck it out and quickly became known for his detailed expertise on sex crimes and sexual killers. He had an inquisitive mind, and his willingness to ask questions made him a perfect fit for the BSU. These qualities also made him a natural for doing research. And just a few months into the job, while reviewing the infamous Harvey Glatman case* for perspective on a current case, Hazelwood started asking questions that no one seemed able to answer: Why did Glatman tie his victims in various positions and take photographs in various stages of undress? Where did he learn such things and why was he aroused by them? Why did he tie a victim's legs entirely instead of just her ankles? As Hazelwood dug through a box of FBI case files, he felt there was still something to be learned from Glatman. He couldn't shake the feeling that there was a reason why people committed acts of sexual violence and that it was important to understand exactly what that reason was. Knowing a killer's past, he reasoned, could offer insights into who they became and why. He found a clue in Glatman's childhood.

One document within the files described an incident in which Glatman's mother had found her young son with one end of a string tied to his penis and the other end shut in a dresser drawer. Years later, when he was still an adolescent, Glatman's parents found him again practicing autoerotic asphyxia, this time in the bathtub, with both his penis and his neck tied to the faucet. During the original investigation, no one had connected these early behaviors to the sexual killings Glatman committed later in life. But to Hazelwood, the connection was clear.

In 1979, at a group meeting, Hazelwood asked BSU chief Larry Monroe for permission to study autoerotic fatalities and see how they connected to other atypical behaviors. Monroe was silent. Hazelwood tried to explain the importance of the work but was

---

* Glatman was a serial killer who was active in the late fifties and was known for taking photos of victims as he sexually assaulted and then killed them.

quickly interrupted with a sharp question: "Why would studying such a rare phenomenon [about fifteen hundred deaths a year] merit the FBI's time and resources?" Hazelwood gave two reasons to support the study. On the one hand, it would bring closure to the families of the victims, who were often devastated by the circumstances of these types of deaths. On the other, police departments needed to differentiate between homicides, suicides, and accidental deaths. Mistaking an autoerotic death for suicide was an avoidable mistake that could save more time and resources than his research would ever cost. Monroe nodded and Hazelwood was given approval, with the condition that he'd make his findings available to the greater law enforcement community.

Hazelwood dove right in to his research. He requested law enforcement students at the Academy find and submit cases representing autoerotic fatalities that had occurred since 1970. He asked that they include investigative reports along with either a description or photographs of the scene of death. Within three years, he received reports of 157 autoerotic fatalities. He asked me and Nick Groth (a psychologist who worked in correctional settings and was lecturing on rapists at the FBI Academy) for our help. We were interested, but neither of us knew what autoerotic fatalities were. In fact, no one seemed to know much about them at all. Hazelwood was the only person who'd given any thought to the issue. He'd had to develop his understanding of these cases from the ground up, categorizing them as accidental sexual deaths attributable to airway obstruction, chest compression, chemicals or gas, or electrical stimulation—all in service to sexual stimulation.

After Nick and I agreed to assist, the three of us spent evenings at Quantico designing a data assessment survey that could be applied to each case. We ran into a problem early when Nick realized he couldn't bring himself to look at the photos of dead bodies. But my curiosity outweighed my apprehension. And my experience of working with victims of rape had taught me how to focus on the data rather than the horror—I'd learned to stomach the trauma because I knew I could help. So we divided the work in such a way that I'd view, analyze, and sort the photos into specific categories while Nick entered the data.

Once we had assessed all 157 cases, we went on to make our findings available to law enforcement just like Monroe had asked. But it wasn't easy to spread the information on this little-known topic. When lecture requests came in from local police departments, Hazelwood—now recognized for his unique understanding of the connections between self-stimulating behaviors and acts of violence or death—would list the topics on offer, making a point of emphasizing the topic of autoerotic fatalities. One police chief, in particular, took a moment before saying: "We don't have too many traffic deaths down here."

Hazelwood's office may have been a converted mop closet, but things could have been worse. Ken Lanning was proof of that. As the most junior member of the team, Lanning had to make do with a former storage space that didn't even have a door. What it did have, however, was the good fortune of being located directly across from Douglas and Ressler. That's how Lanning learned the ropes. He spent days and weeks listening to the two senior agents analyzing all the details of their cases. Like a sponge, he took in everything they said. And over time, case by case, those sessions built his education as a profiler. He once told me it was the best training he'd ever had.

Lanning grew up in the Bronx and spent most of his childhood involved in a government-sponsored FBI youth club, of which he notably became president when he was only ten years old. He did well in school, was a star competitive swimmer, and graduated from Manhattan College just as the war in Vietnam was intensifying. He knew he had to make a decision, so he enlisted in the Navy and qualified to attend its Officer Candidate School, where he took on additional responsibilities by volunteering for a specialized program that involved dismantling underwater munitions and improvised explosive devices. That's where Lanning crossed paths with the FBI. Two agents from the Bureau's Explosive Unit witnessed Lanning's skills firsthand while visiting the Navy's Explosive Ordnance Disposal program at Indian Head, Maryland. They kept tabs on him. And after his three years of service were up, Lanning received a recruitment letter for a probationary appointment as an FBI special agent—pending testing—with a starting salary of $10,252 per year. It was the job he'd always wanted.

Over the next ten years, Lanning gained considerable experience as a field investigator in offices all around the country. He excelled at his work and was valued for his dedication. This paid off in December of 1980, when Lanning was assigned a supervisory special agent position with the BSU at the FBI Academy. He saw the upside immediately. He could now develop his own research, offer case consultation, or lecture incoming agents on what he'd learned over a decade in the field. But despite all of his plans, his doorless office set him on a different path instead. It prepared him to become a highly skilled criminal profiler.

Lanning's personality was inseparable from his work. He was even-keeled and professional, a deep thinker who always had his brain in gear before he opened his mouth to talk. And his calm temperament made him well suited to handle exactly the type of disturbing crimes that the BSU was known for solving. So, in early 1981, when Hazelwood approached him about collaborating on a research project to understand why criminals committed acts of sexual violence, Lanning accepted without hesitation. This was his chance to make a name for himself in the BSU. Other agents were taking on similar projects, and Lanning saw this as his ticket to prove he was more than just the new guy learning the ropes. Still, I sometimes wondered if Lanning truly knew what he was getting himself into. He agreed to focus on child cases, while Hazelwood specialized in cases of adults. And though both of these crimes are the stuff of nightmares, I knew from my own experience that child cases were unmistakably the most difficult to bear.

The central focus of Lanning's work was a behavioral analysis of child predators. He looked at the demographics and individual histories of these individuals, then analyzed the patterns of their motives and actions to develop a typology—he was determined to resolve the confusion of the terms *child molester* and *pedophile*. This research led to a new understanding of the highly predictable behaviors of child offenders, which Lanning categorized into two types: situational child molesters and preferential child molesters. Over time, the insights from Lanning's research became extremely valuable tools for investigators of child cases. And his work led to a new frame of reference for an often-underreported crime that was extremely difficult to prosecute given the "he said, she said" nature of testimony from a child versus from an adult.

I always felt that one of the greatest contributions Lanning made to the field was realizing how traumatic it was for children to testify in open court. For that reason, he stressed the need for law enforcement to build their cases independently of the victim, compiling enough evidence that the perpetrator would plead guilty without undergoing a trial at all.

Lanning's work ethic and steely exterior eventually earned him a reputation as the Bureau's expert on crimes against children. He taught a course that explained the behavioral analysis component of these types of cases, and he became a sought-after resource for field agents working on similar crimes. His work was specifically noticed by the National Center for Missing and Exploited Children (NCMEC). They wanted him to develop a set of resource materials outlining what he'd learned so that it could be shared with law enforcement, prosecutors, social workers, healthcare professionals, and others for educational and training purposes. Lanning was interested, but he had no reference for how the process would look or what was involved. He asked if I'd help, and together we wrote an article for the *Law Enforcement Bulletin* on child pornography and child sex rings. From there, Lanning developed a monograph for the NCMEC that broke down the signs and behaviors of child molesters through a deep and comprehensive analysis. It introduced new concepts such as "grooming" and "seduction." And it quickly became an important investigative tool used by law enforcement around the country.

Lanning was always quick to credit his success to the BSU's "group of dedicated, intelligent, self-motivated, overachieving, and egotistical agents who were able to achieve in spite of upper management that often did not understand, care about, or agree with what the agents were doing." And despite his frustrations with the higher-ups at the FBI—something we all experienced at one point or another because of the novel nature of our work—this description of the team rang true. Especially the part about "egotistical," which I'm sure was a friendly jab at his neighbor in the office across the hall.

John Douglas was another New Yorker. But his family moved from Brooklyn to the suburbs when he was only ten years old to escape the city's rising crime rates. He was a talented high school athlete who went on to study at Montana State University. His grades ended up becoming an issue, though, and Douglas "bombed out" (his words) before moving back home to New York. He was quickly drafted into the Air Force, completed a tour of service, finished his undergrad degree, and was then accepted into a graduate program for industrial psychology at Eastern New Mexico University. In the absence of a social life, Douglas joined a gym near campus, where he met FBI field agent Frank Haines. Frank took a liking to Douglas right away. He told stories about being an agent and encouraged Douglas to apply. Douglas did, but despite the strength of his application and the fact that he was in excellent physical shape, he was considered ineligible until he got his weight down below the Bureau's limit of 195. He claimed he spent two weeks eating nothing but Jell-O and hard-boiled eggs—plus three haircuts to look the part—until he was deemed presentable enough to sit for an ID photo. It was 1970 and Douglas was only twenty-five years old, which was considered young for an agent at the time.

Douglas possessed a combination of sincerity and bravado that was easy to gravitate toward. He was generally well liked, but his strong personality offered very little middle ground, and his detractors were often vocal in their opinions. His work, however, was beyond reproach. He put in long hours, studied every case he could, and was constantly questioning and trying to improve processes and procedures. This reputation for getting things done led to an assignment as a special agent with the BSU in June of 1977. The job came with an orientation period during which Douglas was eased into the unit through an apprenticeship of sorts with senior agent Ressler. The arrangement wasn't punitive by any means, it was just how the BSU operated—senior members took new recruits under their wing and led by example. And besides, it not only was effective for training new agents quickly but also helped develop a strong sense of trust between newer and veteran members of the same team. This unique sense of cohesiveness, I noticed, was a defining characteristic of the BSU. It was impressive to see. And I was certain it would pay dividends in the challenging days that were sure to lie ahead.

As part of the apprenticeship process, Douglas and Ressler were required to complete a series of two-week road school assignments to provide training to selected law enforcement groups around the country. These sessions were in high demand, and the backlog of requests was several months long. Most of the agents, however, were less enthused about road school. It was monotonous. They taught the same classes on the road that they taught back home in Quantico. So, as Douglas and Ressler racked up hours traveling across the country to teach local agencies about applied criminal psychology, they welcomed opportunities for distraction. This usually took the form of beers and small talk with local police after class. And it was through this that Douglas and Ressler began hearing stories about unusual homicides that the small-town authorities had been unable to solve. Many of these cases were bizarre. None of them made sense. And the majority were dismissed as random acts of violence. But Douglas thought differently about these cases. He thought there had to be some sort of reason behind them. Some sort of logic that would make sense if he could just figure out what it was.

Douglas decided the best way to do this was to go directly to the source—to visit prisons and speak with similar offenders who'd already been caught. Ressler, who was already in the habit of interviewing prison inmates to learn about their crimes, told Douglas he was welcome to tag along. That was in 1979. They knew then that there were answers locked away inside convicted criminals' heads, but they didn't know what questions to ask or how to make sense of all the violent stories told in gleeful remembrance. They spent the next few years struggling to figure it out.

Robert Ressler was born and raised in Chicago. He was active in the ROTC program at Michigan State, graduated, and then moved back home to join the Chicago Police Department. But he was told that the force "wasn't interested in recruits with too much schooling, because they might make trouble." Frustrated, Ressler decided to take a post with the Army as provost marshal of a platoon of military police in Germany. He was good at his job and stayed for a second assignment that involved undercover work infiltrating groups that were resisting the Vietnam War. He even grew his hair long and portrayed a disgruntled veteran at protest meetings to blend in. His plan was to stay in the military for the rest of his career, but friends in the FBI convinced him to join the Bureau in 1970.

Ressler brought high-level military experience to the Bureau. He was recognized as smart, disciplined, and a natural leader. These traits caught the attention of Howard Teten and Patrick Mullany, two senior agents with a reputation for using the unconventional strategy of profiling to narrow in on criminal suspects. Teten and Mullany were pioneers in an early form of criminal profiling that hypothesized that crime scenes offered more than just physical clues about the responsible offender. The two of them had created a training course known as the "criminal psychology program." And in 1972, they helped establish the Behavioral Science Unit. But Teten and Mullany favored instinct over methodology. They saw profiling as a process that was fundamentally grounded in how much experience an agent had. To them, it was case reports that mattered most, not research. And they made a habit of leaning on untenable assumptions, such as defining unsubs by their likely mental disorders, which tended to do more harm than good.

Regardless of these early flaws, Teten and Mullany were convinced of the merits of their work. They saw its potential and wanted to develop it further by testing it on an active case. And in the mid-1970s, they brought in Ressler to help them do exactly that. Ressler, with his background as a military investigator catching criminals for the US Army, joined the BSU as a supervisory special agent. It was an ideal fit.

Ressler absorbed what he could from Teten and Mullany. But profiling was something he had to squeeze in behind a long list of more immediate topics tasked to the BSU: applied criminal psychology, contemporary police problems, abnormal psychology, sex crimes, hostage negotiations, criminology, and interviewing techniques. The newly formed unit had its hands full. This meant that, for the time being, profiling remained academic—relegated to informal case colloquiums in the late evenings after work, when young agents and students would speak with Teten, Mullany, and Ressler about their most unusual, unsolved crimes.

But that all changed when Douglas and Ressler finally crossed paths in 1977. The two clicked. And when Ressler described his new vision of criminal profiling as the use of psychology to understand "the force that takes a hold of a person and pushes them over the edge," Douglas was hooked. Shortly afterward, the two of them began spending their nights and weekends interviewing convicted killers to learn how they thought. But their progress was slow. That's why Ressler took an interest in me. He saw value in my experience studying and analyzing rape, as well as my work with Hazelwood on autoerotic deaths. Profiling needed that same systematic approach if it was ever to reach its fullest potential. Ressler understood this, and he saw that I could help.

A few other agents belonged to what became known as the first generation of profilers, but I rarely worked with them—and they rarely worked with the other profilers—because of a lack of overlap in research interests. One was Unit Chief Roger Depue, who was too busy trying to manage the unit to take on any of his own research. Also, for a brief period before their retirements, my time at the BSU overlapped with Mullany's and Teten's. And then there were partners Richard (Dick) Ault and Jim Reese. Both Ault and Reese became excellent profilers who believed in the importance of their work. We shared an equally mutual respect. And although we never formally collaborated, they sometimes asked for my opinions on their research, which focused on educating the police community about the concept of profiling and the importance of considering the psychological aspects of any crime. They were practical and evidence-based in their approach. And they were funny, too. They once concluded an article with a disclaimer that "profiles are not the result of magical incantations and are not always accurate."

My role on the team was different for more than a few reasons. Most importantly, I was an outsider. I wasn't an agent or a profiler. I'd simply been a quick-fix solution enabling the Academy to address a lack of understanding of rising trends in sexual crimes. But chance is a funny thing. I'd spent years being told that my interest in the psychology of victims and their offenders was "taboo" or "dangerous" or "not a place for women to get involved." And from what I knew about the male-dominated world of the FBI, I expected my lectures to be met with more of the same. But in many ways, the BSU was a cast of outsiders, too. They were the rogue agents, the idealists with big ideas, and they wouldn't let the limits of convention or bureaucratic traditions stand in their way. In me, they saw an ally.

For my part, from my unique vantage point of coming in from the outside, I saw the group's unrealized potential to accomplish something important. I knew what a rare opportunity we had if we could just come together as a team. And whenever I could, I tried to encourage a sense of solidarity. But it wasn't easy. Basic Bureau rules discouraged discussion of personal issues and strictly forbade gossiping. Even certain working information was limited to a "need-to-know" basis. So many layers were stacked between us.

Still, at their core, the agents saw their work as a mission, and they understood we were in this project together. The Bureau had invested in us and taken a chance on our collective success. In turn, we were determined to prove the merits of our work through long days and a tireless resolve.

By the early eighties, I had taken a position at the University of Pennsylvania as the van Ameringen Chair in Psychiatric and Mental Health Nursing. It was a quick commute to Quantico, and so I found myself making the trip more regularly, working with the agents side by side. We met for breakfast each morning in the Academy's cafeteria to focus on the day's tasks, went back for lunch to assess what was accomplished and what remained for the afternoon, and often stayed well past five to tie up any loose ends. At the end of most days, we gravitated to the Academy's pub, where the rule was "no talking shop." This was the ritual. There was beer on tap and a relaxed atmosphere. The talk focused on sports and exciting cases from the past. The agents listened to my stories about the rape study, and I listened to their stories about elusive criminals who almost got away. Then, slowly, one by one, we got in our cars and left. The agents didn't take their work home with them. Their wives had no idea about the horrors that consumed their days. The secrets of the project went unspoken. And it was those secrets—the ones among us and the ones we carried on our own—that bound us together. In everything we couldn't say, we became a team.

CHAPTER 4

Reading the Crime Scene

Every investigation starts at the crime scene. It's a record of what happened, how it happened, and who was involved. But the language of a crime scene can sometimes be difficult to understand. It's shaped by discord and violence and the impermanence of the past. It's an echo. And although investigators have been aided by paradigm-shifting advances in technology within the last hundred years—such as high-tech cameras, fingerprint identification repositories, and machines capable of DNA analysis—criminals have become equally skilled at leaving behind fewer traces of themselves. It's an arms race, a game of cat and mouse where the thrill of the chase often stimulates offenders as much as the crime itself. But an unexpected shift in the offender–investigator dynamic began taking place in the late 1960s. It started with a few individual investigators applying basic elements of criminal profiling to their work. They realized that crime scenes could shed light on an offender's defining characteristic, even in situations where little traditional evidence was left behind.

At its core, criminal profiling is well grounded in traditional understandings of psychology, behavior, and the mind. It just applies these understandings differently by using action to predict character rather than character to predict action. It takes the approach that a person's way of thinking—their pattern of thinking—directs their behaviors in predictable and quantifiable ways. Therefore, a deliberate and structured analysis of an uncompromised crime scene can reveal critical factors that suggest the offender's likely motive, which, in turn, helps characterize the specific type of person who committed the crime. In other words: if you know how to read the crime scene, you can better understand the criminal who left it behind.

Informally, investigators had been analyzing crime scenes to find clues about perpetrators since the late 1950s. That's when the FBI recruited James Brussel, a former Bureau counterespionage ace turned Freudian psychiatrist, to help them solve New York's infamous "Mad Bomber" case. The city was under siege with bombs in high-profile locations: Grand Central Terminal, the New York Public Library, and Radio City Music Hall. Flurries of attacks would be followed by long stretches of inactivity. Local police were stumped. Brussel, they figured, was at least a fresh pair of eyes. So, in December of 1956, NYC bomb squad commander Captain Howard Finney took the unprecedented step of handing Brussel sixteen years' worth of materials—crime scene photos, case reports, and letters from the bomber himself—to see if anything stood out.

For his part, Brussel was confident he could help. He had a theory that serial offenders revealed glimpses of their identity through their behavior. He called his approach "reverse psychology" and saw it as a way of finding logic in a killer's head. Brussel did this by combining deductive reasoning, intuition, a careful review of the evidence, and Freudian theory to piece together a description of who the police should be looking for. In the case of the Mad Bomber, Brussel saw the misshapen curve of the capital *W*s in the handwritten letters to be a breast-shaped symbol of sexual frustration. He reasoned that the offender's clunky writing style pointed to an individual who was foreign-born. And he added that the use of bombs as the killer's weapon of choice could be culturally tied to someone of eastern European descent. He described the offender as a middle-aged man, foreign-born, unmarried, likely living with his mother. Then, in what would later be considered an iconic moment of prescience for future BSU agents, Brussel offered a final clue: "One more thing. When you catch him—and I have no doubt you will—he'll be wearing a double-breasted suit. Buttoned." One month later, police arrested George Metesky in connection to the New York City bombings. He matched Brussel's description in almost every way, right down to the neatly buttoned double-breasted suit. It was uncanny.

This first act of criminal profiling in which an investigator used only case materials and his own rationale to create a detailed description of who'd committed a crime stood alone and unrepeated for more than a decade. But in 1972—the same year the FBI finished construction on the new Academy in Quantico, Virginia— the Bureau showed renewed interest in the technique through the launch of its Behavioral Science Unit and by tasking the new team with, among other things, "the development of profiling." This was a small step with big implications. For starters, it was the first time the FBI had officially recognized criminal profiling as a viable investigative strategy. And despite the fact that profiling was only one part of the group's broader directive, the BSU's newly minted unit chiefs— Howard Teten, a former California detective, and FBI instructor Patrick J. Mullany—could see its potential bubbling just beneath the surface. So they ran with it.

Teten in particular had a great admiration for Brussel's reverse psychology technique and the success it had on the Mad Bomber case. He read every article he could find—many of which referred to

Brussel as "the Sherlock Holmes of the couch"—with the hopes of gaining insights into how the process worked. But none of the articles could explain the process. So, in 1973, he drove from Quantico to New York to visit the then-retired Brussel with an offer: Teten would pay the psychoanalyst's hourly rate in exchange for lessons on how reverse psychology worked. Brussel laughed. He said the FBI couldn't afford his rates, but he agreed to help regardless. The sessions that followed set the course for Teten and Mullany's tenure at the BSU. They saw Brussel as a visionary. And they wanted to develop his technique into an investigative tool that could benefit the Bureau agencywide.

Despite the enthusiasm of its new unit chiefs, the FBI's decision to institutionalize profiling—as small and minimally funded as the new BSU was—wasn't without criticism. Public perception at the time considered the technique to be more artifice than science. Newspapers quoted Brussel himself as saying: "I closed my eyes . . . I saw the Bomber: impeccably neat, absolutely proper. . . . I knew I was letting my imagination get the better of me, but I couldn't help it." And much of the old guard within the Bureau cracked jokes about not needing a profile to know who was mentally ill. But perception didn't dictate need. Field investigators across the country noted a disturbing rise in violence and clamored for new techniques to help them better understand what was going on. Their reports described cases as more bizarre, more unpredictable, and much more complex. This was especially true for violent crimes against strangers, extremely difficult cases to solve which were occurring more frequently than ever before. It was clear that criminals were changing their approaches. Investigators needed to change theirs as well.

Teten and Mullany saw criminal profiling as the answer to this new wave of irrational crimes. They'd seen how Brussel's technique could ascertain behavioral patterns and characteristics of an unknown serial offender; they just had to clearly establish a process for how the technique could work. What they developed was a method for linking crime scene evidence to the specific type of perpetrator likely involved. It was a somewhat crude approach—relying too heavily on assigning mental disorders to potential suspects—but it was promising in how it helped investigators create a rough composite of a suspect's physical, emotional, and social traits, such as age, occupation, and past criminal record. The technique showed early success in helping local police solve a difficult stabbing case; Teten looked at the evidence and correctly pointed investigators to an adolescent who lived close by. And when this early accomplishment gained the attention of the FBI, Teten and Mullany were given an opportunity to further prove the efficacy of this technique with a case of their own.

The BSU's first profiling assignment involved a child abduction near Bozeman, Montana. In the summer of 1973, seven-year-old Susan Jaeger was taken from a campsite at a popular state park. The offender cut right through the fabric of the girl's tent and abducted her while her parents slept in their own tent nearby. Local investigators had performed an extensive search over the course of several months, but they failed to locate the missing child. By 1974, the case went cold, and it was reluctantly turned over to the BSU—a decision made more out of desperation than confidence. It was now in the hands of Teten, Mullany, and the unit's newest recruit, Robert Ressler.

The BSU team used their primary principle of profiling ("behavior reflects personality") to characterize the kidnapper as a young white male who lived locally in the Bozeman area. They described him as a homicidal Peeping Tom, a sex-motivated killer who would mutilate his victims after death and sometimes take body parts as souvenirs. Mullany later recalled that, based on growing experience with these types of cases, "we felt the killer was a subtle combination of simple schizophrenia and a psychopath, murdering for the sheer purpose of exploring body parts." The description matched the investigation's main suspect, David Meirhofer, a twenty-two-year-old Vietnam veteran who was known to local police for his obsessive interest in staring at children as they played games in the street.* But there was no strong evidence linking the suspect to the crime. Without evidence, the investigators' hands were tied.

The break in the case came several months later, when eighteen-year-old Sandra Dykman Smallegan went missing from the same area. Smallegan had gone on several dates with Meirhofer, but, somewhat abruptly, she began refusing his advances. After an intensive two-day search, pieces of her body were discovered in a barn on the outskirts of town. She'd been severed into parts, burned, and her remains were then concealed within a barrel. When Meirhofer was brought in for questioning, he denied any involvement and even volunteered to take a lie detector test while under the influence of sodium pentothal, a commonly used "truth serum" of the time. He passed the test with flying colors, and this seemed to exonerate him in the eyes of the local police.

The BSU, on the other hand, was less convinced of Meirhofer's innocence. They considered him to be a calculating psychopath with enough control over his emotions that he could pass a simple polygraph test. They were convinced that Meirhofer was somehow involved. His actions followed a familiar pattern. After all, experience had taught the BSU that killers often sought out ways to insert themselves into the investigation, as Meirhofer had done by readily volunteering to take the lie detector test. It was how killers monitored the progress of their case and tried to stay ahead of the investigators. But their interest also exposed them.

On the basis of Meirhofer's obsession with watching local children,

---

* Police logs showed numerous records of neighborhood parents complaining about Meirhofer's "unusual interest" in their children.

his history with the second victim, and his eagerness to insert himself into the case, the agents set to work refining their original profile of the unsub—a new step for the team, and one that would become important to the process. Upon a second look, they added a key new detail: as an obsessive, the offender would likely enjoy reliving his crimes over and over in his head. That accounted for Meirhofer's interest in following the investigation. And it helped explain the serial nature of the attacks. So, on a hunch, they made a prediction that the killer would likely call the victim's family on the anniversary of the kidnapping because of the date's emotional significance. Teten's rationale was that "because the kidnapper would covet the girl for himself, he'd call the family." This vague explanation for such a specific prediction—one clearly grounded in instinct rather than methodology—showed how undeveloped profiling was at the time. Nonetheless, Teten told the Jaeger family to be prepared. He recommended that they keep a tape recorder next to their telephone, just in case.

As it happened, the killer did call on the first anniversary of the kidnapping. His tone with Mrs. Jaeger was full of disdain and superiority as he teased the bereaved mother about buying the now eight-year-old Susan a birthday present and implied she was still alive, far away in Europe. He even included a detail about the girl's birth defect of "humpy fingernails" to prove he was the abductor. The profiling team immediately recruited an FBI voice analyst to review the tape. The analyst concluded that the voice was likely Meirhofer's, but this FBI-backed conclusion wasn't enough. At the time, the laws in Montana didn't consider this assessment as justifiable evidence for issuing a probable-cause search warrant or making an arrest. Frustrated, the BSU shifted their strategy and ventured into unfamiliar terrain. As Mullany later said, "It was a last-ditch thing. But after listening to that tape, I felt that Meirhofer could be woman-dominated. I suggested that Mrs. Jaeger go to Montana and confront him." This proactive approach, they hoped, would get Meirhofer to break down and confess to the crime.

Mrs. Jaeger agreed, and the meeting was easily arranged. But despite Mrs. Jaeger's pleading for answers about her daughter, Meirhofer remained calm and barely spoke. Several hours after returning home, however, Mrs. Jaeger received a collect phone call from a "Mr. Travis," who tried to explain that he knew about her daughter's abduction. But before the caller could utter another word, Mrs. Jaeger interrupted and said plainly, "Well, hello, David. What a surprise to hear from you." Confronted at last, Meirhofer began to weep, then hung up.

In the days that followed, Mrs. Jaeger gave a sworn affidavit describing the similarities between the anonymous calls she'd received and her meeting with Meirhofer. With her witness testimony in hand, investigators finally had enough to obtain a search warrant. In Meirhofer's home, they found hidden remains of multiple female victims, including the fingers of Meirhofer's ex-girlfriend. There was no hiding anymore. Meirhofer was arrested. He showed no emotion as he confessed to both killings, as well as to the murders of two young boys who'd disappeared several years back. Within days of his incarceration, Meirhofer hanged himself with the towels from his cell. His transition from showing no emotion during his confession to suddenly killing himself—a display of absolute emotion—indicated a preplanned motive to commit suicide if he ever got caught. Ultimately, he had emotions only for himself.

The Meirhofer conviction marked the first time a serial killer was arrested with the aid of the FBI's new profiling technique. Its shoot-from-the-hip approach may not have been the most correct textbook example of profiling, and there wasn't always a clear connection between analysis and prediction, but the case was validating, nonetheless. It proved that behavioral analysis had the potential to one day be a viable investigative tool.

"If it wasn't for profiling," Ressler said, "we never would have identified the most likely suspect in this case. He would have just kept killing. There were so many reasons for the field agents to give up on Meirhofer. But this was the right answer."

Still, although Meirhofer generally fit the profile of the unsub investigators were looking for, the overall methodology and execution of the technique needed a lot of work. Those who looked closely at the case found it difficult to see any clear connection between analysis and the profilers' predictions. In fact, many aspects of the case seemed to be made up on the fly. Comments, such as Mullany's remark, "I felt that Meirhofer could be woman-dominated," showed how much the agents still relied on the conviction of their own beliefs rather than any guiding systematic approach. To a degree, they were simply buying in to their own myth of infallible G-men—convinced that instinct and experience could overcome any gaps in understanding or knowledge. That was the Bureau's culture in the seventies. Few people bothered to question it.

But Ressler was an exception. Early on, he saw past this stylized bravado and understood that profilers needed more than just instinct to carry out successful investigations. They needed a frame of reference to draw from. He saw firsthand that the more information the BSU amassed on violent criminals, the better the agents became at their work. Past cases could offer a baseline of understanding for current cases. This was part of the reason he took on Douglas as an apprentice in the late seventies—it was an opportunity to share knowledge and information with a brand-new profiler who had no preconceptions. And it was the same reason he took an interest in me soon thereafter. Ressler recognized that the questions embedded in my work on the rape study were aimed at uncovering the motivation within a crime. He was impressed by how I'd managed to ground an infinitely complex human trauma into quantifiable data and research. And he believed I could apply these same methods to understanding the seemingly irrational nature of serial killer minds as well. More importantly, he believed in me.

⬥ ◦ ◾ ◦ ⬥

Ressler and I hit it off right from the start and quickly developed a mutual appreciation for each other. I valued his vision for criminal profiling, and he valued how meticulously I approached the behind-the-scenes research that informed every aspect of how profiling worked. We were in constant communication to help close the gap between analysis and investigations. And when the stakes were at their highest, he trusted me as a confidante more than anyone else. That was the situation we found ourselves in one May morning in the early 1980s. Ressler and Unit Chief Depue had a status report meeting with Deputy Director Josephs and a few other higher-ups later that afternoon. The purpose of the meeting was vague, and Ressler was worried that our project might get shut down. He needed proof that interviewing thirty-six serial killers as part of the criminal personality study was starting to pay dividends.

"Hey, Ann," he greeted me first thing that morning. "Remind me again about the data tool. I need a quick summary of how exactly that helps with evaluating the individual killers in the study."

Ressler was wearing a new suit and a freshly starched collared shirt. He looked sharp, but I could tell he hadn't slept.

"We collected quantifiable descriptive data on the subject's demeanor, emotional state, style of conversation—"

"Whoa," he interrupted. "This isn't for a bunch of academics. These guys aren't interested in all that. Just give me something I can use."

"All right, all right, let me think," I said. "Okay, we basically developed an assessment-style form that allowed us to collect data on each killer in the same standardized way. We needed a method of comparing each killer to all the rest, and that's what the data tool gave us. It painted a detailed picture of who these individual killers are. It made them measurable, so to speak."

"That's good," Ressler said. "What else?"

"It might be helpful to explain that we designed the assessment tool as a way to learn about several main things: the killer's personality, their background, their actions during the offense, specifics about their victims, and a detailed review of the crime scene," I added. "Also, that we've only been doing a few cases at a time, which allows us to refine the tool to determine its future relationships to other offenders. I think that's important because it shows how comprehensive our approach has been. It's how we've created and defined new categories of specific types of violent criminals. And it's been a major point of reference in all the profiling work that's followed."

"Yeah, I'm not sure about that last part," Ressler said. "It might be best to ease into the profiling update. I'm just not sure that's as far along as it needs to be yet."

Ressler was one of the smartest agents I knew. His vision and efforts were what led to the concept of the criminal personality study in the first place. He'd been actively involved in its development every step of the way, and he understood its methodology inside and out. But he was also a perfectionist. He never walked into a meeting without a plan. This style of back-and-forth questioning was just his way of making sure every possible avenue of thought had been explored and given the full consideration it deserved.

"You could bring up the National Institute of Justice grant," I reminded him. "The NIJ certainly sees the potential in our work."

"Come on, Ann. The Bureau's not interested in research and theories. You know that better than anyone," Ressler countered. "The brass is going to want proof. We'll need results and analysis from at least fifteen or twenty cases before they'll consider profiling a success."

"So, what do you have in mind?"

"I'll tell them about the first part of the study and how we came up with categories for the different types of serial killers," Ressler said. "I figure, if I lead with enough strange details about the killers, they'll be more interested in that than the quick update on profiling I save for the end."

Early on, after I'd pointed out how complex the criminal personality study was, we'd agreed to break up the research into three phases, each of which would build on the one that came before it. And because virtually no one had ever sought to understand the psychology of serial killers' minds, we had to make sure each phase could stand independently on its own merits before it could be applied to the next.

The first phase was a continuation of Ressler and Douglas's work toward understanding crimes that had no apparent motive.[*] Our goal for the first part was to create a way of cataloging different types of offenders so we could compare their similarities and differences. The second phase, the serial killer phase, was specifically focused on analyzing data from police records, court cases, and, most importantly, agent interviews with thirty-six convicted killers who had incorporated rape or sexual violence into their crimes. The goal for the second phase was to systematically drill way down deep into the minds of these killers so we could glimpse the truest essence of

---

[*]   We quickly learned that these crimes weren't so motiveless after all—they tended to have a sexual motive that was often overlooked during the original investigation.

who they were—the building blocks of their identities—as defined by their patterns and behaviors. We reasoned that these thirty-six convicted killers would become our frame of reference as we profiled serial killers who were still at large. They would essentially compose the "control" section of our database, a resource we could tap over and over again to see what past killers could tell us about present offenders.

The third phase was the development of criminal profiling itself. This would be a culmination of everything we'd learned in phases 1 and 2. Once we understood how a killer's mind worked, once we'd reduced it to its most basic elements of psychology, behavior, fantasy, and intention, we could apply these findings to the process of profiling—chiseling away at everything an offender wasn't until we were left with who he was. That was our goal. Because, by their very nature, serial killers adhered to a pattern. They acted with purpose. Even the most irrational minds start making sense if you look closely enough.

One of our initial findings within the criminal personality phase of the study—phase 1—was that crime scenes themselves often followed patterns, falling into one of three categories. They could be defined as organized (planned, well-thought-out offenses), disorganized (spontaneous, random offenses), or mixed (with features of both organized and disorganized scenes). The difference in the types of killers who left these scenes behind had to do with the presence and development of the murder fantasy. The organized killer always had a clear plan in mind and would wait for the victim of opportunity. The disorganized killer would be involved in a scenario that triggered impulsive aggression. Mixed killers tended to have something go "wrong" during their predetermined offense, which then caused them to become disorganized and kill more suddenly than they'd planned. These classifications became a foundational element in how we defined personality types and behavioral patterns. And they gave law enforcement a clearer way to speak about and understand the types of violent crimes they were seeing with increased frequency.

Once we had established these categories, we were then able to sort the thirty-six convicted killers by type—organized versus disorganized—to find more detailed patterns and characteristics within those sets. This revealed stunning consistencies. Organized offenders, for example, tended to have average or above-average intelligence but worked menial or low-status jobs. They tended to have grown up in a fairly stable family, had strong social skills and relationships, and were sexually competent. When it came to their crimes, organized offenders showed a heightened self-awareness of their methods and made a point of averting detection. Their attacks could usually be traced back to stress or a triggering event, but they maintained enough caution to prey on strangers—almost always a solitary female. The majority of organized offenders also made a habit of taking "souvenirs" from the victim, and they often collected newspaper clippings and other mementos that helped prolong the satisfaction of their crime. In most cases, the longer these organized offenders avoided detection, the more aggressive and frequent their attacks would become.

Conversely, disorganized offenders tended to be of below-average intelligence, came from unstable families, were in and out of work, and usually lived alone or with a parent. They felt socially inadequate, were obsessive in nature, and were sexually incompetent or had sexual aversions. They committed their crimes impulsively and with little to no thought about avoiding detection. They often knew their victims. And they could be extremely brutal both in their method of attack and their mutilation of the body afterward. However, their lack of planning and the clues available from post-crime behavior made them easier to catch.

Having two distinct categories of offenders, as well as thirty-six unique examples of killers—complete with data, context, and the real-world investigation of their crimes on record—spoke to phases 1 and 2 of the criminal personality study. This also gave us a basic template of a profile that we could use for unsolved cases to avoid starting from scratch. The challenge was translating this information to the third phase. We still needed a method for profiling that took everything we already knew about criminals, combined it with the investigative information of an ongoing case, and then pooled this information together to accurately state the motive and characteristics of the person who committed the crime. The pieces were all there, we just needed more time to fit them together.

CHAPTER 5

A Female Killer

Even in the mid-eighties, there was still a misconception in the FBI that profiling was based more on instinct than technique. It was hard for me to understand this stubborn insistence on ignoring the research involved in developing new methods of investigation. And it also made my job a lot trickier. Because, despite the fact that profiling was tallying up more and more successful cases—and despite how elusive each of those individual cases had been before the BSU got involved—the future of our work remained uncertain. Continued funding for our criminal personality study wasn't guaranteed, and the Bureau's upper brass remained noncommittal to both the research side of profiling and the act of profiling itself. And yet, in the three years since our initial success with the Joubert case, we'd seen an overwhelming increase in the number of requests from outside agencies asking for our help—starting with fifty in 1981, then doubling each year after that. There was clearly a need for our work, so why weren't we getting support? Ressler's answer was simple: "The Bureau has a habit of getting stuck in its own mess of red tape."

For the most part, I learned to ignore the uncertainties surrounding the criminal personality study and simply focused on the day-to-day tasks at hand. After all, research in general—whether in academia, hospitals, or, apparently, the FBI—was uncertain by nature. There were never any guarantees. But the act of profiling itself was a different matter entirely. As word spread about the success of our methods, our small team faced growing expectations and pressure to help law enforcement build criminal profiles for their most pressing cases. It was all we could do to keep up with the requests. Add this to the unit's already heavy workload of teaching, road school, and overall lack of resources, and something had to give.

Relief came in January of 1984. Finally, after an impassioned request from Unit Chief Depue, the Bureau stepped in and approved four new agents to join the team. But it wasn't just agents we got. Leadership at the FBI also sent over a long list of questions: Could we make profiling more consistent? Could we speed up the process? Could we apply it to a wider range of cases? And although I wished I could say that my answer was a simple yes up and down the board, the truth was I had no idea. I believed in our work, and I believed in the agents. But profiling was unlike anything the world of criminal investigations had ever seen. The technique was still in its infancy. In my mind, the profiling process made sense because of similarities I saw between it and the techniques I used to diagnose psychiatric patients—all the clues for identifying the disease or condition were there, you just needed to know where to find them and how to connect them. New agents, however, would be coming from a completely different background. They needed their own way of thinking about how profiling worked—an evidence-based approach grounded in the insights gained from the criminal personality study. I realized the opportunity this presented. If Douglas, Ressler, and I played our cards right, we could create a training program for new agents that also helped validate the research side of profiling in one fell swoop. So, at the start of summer in 1984, I took a break from academia and gave my full attention to the team at Quantico and our development of profiling.

I didn't have my own office in the subterranean depths of Quantico. But the agents didn't want to distract me with their nonstop chaos of noise—shouting down the halls, constantly ringing phones, and the screeching of our new analog fax machine. So I was given a small desk in a large conference room at the intersection of two halls. The room was dominated by six industrial-sized filing cabinets that were each stuffed with chronologically arranged binders full of BSU case records and their connected newspaper indexes. The setup was perfect. It felt like here, in this space, I was at the center of the hive, surrounded by the collective investigative knowledge we had of serial killers and their crimes. I had everything I needed to untangle the cluttered mess of criminal minds and find the common threads among them. This was my chance to add nuance and depth to the criminal personality study and to then apply that knowledge to profiling in ways that would make the process faster and more consistent.

I started with the data. At that point, we'd recorded prison interviews with more than fifty notorious killers—the thirty-six from the original study, plus the others we'd recorded since—and none of them had been shy about opening up. They readily talked about how they chose their victims, what happened during the assaults, what souvenirs they took, what role pornography played, what they did after the crime, what they thought about over the days that followed, and a whole range of other questions intended to shed light on their criminal predisposition. The consistency among their answers was fascinating. Studying these answers revealed common denominators among crime scenes and criminals that stayed true across time and distance and showed that these were far from individual acts of random violence. Fifty-one percent of the killers we interviewed, for example, displayed above-average intelligence, while 72 percent had an emotionally distant relationship with their father and 86 percent had a prior psychiatric history or diagnosis. This background data showed, for the first time, clear patterns in serial killers' behaviors when compared to human behavior at large. And it grounded criminal profiling in measurable research that further validated our results.

When I first showed Ressler my findings, he sighed with relief.

"I've got to tell you," he admitted, "my biggest fear was that the data would be totally, diametrically out of kilter with what I've been doing here for the last couple of years."

I knew exactly how he felt. The work we did, putting ourselves in the mind of an offender to understand the nature of their crime, came with serious risks. It was a raw confrontation with horror. Weight loss and chest pains were common among agents at the BSU, with Douglas being the most notorious example. He was working a case in Seattle in 1983 when a medical emergency caused him to be hospitalized, unconscious, with a near-deadly case of meningitis. It took months of rehabilitation at home in Virginia until he finally got back on his feet. "I felt it was payback for six years of hunting the worst men on earth," he told me. After that, I made a habit of regularly meeting with the team to review the emotional toll of the cases we were taking on. We had to reassure and support each other in whatever ways we could.

That brought me to my second focus during the summer of 1984. It wasn't just criminal psychology I was interested in understanding. I wanted to learn how the agents' minds worked, too. If their goal was to think their way into an unsub's head, then I needed to understand their exact step-by-step approach so I could better refine profiling as a methodological process. So, I paid attention. I focused on their individual patterns and behaviors, and I jotted down what I saw.

Some were visual thinkers, crafting pictures in their heads about the crime. Some organized their thoughts into a series of mental checklists. And some started each session with an open mind, meticulously shaping an opinion as they challenged the analysis of others. Yet, despite these differences, the agents arrived at the same conclusions more than 80 percent of the time. It was uncanny.

For example, in trying to determine the size and weight of the unsub later identified as John Joubert, Ressler thought the suspect would be slim because he dropped his victim close to the road—the implication being the unsub couldn't carry the victim any farther. Hazelwood also believed the unsub would be slim, but his reasoning came from observing that the suspect's footprints were close together. Both agents described the unsub as "slight of build," which he was, but their mode of understanding was different, likely because of different investigative experiences from earlier in their individual careers.

This convergence raised several questions: Which parts of profiling could be taught, which parts could be refined through experience, and how could we assess a potential agent's aptitude for profiling? I wasn't sure, but the timing was right to find out. With the second generation of profilers—Ron Walker, Bill Haigmier, Judson Ray, Jim Wright, and new recruit and profiler apprentice Greg Cooper—just starting to participate in active cases, we'd have our answers soon enough. Their development and contributions would have far-reaching implications for the future of profiling. If these newest members of the team could learn to successfully analyze, reconstruct, and classify the behavioral characteristics of an unsub based on the available information of their crimes, then we'd know that profiling could be a learned skill. It would set a precedent for how we trained new agents and law enforcement officers moving forward. This would be the blueprint.

For the moment, though, just having four additional agents and an apprentice around was a huge relief. Not only did they allow us to take on a greater number of cases than ever before, but they also broadened the scope of cases we could tackle. Up until then, all of our profiling work—both in the study and in active cases—had involved multiple killings by male offenders between the ages of eighteen and thirty-five, most of whom were white. The killers' methods and motives showed a range of differences, but their demographics were largely the same. In part, this was simply the reality of known serial killers at the time. But it also spoke to a general shortcoming in the overall culture of law enforcement. In the late seventies and early eighties, cases with white victims were more thoroughly investigated than cases involving minorities. It was a shameful truth. And it was also a weakness, limiting our potential to understand the full spectrum of criminals and their crimes.

In my position, one of still only a few women at the Academy, I was perhaps more acutely aware of prevailing social issues than anyone else. I knew what it felt like to be the odd one out, and I'd learned to see the value in that perspective. This was something I often stressed to the team—explaining how agents with diverse backgrounds could help us better know and reflect the diversity within crime—and normally this would get me a couple of agreeable nods, but not much else. But that finally changed when Judd Ray joined the BSU as part of the second generation of profilers. Ray was the first Black agent on the team, and the two of us quickly became allies. He understood the importance of pushing the BSU out of its comfort zone. He agreed that profiling could be effective beyond just one narrow demographic of killers. We just needed to prove it. We needed a case that highlighted our technique and its novel reimagining of the investigative process, no matter how unexpected the killer's identity might be. We needed a case to serve as undeniable proof of profiling's transformative potential. That case landed on Agent Ron Walker's desk one afternoon in 1984.

Six of us gathered in the bomb shelter early the next morning—I made sure Ray would attend—with Walker in the role of lead profiler. The room was set up when we arrived. And as he gave us a few moments to review key details of the case, I decided I'd treat this session differently. I wanted to focus as much on the specifics of the case as I did on the method itself. I knew that the agents each approached profiling from their own unique vantage point, but I'd never considered how these differences affected the end result. This context was crucial. By observing how agents asked questions, processed information, and oriented cases toward their own area of expertise, I could better understand profiling as a methodological process. In other words, the observations recorded by each agent were the nuts and bolts of how profiling sessions worked, and by seeing how each agent operated, I could piece together how they approached and analyzed the subject of a given session. The agents themselves were a point of data that needed to be considered within the greater work.

"This one might be a first for the team," Walker said, pressing record on the tape drive to record our conversation for future reference. "There's a witness who saw the attack. Apparently, the unsub's a female." He then clicked off the lights and aimed the projector at the far wall.

On Saturday, June 23, 1984, in the upper-middle-class suburb of Orinda, California, fifteen-year-old Kirsten C. was home alone, waiting for a ride to a secret initiation dinner to join the exclusive Bob-O-Links civic group, known locally as the "Bobbies." The Bobbies were a big deal. Membership was a sign of social status that extended beyond just the immediacy of high school. So, when Kirsten's mom had earlier received the call from an unidentified female who explained that the dinner was a secret and that she'd pick up Kirsten at 8:30 p.m., the whole family got excited.

That evening, Kirsten's parents and her twelve-year-old brother left the house to attend a baseball banquet, and Kirsten waited for her ride to show up. At 8:20 p.m., Kirsten's mom called to wish her daughter good luck. Soon after, a car honked in the driveway, and Kirsten raced out the door and into the passenger side of a beat-up two-tone orange Ford Pinto. The Pinto cruised over to a nearby Presbyterian church and parked out front, resting for about thirty minutes with the two passengers staying inside. Then, Kirsten stepped out of the car and walked five hundred yards or so to the nearby home of family friends, the Arnolds, at the end of a cul-de-sac. Mrs. Arnold opened the door and listened intently as Kirsten explained her predicament: "Jell, my friend, is acting really weird and she won't take me home." She then asked if she could use the Arnolds' phone to call her parents. At this point, Mrs. Arnold noticed a teenage girl with light brown hair standing on the sidewalk. It struck her as odd, so she invited Kirsten to come in. After calling home but failing to reach her parents, Kirsten accepted Mr. Arnold's offer to drive her. They left at about 9:40 p.m.

Throughout the three-mile drive, Arnold noticed an orange Pinto that was clearly following them but keeping some distance back. He turned to Kirsten and asked her point-blank: "Is that the girl you were with?" Kirsten confirmed that it was but reassured him that everything was okay before calmly changing the subject to things about school and her friends. Once they arrived at the C. family home, Kirsten noticed that her parents still weren't back yet. She told Arnold that she was going to wait at the neighbor's house next door. Arnold said he'd watch to make sure she got inside safely. Moments later, though, through the passenger-side window, he spotted a female figure racing across the neighbor's front lawn toward where Kirsten was standing at the entrance of the porch. Arnold heard an altercation and then saw Kirsten fall to the ground. Screams followed. Moments later, he watched the assailant run back down the driveway, jump into the Pinto, and hit a curb as she made a sharp U-turn before speeding away.

There were multiple witnesses to what happened next, but much of it was sheer chaos. Porch lights flicked on. Neighbors ran outside in the direction of the commotion. And Kirsten got up and stumbled past Arnold's car, screaming for help, her bloody hands leaving thick crimson prints where she held onto the trunk of the car for support. Arnold took off after the speeding Ford Pinto, then reconsidered and drove back to the crime scene to see if Kirsten needed help. He saw paramedics rush Kirsten into an ambulance. Then he found a police officer and described the Pinto he'd been chasing and Kirsten's comment about her weird friend.

In the midst of everything, the C. family arrived home. The scene turned from chaos to pin-drop silence, then back to chaos again as the family glimpsed their daughter on a stretcher in the back of an ambulance. She was covered in blood. Paramedics slammed the doors, blared their siren, and cut a path through the gathering crowd. They raced Kirsten to a nearby hospital, where an hour later, she was pronounced dead. It was 11:02 p.m.

The investigation started immediately, with the primary focus on the investigators' main lead: the killer's Ford Pinto. Police looked into over 750 yellow and orange Pintos, but they still couldn't nail down any definitive evidence connecting one particular Pinto to Kirsten's murder.

From there, the police searched for additional witnesses. They found three. The first was a neighbor of the Arnolds who saw the Pinto parked in the cul-de-sac while he was out on an evening walk. He observed that a female was driving the car and that she was upset, so he went up to the window to ask and see if she was okay. The driver waved him off, saying, "I'm fine, just leave me alone." Their interaction ended with that.

The second and third witnesses were a young couple. They were also parked in the church's lot—a local hangout for the area's high school kids to party, smoke pot, and have sex—when they saw the Pinto pull in and park for about thirty-five minutes. Unfortunately, the couple said they didn't recognize Kirsten or the driver, and they didn't get a good look at what happened inside the car.

"That's where the case stands." Walker turned over the last page of his files and looked across the table at us. "It's been months with no further leads. The case has gone cold. But let me just add that forensics shows five stab wounds and a defense wound to the right forearm. Two of the wounds went deep into the victim's back and punctured her right lung and diaphragm." Walker rapidly clicked forward a few slides on the projector. "Then there's the autopsy. These photos show where one wound lacerated her liver. And the other two wounds on her chest, which are about fifteen centimeters long and penetrated her left lung. She seems to have choked to death on her own blood. There were no indications of physical or sexual assault.

"All right. Let's open this up for questions."

"What about the witnesses' descriptions?" Ray asked.

"See, that's part of the problem." Walker shook his head. "Arnold isn't much of a witness. He got completely overwhelmed. He couldn't recall the license plate number, and he couldn't give a description of the person that ran by his car. All he said was that she was female, with dirty blonde hair, dressed in what appeared to be jogging-type clothes. He couldn't even give us an age, just that 'she wasn't old, she wasn't young.' They even tried to hypnotize the guy and he wasn't able to come up with more than that. The other witnesses, the couple making out in their car, they were parked all the way in the far corner of the lot. They only saw the victim get out of the Pinto and walk away."

"And you're sure it was the Pinto?" Ray asked. "The same one that picked her up at her house and the same one Arnold chased after that?"

Walker flashed a look of frustration. "The car that picked her up was an orange Pinto. It was an orange Pinto seen at the church parking lot. It was an orange Pinto seen here, and here. It was the same car. If you need more proof, we have multiple witnesses describing it as banged up and dented looking. It's not in good shape."

Out of the corner of my eye, I saw Douglas smiling. I knew what he was up to. He was going to crack a joke or make some other remark to smooth out the tension in the room.

"Geez, Walker. Now I'm a little afraid to ask the obvious," Douglas raised both hands in a surrender-type gesture, "but was there even an initiation dinner that evening?"

"No, no initiation that night. That goes back to the Bobbies again. The club's main officers were all out of town on an annual field trip to Hawaii. You've got to remember, this is as much of a civic group as it is a sorority of sorts. It's a social club and social organization that provides assistance at the local hospital, sort of like candy striper–type assistance. The club itself is restricted to the in-crowd. And its members are generally wealthy. That's what the field trip to Hawaii was all about and why the only ones left in town were the initiates and nonofficers, and that's not a whole lot of them. It's not a very big organization. Maybe twenty or thirty girls, and about half of those hold some sort of official position. So most of them were away while this was happening."

"Tell us more about the weapon." Ressler refocused the conversation. "Did they ever find it?"

"It was never found, no. Our best determination is that the weapon was a large, single-edged blade, probably a typical hunting knife. That's unconfirmed though. The witness didn't see the knife. We just have the coroner report, which attributes the wounds to a single-edged weapon of fairly good size—an inch and a half blade at least. Investigators found a butter knife at the scene, but that had nothing to do with the attack."

"Besides the butter knife, did forensics recover anything else?"

"Nothing useful," Walker said. "They did find one bloody fingerprint on one of the porch rails at the site of the assault, and it wasn't the victim's. Unfortunately, it was just a partial, not enough to get any points of comparison off of."

"Can we go back to the victim?" I pivoted. "What was her demeanor in all this? How did the witnesses describe her?"

"She wasn't panicked. Arnold and his wife described her as worried and a little upset. That's it."

"And what about victimology and the victim profile?" I asked.

"Let's see." Walker flipped through his notes. "What you have here is a fifteen-year-old high school student. She's very popular in school, belongs to the in-crowd, sort of a little princess in her own household, her every whim is catered to by her mom and dad. She does have other siblings in the family, but she's the oldest daughter. She's a very attractive young lady. Victimology-wise, there's nothing in her background that puts her at high risk. She relates well to her girlfriends, she relates well to guys in the school, she relates well to adults. There's no sexual promiscuity on her part that we know of. She's described by her peers as being sort of a tease, the type who would lead the boys on in a way, but she always cut the guy off when things started to get serious. The only thing in her background that's a little unusual—well, it's not unusual for California, but typically would be unusual for a fifteen-year-old girl—is that she likes to toot some drugs every now and again. She also smokes marijuana and likes to drink a lot of beer, to the point of getting intoxicated. This is not habitual with her, but she does go to parties, she drinks beer, and she certainly never passes up the opportunity to toke a joint. Again, this isn't unusual for the California high school kid. But it's what she was into."

"The guy that drove her home, Arnold . . . are we sure he wasn't involved in this? It's pretty unusual he couldn't give a better description of the unsub after being so close to the attack," Ressler said.

"He was just spooked. The whole thing was too much for him to handle."

"See, that feels off to me," Ressler continued. "It makes me wonder if he knew the unsub. Maybe it's another high school kid he's trying to protect."

"Hold on a second," I cut in. "Before this gets into profiling, can you clarify something? You said the victim was a popular girl, right? So, did she have any friends in the club that she talked to about the initiation? Wouldn't they have told her that nothing was going on that night?"

"Now, that's an interesting question," Walker agreed. "The victim did call one of her friends to talk about the initiation. The friend, who also happens to be one of the Bobbies, knew nothing about the initiation. However, the victim and the friend sort of agreed that, well, there could be something going on, there could be an initiation, we just don't know about it. It's sort of a secret club, remember. So she agrees to go."

"That makes our unsub one of the Bobbies," Hazelwood said. "Or else why would the victim get in the car and go with her? Not to mention sitting in the parking lot with her for all that time."

"So, we're getting into profiling now," Walker said. "That's fine. But the problem with saying it's definitely one of the Bobbies is that the original call went to the mom, not the victim herself. That strikes me as deliberate. That's using a disguise of some sort. At the same time, we know that whoever made the call is someone who knows very intimately how the Bobbies set up their initiation process. So, yes, you're probably right. Because it's unlikely that the victim would have gotten in the car if she didn't recognize the driver as a known member, since the Bobbies don't use nonmembers as part of the initiation process."

"This is how I see it," Douglas laid out his theory. "It's the opinion of this profiler that the victim and her assailant were acquainted and possibly shared an association unknown to the victim's family and friends. A lot of what went on here indicates, as Walker pointed out very aptly, that the person was a member of or at least familiar with the Bobbies organization, so it must be a female. That the person is familiar with the area is very obvious, too, because the driver of the Pinto took the victim to an area frequented by the local teenagers. There's obvious planning that went into the situation. A younger girl couldn't do that, so maybe it was a high school junior or senior. Or maybe somebody recently graduated that's still hanging around the town and feeling kind of angry about being stuck there but not part of things anymore. But what's conflicting is that there was a lot of organization that went into the planning of the crime, but the way the crime went down was totally disorganized. Running up in front of a witness that's sitting in the car and stabbing the victim and passing by that witness twice, once on the way to the victim and once on the way back from the victim. It's thoughtless."

"That element of planned but disorganized is important," Hazelwood agreed, picking up on Douglas's train of thought. "But you have to wonder what the unsub's plan really was. I don't think it was homicide, and the reason I say that is there was a lot of opportunity, at least thirty-five minutes while they were parked in the parking lot, plus the whole ride in the car before that."

"Makes sense." Walker nodded in agreement. "Something happened in the parking lot that caused the situation to deteriorate. There was a confrontation of sorts. The victim leaves the Pinto and says something like: 'The hell with this. I'm leaving. You're weird.' And so whatever transpired there is causing this driver of the Pinto a lot of grief, anxiety, anger, rage, to the point where she follows the victim home, gets out of the car, and assaults her."

"It's a very disorganized, impulsive type of act," Douglas said. "All of this wasn't planned for the purpose of murder, it was simply to be with this girl for one reason or another. Possibly with romantic intentions."

"So if we're building a profile around a high school–aged female, which it sounds like everyone agrees we are," I looked around the room and counted several confirming nods, "then how does the hunting knife fit in? If it's only a weapon of opportunity, why does a high school girl have it in her car?"

"Well, we don't know if the driver owned the car or had the habit of borrowing it from friends or family," Walker said. "And if it's that second option, then the knife was likely there independent of the unsub or her intentions."

"If we're building on victimology, I think the vehicle's age and condition are another significant factor here," I said. "It points to a lack of economic capacity. That's a big difference from the general affluence of the area in which the crime occurred. The condition of the unsub's car signals a lower economic status, which probably adds to anxieties about not fitting in."

"Let me say something I think is extremely important," Ressler interjected. "Forget the car for a second. We've got an elaborate scheme to get this girl away from her home, and then she's murdered with a knife—a weapon that would generally indicate a planned homicide. And yet we also have the victim and unsub alone for a considerable length of time, and there's no trauma to the victim's face or tearing of the clothing. But now some of you are saying it wasn't a premeditated homicide, and therefore the weapon becomes a weapon of opportunity instead of a weapon of choice. That's a hell of a differentiation to make when you have all that planning and a girl stabbed to death."

"Maybe there's something else involved we haven't accounted for yet," Douglas pushed back. "Something that could explain the time in the car and the impulsiveness of the attack."

"Let's focus back on the profile," Walker switched gears. "We agree on the category of disorganized. We also seem to agree that the offender possesses at least a partial high school education and may well have been a student or recent graduate still living in the area at the time of the offense. If they're part of the Bobbies, they have an average to above-average intelligence but may have had only a mediocre academic record due to a greater interest in social standing than their academic success. The assailant either resided or was employed in the area at the time of the crime. And although they must have had some capacity to relate to others—again, assuming they're part of the Bobbies—their economics likely puts them on the lower end of the social spectrum, which adds a whole other layer to why they struggled to make any actual friends. I'd say this points to a likely history of recreational drug and alcohol use that also compensates for anxieties and lower inhibitions. I think age is enough to rule out any criminal history, other than maybe a misdemeanor drug offense."

"That sounds about right," Ressler said. "Although I wish we had a better read on what happened while they were sitting in the car. It had to be a pretty big confrontation between the two to trigger such a violent response."

"Drug use," Douglas repeated.

"Can we do a quick segue into post-offense behavior?" Hazelwood asked. "Ann, this part could really use your insights to help rationalize the psychology involved. You've got an advantage because, even after twenty years of marriage, I still have no idea how women think."

The agents laughed, and I smiled along to play nice. Then I thought better of it. "Talk about your personal life on your own time, Roy. I'm more interested in solving this case."

There was a brief silence before Hazelwood sheepishly and good-naturedly apologized.

"It's a fair point, though," Walker said. "Post-offense behavior is important in this one. The first thing to address is the issue of the weapon. Who wants to start?"

Ressler took the lead. "Based on how disorganized the attack was, it's likely the unsub disposed of the weapon on her drive back home. She probably just threw the knife out the window to get rid of it without much thought. I feel very comfortable saying that the driver got back into the car and drove straight home. I say that because I don't think this person ever committed an act like this before in her entire life, the assailant."

"I'm with Bob on this one," I agreed. "This was a traumatic act, and people not inclined to homicidal behavior—and I don't think this girl was inclined to homicidal behavior—the first thing they do when they commit an act like this is they go someplace safe. They find a warm, supportive environment where they can shut themselves off from what really happened. In this case, if we're looking for a high school girl, she would immediately go back to her family's house."

"That's good," Douglas said. "The knife gets tossed out the window on the drive home. So if police can come up with a list of suspects, they should be able to search the most logical driving routes and come up with the knife."

"The driver would also clean up any trace of evidence inside the vehicle," Hazelwood added. "This is particularly true if the vehicle was borrowed. She might even get up early to take it to a local car wash the next day."

"That's the key time period," I said. "The unsub's personal behavior would have changed noticeably immediately after the offense. She might not have seen anyone that night after she got back. But as a high school girl living with her family, she likely would have seen someone the next morning, and they might have noticed her becoming withdrawn and introverted for at least a few days after the offense. She could have appeared anxious, agitated, nervous, preoccupied with distant thoughts. Her normal daily pattern could have changed, including a change in eating and sleeping habits. Even her physical appearance could have noticeably changed. She could have been less clothes-conscious, less concerned with how put together she was or how she looked."

"Do you know if the local police noticed anything unusual at the funeral, Walker?" Douglas asked. "We've seen this before where the killer attends and exhibits an inappropriate lack of emotion. Usually, they leave the service early too."

"The police have to know who she is," Ressler insisted. "They can't have that many suspects. They probably already interviewed her within the course of their investigation and noticed that she was more anxious and upset than some of the other kids. Maybe she even offered to help in the investigation. What aren't you telling us, Walker?"

"All right, everyone." Walker wrapped things up quickly. "That should be enough. I'll write up the profile and send it back to the Orinda police. We'll debrief if there's an update."

———

That was it. When the session ended, these agents, who were well practiced in these types of transitions, simply flipped a mental switch to click back into their own individual worlds. They jumped from an analysis of violent stabbing in all its graphic details to chatting about weekend plans with the family or politics around the office or what Joe Gibbs was doing with the Redskins. It was startling in a way, but it was also part of what the FBI recruited for. Despite their differences, each agent within the BSU had an ability to empathize without being affected, to compartmentalize the disturbing without becoming disturbed themselves. They had ways of staying detached in order to survive.

My experience was different. Working with victims of sexual violence hadn't numbed me to such horrific acts. Rather, it helped me understand the nature of violence more fully—it helped me recognize patterns and designs. I did this by connecting with victims, relating to their stories, and analyzing the underlying psychology at work. This gave me a unique insight into the victim side of profiling. It was something the offender-focused agents appreciated, particularly because it helped clear up inconsistencies in how repeat offenders treated victims over a series of crimes. I was often brought in on these types of cases to explain the interpersonal dynamics of a crime—such as how victims might fight back or give in as an act of self-defense—or to offer my opinion on how different scenarios could stimulate or upset an offender. But my approach also left me more vulnerable to the emotions of the cases. They stuck with me. I'd often find myself replaying the details and nuances of a crime to better understand what motivated an offender and who they might be. And when profiled offenders were finally captured, I felt proud of our work—but more than anything, I felt relieved.

This was especially true of the Bobbies case. Of the dozen or so profiling sessions the team had worked on since the start of the 1980s, this was the first female-on-female case. If we got this one right, it would serve as a resounding yes to the Bureau's as-yet unresolved question: Can profiling be applied to a wider range of cases? The answer came a few months later, in December of that year. Walker told me that an arrest had finally been made. He added that he was scheduling a debriefing with all the agents involved in the original profile, and he suggested I join them.

"So, here's what I didn't tell you at our last session. Even before we started profiling this one, the investigation had a pretty narrow suspect list. They even had one suspect who had access to an orange Pinto, was a friend of the victim, attended the same high school, was a member of the Bobbies, and had an unexplained absence from her house for the two-hour period that encompassed the event." Walker quickly cut us off before anyone could respond. "I know, I know. But they ruled her out after passing a polygraph examination, because there wasn't a single deception noted on the results."

"What was the alibi she gave for the missing two hours? Did the polygrapher ask her about that?" Douglas asked.

"She said she was babysitting. That's how she got access to the car—the Pinto was her older sister's, by the way. She conned her sister and parents with the babysitting story."

"Clever," Ray muttered.

"Here's the thing, though. When I heard about the polygraph, I asked them to fax a copy and had it reviewed by one of our own guys. And he said it was a lousy test. He said that, if the questions had been asked differently, or if the right questions had been asked, the results would have been inconclusive. That alone would have been enough to keep the suspect on the list."

"Clearly, the local boys in blue don't see a lot of murder investigations," Douglas observed.

"So the next step was to put together our profile so I could show it to the investigators and point out all its overlaps with the suspect they'd ruled out. But the problem would be the suspect herself. By then, she'd have had enough time to rationalize the attack. She'd feel justified in the killing. We've seen it before. The unsub goes through a psychological self-defense mechanism, with thoughts like: 'She deserved what happened to her, she's a brat, she's a snob. I don't give a shit about her. She deserved to die.'"

"Devious," Ray remarked.

"That's why I wanted Ann's help with the post-offense behavior in our last profiling session. I knew I could get the investigators to interview the unsub again. But we needed something to get her to crack. We had to walk her back through everything that happened that night, including her own thoughts and actions, even the ones she'd kept exclusively to herself. Otherwise, the investigators had nothing. We needed this girl to come out and fully confess."

"So you *do* listen occasionally." I laughed.

"I gave the investigators the profile. The investigators found the suspect again. And she agreed to come back for a second polygraph that upcoming Friday evening. Here's what was strange, though: it's a four-hour pre-polygraph interview, followed by the polygraph itself, and then, even after all that, the girl was reluctant to leave. She kept hanging around and wanting to talk to the polygraph examiner. And when she finally did, she said to him: 'I think you believe I did it.' And he says: 'Yes.' And then she asked for his name, and he says: 'Ron Hilly.'

"Anyway, the test showed deception in two key areas and was inconclusive on a number of others. But there still wasn't enough for further investigative action."

"You were right," I said. "She had enough time to build up her defenses and justify to herself what she'd done."

"That's what I thought on Friday night after the results were in and the girl finally went home. But what happened next—I only learned about this after the fact—was that Saturday and Sunday, the girl kept trying to talk to her mom, but her mom was too busy to give her any time. Then on Monday morning, as the girl got ready for school, she pointed to a note on her dresser and said, 'Mom, you better read that while I'm at school.' It was a signed confession for the murder of Kirsten C."

"That's interesting," I said. "It's as if she handled the confession in a way that still gave her some element of control. She couldn't get her mother's attention earlier, so she created a scenario where her mother was forced to get involved. Can we see the note? I bet that spells out her motivation to confess pretty clearly."

Walker nodded, then picked up a piece of paper and started to read.

"'Dear Mom and Dad. I've been trying to tell you this all day, but I love you so much it's too hard. So I'm taking the easy way out. The FBI man … thinks I did it. And he's right. I've been able to live with it, but I can't ignore it. It's too much for me, and I can't be that deceiving. Please still love me. I can't live unless you love me. I've ruined my life and yours, and I don't know what to do and I'm ashamed and scared. P.S. Please don't say how could you or why, because I don't understand this and I don't know why.'"

On the morning of December 12, 1984, after reading her daughter's note, Bernadette Protti's mom raced to school, picked up her daughter, and drove her to the Miramonte police station. Sixteen-year-old Bernadette refused to speak to anyone except polygraph examiner Ron Hilly, with whom she'd established a rapport the previous Friday. In her confession, Bernadette explained that she hadn't planned the murder, that it was a misunderstanding, and that all she'd ever wanted was to fit in.

According to Bernadette's confession, everything revolved around a party planned for the night of June 23. Bernadette hadn't been invited, but she knew that Kirsten C. had been, which inspired her to concoct the scheme of a Bobbies' initiation night to get Kirsten out of her house. Bernadette explained that she thought if she showed up at this really in party with one of the most popular girls at school, she would finally be accepted.

So, after the two of them arrived at the church parking lot and it eventually became obvious there was no initiation, Bernadette said, "Well, I guess there's no initiation. I know of a great party. Let's go to that." And although Kirsten initially agreed, something transpired in those moments—something that was never fully explained or made clear—that caused her to change her mind, to call Bernadette an asshole, and to get out of the car.

That's when Bernadette decided she had to do something about Kirsten. She was afraid that Kirsten would tell everybody at school that she was weird because she wouldn't get high, and she couldn't handle the thought of rejection from her peers.

As for the knife, Bernadette explained that her older sister had left it in the car. The sister had originally put the knife in the car before going with some friends to a sub shop. The sister used it to cut the subs in half, and she just forgot to take it out of the car afterward. That was her explanation, anyway, believe it or not.

At the end of the debriefing, I asked Walker if he had a minute to chat. He was still new to profiling and the BSU, and I hoped I could learn something by hearing his perspective.

"That was a good outcome," I said. "It will give the family a little peace."

"They probably wouldn't have caught her if she didn't give herself up."

"Maybe. But it's hard to say how much of an impact your

re-interview strategy had," I continued. "That's not what I wanted to talk about, though. I'm curious about your overall impressions of the case. And why'd you choose to focus on her in the first place?"

"There were things in her polygraph that stood out," Walker said. "Especially that one question she asked, the thing about 'Do you consider the publicity is more important than the murder,' that jumped out at me. It was like she felt justified in her actions and used that emotion to help her pass the polygraph. Which, by the way, I found out that Ron Hilly ran a 'check attention'–type polygraph, asking specific questions only the perp would know and then watching for a reaction. Those aren't easy to pass."

"Makes sense. What else do you think?" I pushed him to continue. "Was this simple jealousy and fear of rejection?"

Walker tipped his head back slightly and paused a moment before answering. "I think there are parts that don't add up. But that's for the courts to figure out. My opinion doesn't matter anymore."

"It does if we can still learn something from it. It might matter a lot to the next case we see."

"All right," Walker said, choosing his words carefully. "I think— and this is looking at it in retrospect—I think there's a lot we still don't know. Take the confession, for example. The subject describes the victim taking marijuana out of her purse, but the victim's parents said she wasn't carrying a purse that night. Also, look at the alibi from the eighteen-year-old sister. The sister lied. She tried to cover for the subject during the time she was out of the house. I think the subject also lied about the knife. I get the impression that the parents lied, too. But not because they knew anything about their daughter committing murder, they lied because they knew she'd been driving without a license. My guess is that, when the parents initially got a call from the police, they thought their daughter might have been in a traffic accident. They covered for her without knowing what she did."

"So, what do you think really happened?" I asked.

"Honestly? I think the girl did take the knife out of the kitchen and put it in the car that night. How else would she have just found it under the front seat? That's bullshit—sorry for the language. But I also don't think she intended to commit murder. I think what she did was she, because of her envy and the jealousy she felt, I think she maybe wanted to frighten the victim or scare her by using the knife as a big display. But it's easy to guess what happened next based on the subject's patterns of behavior. Her fear of rejection controlled her. The only thing that mattered was fitting in."

"Why didn't you mention any of this in there?" I asked.

"Because those guys are all veteran agents. The subject in this case wasn't a big-name serial killer. It was just a one-off. They've got bigger fish to fry."

In that moment, I wanted to tell Walker that his case mattered for exactly the reasons he thought it didn't. For every big-name serial killer that the BSU tracked down, there were hundreds, if not thousands, of one-off cases that never got solved. By sheer numbers alone, *these* were the cases where we could make the biggest impact. And for profiling to work on that scale, we couldn't limit ourselves to one way of thinking or one simple approach. We needed to throw everything we had at these cases: our different backgrounds, experiences, perspectives. Because that was the real key to methodological profiling. We were at our best when we came together as a team. We solved cases by reducing them to their smallest details, then putting them back together based on everyone's unique understanding of the behaviors involved. Our collective analysis evened out any unknown biases we might have as individual profilers. Collaboration was the BSU's greatest advantage and something we'd need to rely on more and more as new cases came in that stretched us to our limits. Profiling was more than the sum of its parts.

"Every case matters," I told Walker. "They're all important."

On April 1, 1985, Bernadette Protti was found guilty of second-degree murder for taking the life of Kirsten C. She received the maximum sentence of nine years, during which she was denied parole twice before the state Youthful Offender Parole Board released her on June 10, 1992, in a two-to-one decision.

In many ways, the Bobbies case was exactly what the BSU needed. It was prominently publicized, it had a successful outcome, and it proved that profiling could be an investigation's big break, regardless of who the subject was or how many crimes they'd committed. Even throughout their coverage of the trial the media—often critical of the FBI as a whole—was unusually complimentary of the Bureau's "new investigative technique." This positive media attention was another turning point for the BSU. Publicly, it set in motion a new narrative in which profiling was considered a valued part of how the FBI combated violent serial crimes. But internally, where it mattered most, the significance was much deeper. Coverage of the case helped validate our work in the eyes of higher-ups within the agency's echelon—people with decision-making ability, budget oversight, and departmental authority.

The case also helped highlight the importance of collaboration among the lead profilers, agents, and local investigators. These relationships are critical to the development of a solid profile. Information needs to be clear, comprehensive, and unbiased. And there has to be a constant dialogue between everyone involved. This level of transparency and cooperation was almost unprecedented for the time. It was thrilling. And at the same time, we were flooded with more calls than ever before from investigators who needed our help. There were child killings in Atlanta, highway slashings in Chicago, and a series of dismemberments along the California coast. The list went on and on.

The Bobbies case was influential in an operational sense, too. Even with the addition of four new agents, the BSU had only ten active profilers on its team. And none of those ten was profiling full-time—they did so in addition to their teaching responsibilities, training programs, or whatever else they were asked to do in their capacity as agents. But the successful impact profiling had on this case and others like it was becoming too hard to ignore. If the higher-ups wanted profiling to get faster and more efficient, they had to give us the time, space, and resources to really focus on it. Frustrated and nearing a breaking point, Ressler pressed then FBI Academy director James McKenzie about instituting a national center to continue our work. McKenzie moved the idea up the ladder, and later that summer, the Bureau formally announced its establishment of the National Center for the Analysis of Violent Crime (NCAVC).

NCAVC officially became operational in June of 1985. In a way, the establishment of this new center spoke to the BSU's success. Because, as is the case in any governmental bureaucracy, the more success a department has, the bigger and bigger it gets and the more units are added. NCAVC was simply a new name for an overarching entity that allowed the BSU to split into an investigative support unit and a research unit. The center was officially tasked with understanding and finding solutions for violent crimes: conducting research and development initiatives, establishing training programs, expanding criminal personality profiling, and maintaining the Violent Criminal Apprehension Program's catalog of violent crimes. But at its core, we were still the same old BSU. All that really changed was that, after years of being isolated, we were finally getting access to greater resources that helped us integrate into the Bureau as a whole. It made us more efficient. And for time-sensitive cases, efficiency could be the difference between life and death.

CHAPTER 6

My Best Friend Missy

I noticed a curious development in the aftermath of the BSU's success with the Bobbies case. It wasn't just that local law enforcement reached out for our help with a wider variety of investigations than ever before—we'd expected that after solving a high-profile case involving a female killer—it was that the incoming requests were asking for individual profilers by name. I couldn't help but laugh at the irony. We'd been underfunded, underestimated, and buried deep underground in the Academy's bomb shelter. But even that couldn't stop us. Profiling had spoken for itself. Now it was the profilers' opportunity to step out of the shadows to get the credit they'd long deserved. And though it was fun to see the agents fielding more requests and enjoying a new level of fanfare as they traveled from precinct to precinct, I was happy to observe it from a distance. My work kept me busy enough. Besides, ever since joining the BSU, I'd considered Quantico, not out in the field, to be the place where I could do the most good. But that was all about to change.

In the summer of 1985, a child case in Illinois required an

immediate response. It involved a missing seven-year-old girl and a surviving child witness. The event had taken place in broad daylight on Sunday, June 2, 1985, but investigators had few clues to go on. The surviving witness was scared and unable to talk. What the investigators really needed was an expert who could help make the child feel comfortable enough to tell them what had happened.

I got the call on June 11, more than a week after the initial kidnapping. This put me at a huge disadvantage. I knew from firsthand experience that after an incident there was a narrow window to find the missing child unharmed, and an even smaller window to find her harmed but still alive. After that, the likely outcomes went from bad to worse. It was a race against time.

"Why'd you wait so long?" I asked the Chicago-based agent on the other end of the line. I was frustrated, but I tried to rein it in.

"It's not easy finding someone with experience interviewing child victims of trauma. We didn't realize the BSU had one of their own. And to be honest, no one even thought about talking to the girl [the witness] after that first interview with the police."

"All right." I sighed. "What's the case and who's involved?"

"The victim is a seven-year-old girl named Melissa A.," the agent explained. "Everyone calls her Missy. She was bike riding with her friend Opal Horton on a road near the local school. Opal, who's also seven, saw the whole thing happen. She was almost abducted too."

"What about suspects?"

"That's less clear. What we know is that some guy pulled over and asked the girls for directions. He got out of his car, saying he couldn't hear them, walked right up to them, then grabbed Opal by her neck and threw her into the front seat. He went to get Missy next, but while he was distracted, Opal escaped by climbing out the driver's-side window. She ran to a nearby John Deere dealership and hid in a tractor tire. Missy's face was pressed against the back window as the car disappeared down the road. But we got all that from witnesses. The girl—Opal, I mean—isn't willing to talk."

"Let me talk to the unit chief," I said. "In the meantime, don't upset the girl with more questions. Just keep her safe."

I was given approval to leave the next day. And the following morning, June 12—Missy's eighth birthday—I flew commercial into Chicago's Midway Airport and then jumped into a small four-seater Cessna used by the local law enforcement agencies in the area. As my flight approached the small airport just outside Somonauk, Illinois, I realized why Missy still hadn't been found. Dense forests and raw terrain stretched as far as the eye could see. Missy could have been anywhere. But she did have one advantage: Opal. Opal had been a direct witness to the kidnapping. Her memory could provide invaluable insight into the offender's mental, emotional, and physical characteristics, which in turn might help us figure out who he was and where he was hiding. Opal was Missy's best chance at being found alive.

I was greeted by agents from the FBI's Chicago Field Office, Candice DeLong and Dan Cantella, at their temporary command center within the St. John the Baptist Catholic Church in Somonauk. I knew Candice from a brief meeting in 1980 at her FBI training for new agents. She was one of only seven female recruits. And she had a similar background to mine: she'd been a psychiatric nurse before entering the FBI. It was a relief to see her. She was the right agent for the case.

DeLong and Cantella immediately got down to business, telling me everything they knew about Missy, Opal, and the other witnesses. They also told me about the A. family, adding that now wasn't a good time to meet them because a "Happy Birthday" balloon had been sent to their home earlier in the day by a well-intentioned but out-of-the-loop family friend.

At the time Missy disappeared, the tiny town of Somonauk had a population of only thirteen hundred residents. It was a farming community—checkered with corn and soybean fields—located off Highway 34, 270 miles east of Mendota, Illinois, and 4 miles west of Sandwich, Illinois. The town itself was a grid of evenly spaced ranch houses. Very few trees stood in the yards, and only a handful of church spires broke up the monotony of the vast open sky. Neighbors knew one another, and the community itself had always felt safe.

Investigators determined that late in the morning on Sunday, June 2, Missy and Opal were riding their bikes in the area of County Line Road when they stopped at the home of their elementary school principal, James Wood, and asked him what time it was. Principal Wood told the girls it was 11:30 a.m., at which point they returned to their bikes and rode off toward the east. Shortly after that, Principal Wood left his home to drive to school. On the way, he observed the girls' bicycles abandoned in the center of the road. The girls were nowhere in sight, but he assumed they were playing somewhere nearby.

At 11:42 a.m., the Sandwich Police Department, which handled police calls for Somonauk Police Department, received a telephone call that Missy A. had been kidnapped. The call came from the residence of Charles Hickey. Charles's son Jeff, who knew both girls, frantically yelled into the phone while Opal—who'd run a half mile to get there—sobbed and gasped for breath in the background. Both the Somonauk Police Department and the DeKalb County Sheriff Department initiated an immediate investigation. They notified the FBI at 6:45 p.m.

On June 3, Opal Horton spoke with FBI investigators and provided the following details of the event: Opal and Missy had just left their school principal's house on County Line Road when a vehicle appeared behind them and passed them going east. The vehicle suddenly stopped, turned around, and slowed down as it approached the two girls on their bikes. The male driver of the vehicle called out to the girls for directions back to town. Opal answered, but the driver told the girls he couldn't hear them. He then exited his vehicle, approached the girls, and asked the same question about how to get back to town. Opal started answering again when the subject grabbed her around the neck, lifted her from the ground, and tossed her through the driver's-side window onto the front seat. The subject then began chasing Missy around and around the vehicle in circles. Opal tried to get out of the car through the passenger-side door, but the lock button had been unscrewed and was missing. Opal tried to jump but sort of fell out of the driver's-side window onto the ground. The kidnapper then came running back around the front of the vehicle, chasing Missy, and tripped over Opal. As the subject fell to the ground, he struck his elbow on the gravel road, then grabbed Missy by the ankle with his right hand, pulling her down to the ground. Opal jumped to her feet and crushed the subject's right hand with her shoe, causing him to momentarily let go of Missy. As he reached for Opal with his left hand, she stamped on it and fled toward some machinery parked in a nearby lot.

From her hiding place, Opal watched the subject grab Missy around the neck and throw her through the driver's-side window of the car. The subject then calmly got in the car and sped off toward the west. At first, she could hear Missy crying out for help, but before long, her screams dissipated into silence. Terrified, Opal only left her hiding place once she was sure the car was gone and wouldn't be coming back. She ran across the schoolyard and kept running for several streets until she reached the home of Charles Hickey.

A second witness, Mike Marquardt, had a partial view of the abduction from where he was standing outside the nearby Turner Funeral Home. Marquardt, a seventeen-year-old boy, had been babysitting the Turner children when the kidnapping occurred. He was playing with the kids in the yard when he observed a blue vehicle speeding away from in front of the John Deere dealership. Marquardt was able to narrow down the vehicle possibilities to a 1976 AMC Gremlin, a 1971 Ford Maverick, or a 1968 Plymouth Valiant.

At the time of the abduction, Missy was wearing a bright pink beaded necklace that spelled out "M-I-S-S-Y," the individual letters of the nickname inscribed on five consecutive hearts. She had on a short-sleeved purple polo shirt with light green trim on the collar and sleeves, and two heart-shaped green buttons, one of which was missing. Over the polo shirt, she wore a sleeveless tank top—light purple with a multicolor rainbow in front. She was also wearing Gitano brand blue jeans, white bobby socks with stripes, and pink tennis shoes with side decorative zippers and faded pink laces. Her two upper front teeth were missing, but her adult teeth were just starting to come in.

The professional part of my brain took all this information in as data. But the rest of me, all the pieces inside that made me who I was, felt overcome with a deep sadness that I struggled to contain. Missy was just a little girl. And no matter what happened next, nothing for her or her family or her best friend Opal would ever be the same.

I took a short break to process all this information. And as much as every second mattered, I also knew how important it was to approach this case with logic and a clear head. After taking a moment to think about Missy first, I shifted gears and focused on the work itself. As I paced up and down the command center halls, I noticed a detailed map of the massive six-hundred-square-mile area in DeKalb County that the search teams had already scoured. It was covered in colored grids showing where police, firefighters, and volunteers had completed their assigned checks. Also, icons indicated where aircraft or canine units had been brought in to aid in searching barns, silos, streams, and ponds. None of this information had yielded clues about Missy or her abductor or where they might have ended up.

"There you are." DeLong stopped me mid-pace. "Are you ready to meet Opal?"

I was anxious to get started, but I wanted to make sure this was done right. "I'd like to speak with her parents first," I said.

"No need," Cantella assured me. "We got their permission."

"That's right." DeLong flashed her partner a look of impatience. "We told them about your experience and that you wouldn't trigger any unnecessary stress or harm. They know you're just asking about things she already remembers."

"I appreciate that," I said. "But I'd still like to speak with the family first. They're dealing with trauma of their own right now. It's important to hear their concerns."

The meeting was set up for later that afternoon. It was held in the command center and took no longer than fifteen minutes. I introduced myself, asked Opal's parents about their experience, and then discussed the approach I planned on using with their daughter. I explained that I'd use a drawing technique that didn't require Opal to say anything. She could just draw and/or talk as much as she wanted. In child psychology, experts often use artwork as a tool for helping kids to communicate traumatic experiences. For many children, drawing can be a nonthreatening medium to express what might otherwise be too overwhelming to say out loud. I then asked Opal's parents if I had their permission to move forward, and they agreed. This step was essential because it helped the family feel a sense of control within the investigation.

The next morning, DeLong and I drove to meet Opal at the command center conference room. It was just the two of us. Of course,

Cantella had also wanted to sit in on the interview, but I explained to him that children tended to respond more openly to female investigators, especially after witnessing a male commit a violent crime. He understood, and he agreed to watch from outside as long as we recorded the session for evidence.

Opal was already seated when we arrived. She wore a short-sleeve pink blouse and navy-blue shorts. Her light brown shoulder-length hair was tucked loosely behind her ears with pink barrettes on either side. She looked at DeLong, then at me, and mumbled "Hi" in a small voice. She was a tiny, sad girl. I hoped I could reach her. I wanted to do anything I could to help her feel safe enough to open up.

DeLong was still setting up the tape recorder when Opal began to talk. She said she thought that "Missy had a plan that day, but it wasn't to be kidnapped." She talked about the day and how it was going well "until that happened." Then she added that she was still scared just thinking about it.

"That's okay," I told her. "How about this. What if instead of just talking, what if we draw and talk a little instead? You can make some drawings for us to keep, and you can make some drawings to take home, too. Would that be okay?"

She nodded and sat up a little in her seat.

"Do you make drawings in school?" I asked, placing a collection of crayons on the table. "What kinds of pictures do you like to draw?"

Opal thought for a while before nodding yes. "We draw dogs," she replied. Then she continued with what's called a thought intrusion—a suddenly overwhelming expression of violent or anxious or sexually explicit thoughts. "I don't know what we've done. It's been a long time because the last two days in school I couldn't remember. I was worried about Missy."

Opal stared across the table with a faraway look in her eyes. It made perfect sense that she couldn't get Missy out of her thoughts, and I was glad she could talk about it. So, I followed her lead. "Maybe we could draw a picture about that, what it's like to worry about Missy. Or how about a picture of your favorite weather?"

Opal looked at the crayons and picked out a blue one. "Rainy days," she said.

"Okay," I encouraged her. "Let's make that our first drawing. You can talk and tell us about what you draw. Is it okay if we ask questions, too? You can just talk about whatever's on your mind."

"When I'm dreaming at night, I think about Missy," she whispered. Then, she concentrated on her work until the first drawing was finished.

The picture showed blue teardrops that spelled out the name *Melissa*. The letters were drawn on two lines, suggesting that Opal's mind was half on rain and half on Missy. Missy's name clung to one side of the paper, a sign of anxiety and disorganization.

"Okay," I said. "That's our first one, that's your favorite weather. How about on that day? What was the weather like then?"

"Hot and sunny," she answered.

I asked more questions, but Opal took a moment to distract herself before thinking back to that day. She looked at the crayons and the paper and shuffled back and forth uncomfortably in her seat.

"I wanted to play with Missy, but Mom said I had to eat breakfast and clean my room," she began. "I took my blue bike and rode to Missy's house. Then we rode to school and saw one teacher." She added that they played on the merry-go-round, went to her baby-sitter's house to use the bathroom, and then rode to the principal's house to ask him the time.

"Did you see anything out of the ordinary?" I asked.

Opal described the rusty blue car driving past them outside the principal's house and mentioned that it was the same car that came back for them later. "It was shaped like a Pinto but was not a Pinto." She said they then left the principal's house and went back to their bikes.

Her second drawing showed the bicycle ride to Missy's house. "It's hard to draw," she apologized. The images were disorganized, with floating bicycles in abstract sizes, but Opal tried to tie it together with arrows and words. The memory wasn't integrated—it wasn't organized like the figures in the first drawing. The enlarged bikes suggested feelings of being overwhelmed, and the bikes' absence of pedals showed an inability to escape or feel control.

I slowed down a little to let Opal draw. I could see that she was struggling and hoped I could pace her through this because I needed to get to the kidnapper memory. I didn't want her to retreat back into herself. She picked out a green-colored crayon. "That's a nice color," I said.

Opal didn't say much between her second and third drawings. She mostly concentrated on the picture in front of her. It showed the principal's house and the kids by the funeral home. The focus of this picture was time—a large brown clock on the house just above the door. She then took a blue crayon and started to draw a car. But she stopped abruptly without finishing it.

"I can't draw a picture like that car because it is hard to do," she told me. Then she shifted back in her chair and gently swung her legs beneath the table. A minute passed. She stopped swinging her legs. Then, very quietly, she spoke again. "He snuck up behind me, grabbed me, and threw me in his car head first."

"What did he look like?"

"He was dark-headed. He had a mustache and things sticking out of his chin like he hadn't shaved." She picked the blue crayon back up and continued with her drawing.

This fourth picture showed the incident of the driver throwing Opal into the car. Despite the violence she and her friend had endured in this moment, she omitted drawing herself or Missy. It was mostly an auditory memory, not visual, and had confused wording that read: *get out of car, got me.* The main image was a man that loomed large and lacked feet—ghost-like—as if he were haunting her.[*]

"What was that like?" I asked her.

"The inside of the car only had a steering wheel, no radio, with the floorboard and seat torn up. The back seat was like the front seat bench."

Drawing number five showed the inside of the car. Opal seemed distressed and fidgeted constantly as she worked, sketching one section and then another in a disorganized rush. She still didn't include herself or Missy. But she did try to explain the drawing's chaos by attempting to label and diagram her thoughts, including the words *shocking, little dirt,* and *jump out.* The result was unique from her other drawings in that Opal used the whole sheet of paper to write words and sketch chaotic shapes. This showed how absolute the moment felt. It showed fear. And despite how crude the drawing was with its tilted words and abstract shapes, it was also intensely powerful. I couldn't help but feel a deep sadness as Opal handed me the page.

Opal returned her blue crayon to the box and took out a black one. I asked her what happened next, and she described waiting until the car took off and then running to the house of a local teacher, Charles Hickey. She remembered crying and telling Hickey that her friend had just been kidnapped. Hickey called 911. The sheriff was the first person to arrive, then her dad (Jim), then Missy's parents, "Mike and Sherri, who were really scared because they just let us go on a bike ride and it happened to Missy."

Opal's sixth drawing represented waiting. She didn't draw Missy, but she showed herself as a tiny figure tucked behind a truck's wheel in the bottom right corner of the page. The large size of the truck suggested she felt a little protected for the first time. But by

---

[*] It ended up being this drawing, along with Opal's description of the man, that later proved to be the identifying components in the forensic artist's composite sketch of the offender.

depicting the kidnapper's car in the middle of the page, the picture still conveyed how anxious and vulnerable she felt.

"How did you feel when the man left?"

"I stopped crying and I was feeling safer. It was really shocking because I never saw that many police. It was scary," Opal said quietly. "The FBIs started coming, brought pictures for me to look at. One looked like Chuck, one of our friends."

In drawing seven, Opal wrote the words *feeling better* and drew herself taking action and looking for help at Hickey's house. She also included a very large police car.

Drawing eight showed Opal looking at police mugshots. There was a tiny face in the upper corner that said *check door*, and at the bottom there was an auditory memory: *father and me home.*

"What were you thinking during everything that happened?" I asked. "What kinds of things were going through your mind?"

"I thought about Missy and what he could have done to her and all these sorts of things, like he could have buried her or killed her or something like that. It scares me and I lay with my mom. The part that really scares me, I think like he's right behind me, watching me, and that's what really gets me scared. I turn around and look behind me and I don't see anybody, but I keep doing that every time I think of him. I think he's really looking for me. I think like he's right behind me, watching me, and that's what really gets me scared. I always walk with my mom."

"What would happen if you did see him? What would you do?"

"I'd call my mom and I would run away and go get the FBIs because I live in that neighborhood close to the FBIs." Opal then lowered her voice to a soft murmur. "If he was behind me, I would tell my mom it looks like him. When I go to bed, I always feel like he is looking in the window. I always sleep with my mom. But it just scares me, it feels like he makes a hole and goes through the machine shop and goes up to our house and he's watching me. I think about it a lot."

I suddenly noticed how thin Opal looked. She was frail and had dark circles under her eyes. I worried that she'd become an afterthought in all this chaos. Because despite how much she could help, she was still just a little girl who needed comfort and support of her own.

"Are you eating?" I asked.

"I'm not eating at all. I haven't eaten breakfast or lunch or anything."

"Why aren't you eating?"

"Because I just don't want to eat. I'm not hungry."

"What could help make you hungry? Anything?"

"Missy," Opal answered. "Missy, she hasn't ate since Sunday morning. I don't think she had breakfast."

I went back to nonthreatening topics to wind down the session. I did this to help transition Opal away from the intense negative emotions of that day but also to see how the experience persisted. I encouraged her to still use the paper and crayons as I asked about her favorite TV shows.

"I watch *Benson*, *The Hugabunch*, and all sorts of cartoons. I get into, like, *Star Wars* and *The Return of the Jedi*. When this is over with, I'm going to start watching scary movies again." Then she had another thought intrusion. "I thought this might be her lucky day or yesterday because it was Missy's birthday."

Opal's ninth and final picture depicted Missy's birthday and consisted of a rainbow with a pot of gold at the end. The pot of gold was miniscule, while the rainbow showcased nine colors. To finish the piece, Opal signed it with her name and the date, and then left the room to return to her family.

By the end of the session, I couldn't help but feel connected to this girl. Opal would forever be defined by this event. It was enormous—the type of experience that no one, let alone a small child, could fully process or rationally understand—and it would change her. I was grateful that DeLong was with me to witness Opal's story and to help guide her through everything that would come next in the case. Opal would always carry this experience with her. But so would I and so would DeLong. In some small way, I hoped that would help.

Four days later, on June 17, a small body was found partly submerged and loosely covered with rocks in a drainage creek on the outskirts of nearby Mendota. FBI agents identified it as Melissa A. She was still wearing the beaded pink necklace spelling "Missy."

It was DeLong who met with Opal to tell her that Missy was gone. The two went for a car ride, talked a little, and then returned to the command center. Opal asked if she could draw another picture, and DeLong laid out paper and crayons for her, giving no directions. After about an hour, Opal had made five drawings and written a letter in blue crayon:

June 18, 1985

Dear Missy,

I wish you wear here on erath. I wish this did never happen at all.
    We love you very much.

Your friend,
Opal Horton and everyone else

After Missy's body was found, the case switched from a missing person to a homicide investigation. Local law enforcement worked with the FBI to conduct a meticulous forensic examination of the body and the creek where it was found, scanning both relentlessly for clothing fibers, hair strands, cigarette butts, ash, or any other physical traces that could lead to a suspect. They also assembled a list of known criminals in the area whose previous convictions were a fit for child cases or sexual assaults. That list, aided by Opal's physical description of the kidnapper and his car, quickly narrowed the search to a single suspect.

On the day of the abduction, about an hour after Missy was taken, Mendota police officer James McDougall had radioed dispatch to report a car with a missing identification sticker. The driver parked and went into a local gas station. Officer McDougall waited for the driver to come out, then approached the car and asked to see an ID. The driver showed him a fishing permit with the name Brian Dugan. McDougall inspected the car but found nothing suspicious, so he made a note of the fishing permit and told Dugan he was free to go, even though he didn't have a driver's license. Later that evening, the county sheriff's police contacted local departments with information about the Missy A. abduction and gave a description of the suspect's vehicle, which the Mendota department connected to Dugan. They ran a report and quickly realized that Dugan's car also appeared on a police report from five days earlier, in which the driver had been involved in an attempted rape of a nineteen-year-old girl. They relayed this back to Central Command and, the next morning, at 6:45 a.m., after learning Dugan was a suspect in several other violent attacks, a team of FBI agents along with officers from several state agencies waited in the parking lot of Midwest Hydraulics—the Kane County plant where Dugan worked—to arrest him at gunpoint as he stepped out of his blue AMC Gremlin.

At the time of my interview with Opal, I already knew that investigators had several suspects in the case, including Dugan. But *proving* Dugan's involvement wasn't easy. He'd already gotten away with too many crimes to simply slip up or turn himself in. Investigators needed hard evidence. My interviews with Opal, her drawings, and her descriptive retelling of what she witnessed that day proved to be the key elements investigators were missing.

After Dugan's arrest in the parking lot of Midwest Hydraulics, he was quickly charged with two unrelated Kane County rapes and was elevated to the main suspect in Missy's abduction. At first, he was interviewed by a local detective but refused to cooperate. That's when the FBI stepped in. They inspected Dugan's car for forensic evidence connecting him to Missy's murder; and while they waited for the results to come back, they began combing through his criminal record and accumulated hundreds of pages of background information—mental health evaluations as well as interviews with his mother, siblings, girlfriends, and coworkers—to piece together a review of his history of violence. Their findings brought to light many similarities between Dugan's history and both the serial killer study and the criminal personality analysis I was doing with Douglas and Ressler at the FBI. Dugan's patterns of crime, starting with theft as a teenager and escalating to rape and murder in his twenties, matched specific variables that our research was just starting to understand. And the connection between his upbringing and preferred expressions of violence helped reinforce ideas of ours that would later become central to a formalized method of profiling. Just like the killers in our study, Dugan could be deconstructed, evaluated, and neatly categorized as a type. His actions showed little reasoning or intelligence, indicating that he was a disorganized offender—spontaneous and opportunistic in his attacks.

Brian James Dugan was born September 23, 1956, in Nashua, New Hampshire, to Genevieve "Jenny" and James Dugan. He was the second of five children and, according to two of his siblings, his life was marred by violence even from birth. Hospital staff had tried to delay Dugan's birth until a doctor could arrive by pushing his head back into the birth canal and strapping his mother's legs shut. The family worried that he had suffered brain damage as a result.

Early on in childhood, Dugan displayed traits that were common among violent criminals. He chronically wet the bed and was forced to sleep in urine-soaked sheets as punishment. He tortured animals—

once pouring gasoline on the family cat, lighting it, and laughing as the creature burst into flames. He burned down the family's garage when he was only eight years old. He also became sexually active at a young age, losing his virginity at thirteen and having an affair with the mother of a friend shortly after.

At around this same time, the Dugan family moved to Illinois so they could all get a fresh start. His mother described those years as happy. In an interview with the FBI after her son's arrest, she said Brian liked to read and play sports, especially baseball. According to Jenny, her son's problems didn't start until he was first arrested in connection with a burglary as a fifteen-year-old high school student. His conviction led to a short stay at a youth home, where he was likely the victim of sexual abuse. The experience changed Dugan, his mother noted. He tried to molest his younger brother shortly after returning home. And his crimes quickly escalated in severity, from petty theft and drug use to obsessive acts of sexual violence. Dugan's first attack occurred on April 21, 1974, when he attempted to abduct a ten-year-old girl from the local train station. The charges were dropped on a legal technicality.

In that same interview, Jenny told the FBI she didn't think her son was capable of anything beyond small, nonviolent crimes. But his siblings felt differently. In their interviews, Hilary and Steven Dugan both admitted that killing Missy was something Brian could do. Hilary didn't believe her brother was able to feel sorry for anyone other than himself. If he did it, she said, "He should get the death penalty." She hadn't forgiven him for the time he threatened to kill her and chop up her son.

The official records noted other risk factors. Both of Dugan's parents were alcoholics. His father, a salesman, was on the road a lot and died of liver cirrhosis in 1975. Jenny was the disciplinarian. She once caught Brian playing with matches and then made him hold a lit one until it burned down and singed his fingers. She would sometimes force him to eat spoonfuls of hot sauce or would beat him as punishment. Still, when questioned about it later, Dugan denied that his mother ever seriously abused him.

The FBI's file on Dugan also included mental exams from his earlier stay in prison after burglarizing two churches. One expert recommended he be placed in protective custody, describing Dugan as immature, extremely unstable, and having a poor self-image. Another categorized him as a sensation-addicted neurotic who drank and used drugs to lessen his inhibitions before committing a crime. These same reports also note Dugan complaining of being sexually abused in prison, just like he'd been abused ten years earlier during his stay at the youth home. This abuse was likely Dugan's trigger.

Six months after being released from Joliet Correctional Center, Dugan went on a two-year binge of violence. It started in late February 1983. Dugan was looking for a house to burglarize when he spotted ten-year-old Jeanine N. through the window of a house on a quiet street. Jeanine, who was home from school sick with the flu, screamed when Dugan kicked in her door. She struggled against the attack, leaving fingernail scratches on the walls of her home, but couldn't break free. Dugan wrapped her in a bedspread and kidnapped her in broad daylight. Her body was found two days later on a popular biking path.* She'd been raped and brutally beaten with a tire iron. Investigators found her head wrapped in a towel bound with tape so she couldn't see. There was nothing personal about Dugan's relationship to Jeanine. He didn't know her at all. Like all of Dugan's victims, she was simply a victim of opportunity and his own dark impulses.

Later that year, on July 15, Dugan spotted Donna Schnorr, a nurse at

---

* Shocked police quickly offered a monetary reward for information aiding their investigation, and just as quickly charged three local gang members with Jeanine's rape and murder after one of their ranks, twenty-year-old gang member Rolando Cruz, offered police false information in an attempt to claim the reward. Dugan remained free to continue his violent spree.

Mercy Center in Aurora, waiting in her car at a stoplight. It was early in the morning. No one was around. Dugan followed her for a while in his car until they were near a quieter stretch of road. He sideswiped her car off into the grass, then forced her into his vehicle and tied her hands together. Dugan drove her to a nearby quarry, where he raped her, forced her to walk out into the water, and drowned her by holding her head beneath the water until she stopped struggling. He watched her body floating for a while before getting back in his car and driving home. Again, investigators didn't identify Dugan as a suspect.

On May 6, 1985, Dugan followed twenty-one-year-old Sharon Grajek to the townhouse where she lived. He told her that her taillight was out and asked if she wanted to go out for food and drinks. Grajek said no, and Dugan then asked if she wanted to have some fun with him for eighty dollars. Grajek again declined his offer, at which point Dugan pushed his way into her car, threatened her with a hunting knife, and gagged and blindfolded her. He told her he would kill her if she didn't get into his car. After a fifteen-minute drive, Dugan pulled over and sexually assaulted her multiple times in the back seat. He then removed her blindfold and told her to get dressed. Dugan re-blindfolded her and began to make small talk as he drove, with questions like: "Where did you go to high school? Where do you party?" At the end, he left her blindfolded in the parking lot of a school near her home. He said his name was Brian, and he threatened to kill her and her sisters if she tried to look at him as he drove away. The victim felt too intimidated by Dugan's threats to report him to the police.

Dugan attempted two other kidnappings that month. The first one was nineteen-year-old Geneva, who was able to run away as he tried to force her into his car. She saw the car's license plate and reported it to the police. A day after that, Dugan coerced a sixteen-year-old girl into his car in Aurora by threatening her with a tire iron. He drove her to a secluded spot, where he wrapped a belt around her neck and raped her, then he took her home. He told her his name, but she was too frightened to call the police. By the time she filed a report, she only remembered his first name and last initial.

Dugan's final act of pure evil was the abduction, rape, and murder of Missy A.

On June 18, fifteen days after the search began, when Missy's body was found, it was taken to a lab in Washington, DC, to undergo a series of forensic tests, which included searching for fibers, hairs, and semen for DNA analysis. Dugan was ultimately connected to the crime through a strand of Missy's hair collected from Dugan's sleeping bag and a clump of dirt on his boardinghouse floor that matched the soil at the creek where the body was found. Since this was back in the 1980s, DNA wasn't completely trusted or admissible as evidence on its own, so it took two forensic tests to confirm the matches to both the hair and dirt samples. The coroners suspected that Missy died a violent death, likely within an hour of her abduction. Dugan was eventually charged and convicted, but he avoided the death penalty by agreeing to confess to the murders of Melissa A. and Donna Schnorr. During plea bargaining, he offered no real explanation for his crimes, admitting, "It might have been for the sex, but I don't understand why. I wish I knew why I killed those girls. I wish I knew why I did a lot of things, but I don't."

The Dugan case marked the first time I was there to witness the trauma of a killer's actions unfold. I spoke with Missy's family. I spoke with her friends. And I spoke with Opal Horton and her parents. The experience was more than just personal, though. It also forced me to reconsider how I approached both the criminal personality study and my work on individual investigations going forward. It made me understand that Dugan and others like him were often genuinely unable to explain why they killed. They didn't have the answers. But this didn't mean their actions lacked cause. They killed for a reason— and I was going to figure out that reason.

CHAPTER 7

Victimology 101

Throughout my time at the BSU, I made a point of continuing to lecture on rape victimology at the FBI Academy as often as I could. It was important to me to get the information out. It seemed important for the agents. And it offered a unique opportunity to further advance criminal profiling at a critical time in its development. This was the mid-1980s, and after being ignored and dismissed for years, profiling was suddenly recognized as an effective tool for criminal investigations. Everyone wanted to see it in action. The problem was, no law enforcement agency outside of our small group at the BSU had the expertise or knowledge to use the technique as it was intended. We were it. And despite our goal of creating a standardized process for profiling so it could be easily taught to other agents, we simply weren't there yet. We were still refining our own understanding of profiling as we worked from case to case.

That's why lecturing was so important, especially when it came to young agents—the ones who believed that instinct and the virtues of their own hard work were all it took to make a case. This group had no interest in thinking about psychology, behavior, or a serial killer's deeply patterned thoughts. They wanted action. And yet, these were exactly the types of investigators who could benefit most from profiling. These were the ones who'd be tasked with confronting new types of violence—stranger, more chaotic, and less logical than anything the Bureau had ever known. They'd be entering a whole new arena where crime had changed. It wasn't a simple game of cops and robbers anymore. The sooner new investigators understood this, the sooner they'd be able to stack the deck in their favor. But they had to see the relevance first.

So, I met them on their level.

I used real-world cases with real-world outcomes to show step by step how profiling worked. I explained the significance of John Joubert's biting and ritualistic carving of young boys, David Meirhofer's habit of keeping morbid souvenirs, Bernadette Protti's obsessive thought patterns, and Brian Dugan's violent upbringing. But mostly I talked about victimology—a method of analyzing crime from the victim's perspective—which, at least at that point in time, was an underutilized way of gaining deeper insights into the mind of a killer. This was something I'd become well versed in during my research on rape. It was also a key component of profiling, and the agents at the BSU considered my expertise a unique advantage.

"Today's lecture's going to be a little bit different," I announced, looking out at the thirty or so agents seated in the Quantico auditorium. "The focus is still on victimology. But unlike our previous sessions, today's case has a victim that's still alive. It makes a big difference when investigators can talk to the victim, ask questions, and get answers about who she is and why she was targeted. It makes things easy, right?"

The young agents all nodded in agreement.

"Except, history shows us it doesn't," I said. "It adds a new layer of challenges that need to be recognized. Let me give you an example. How should you proceed when the victim can be thoughtful and articulate about the rawest details of the attack, but then can't remember if it was raining or not? Or what if they describe the brand and specific color of their assailant's shoes, but struggle with the exact location of where the attack happened? What happens then? Can you trust them? Can you trust their account?"

I wasn't expecting an answer—and I certainly didn't get one—but it was important to let those questions sink in. I wanted the agents to confront their own biases, whatever those happened to be. So I busied myself by shuffling papers and pretending to look at one document in particular. Then I focused back on the auditorium.

"That's what we're going to talk about today," I said, breaking the uncomfortable silence. "Victimology in cases where the victim's still alive. The example we'll use involves multiple violent sexual assaults in the catacombs of Philadelphia's Suburban Station. Let's start with an overview, then we can break down the details. The victim in this case is a woman named Pauline."

Pauline was attacked during a Thursday afternoon in June of 1976. She was changing trains at Suburban Station in the rush of midday traffic. She had just finished shopping and was the last passenger out of the subway car—distracted by thoughts of a long list of chores waiting for her back home—when suddenly, she felt herself pulled backward in a violent jerking motion. She looked behind her, wondering if her purse had been caught in the train door, but as she turned, a gloved hand covered her mouth just as an arm tightened around her waist. She tried to scream, but couldn't. She tried to fight the person off, but his grip was too strong. Passengers crisscrossed around her without seeming to notice—it was the bystander effect in full force. Pauline felt completely helpless as she was pulled across the busy platform and down a ladder into the station's catacombs.

It was dark. The air was noticeably cooler, and she felt disoriented as she was forced onto the rough floor. Her attacker tore off her underwear with one hand while his other hand stayed firmly pressed against her mouth, muffling her cries for help. She was elbowed, hit, and beaten against the cement, then raped—all while the sounds of trains screeched in and out of the station overhead. She never saw her assailant's face.

I became involved in the case in the immediate aftermath of the attack. This was in the late 1970s, and my earlier work on the rape study had already established me as one of the few known experts whose sexual assault testimony carried any weight in court. In this case, Pauline's lawyer had arranged for me to perform a forensic psychiatric evaluation of Pauline to measure the impact the event had had on her life. Pauline and I talked generally at first about her interests and background so I could establish a base-line of her temperament and characteristics. Then I switched gears and inquired about the attack. She hesitated for a moment before carefully recounting the events—the whole while keeping her knees pressed tightly together and rocking herself back and forth in small, measured movements. She described the subsystem's cold floor, the glint of broken glass, and a smell of something like vinegar. She could still smell it, she said. Every time she thought back to that day, that awful smell rushed back into her head.

As the memories bubbled up in her mind, I could tell Pauline was growing increasingly upset, so I redirected the conversation to how she was coping in the aftermath of the attack. Pauline replied that she found herself becoming reclusive, distancing herself from family and friends, and added that she didn't really eat or sleep. Whenever she closed her eyes at night, she dreamed about the gloved hand covering her mouth. She was scared to be alone, and yet, at the same time, she felt isolated in the company of others. Sounds of metal against metal—pots scraping a kitchen stove, the shrillness of hinges on a loose door—reminded her of trains pulling in and out of the station as she was raped just a few feet below. She replayed the memory often. She said she hated thinking about it, but there were details she needed to remember, moments that flooded her mind in a disorienting kaleidoscope of shapes, colors, and sounds. She needed to get the memory straight to move on with her life. She needed to confront what happened. She needed to take back control. But she hated going back there, to those sounds, sights, and that awful, awful smell.

"Here's the thing," I explained to the agents. "It's these types of sensory details that victims tend to remember with extraordinary clarity. They're vivid and perfectly intact. Whole. But in Pauline's case, when I asked her about peripheral details of the day—the weather or visual markers within the station—she became confused and sometimes recalled details inaccurately. Still, that inability to remember certain details doesn't negate someone's credibility. In fact, in Pauline's case, she openly admitted to what she knew and what she didn't. The key thing here is that this is just the brain's way of processing trauma. It's a universal coping mechanism, whether someone's a combat soldier, a survivor of an accident, or a victim of a violent crime. Your job is to know this and to account for these types of psychological mechanisms when you're talking with victims. It's all about organizing the chaos to make crimes make sense."

"I have a question." An agent in the front row raised his hand. "How do you know who you can trust and who's just lying to you? Like, what if they're making the whole thing up?"

"That should be pretty far down on your list of things to worry about," I responded. "I'd suggest not leading with assumptions. It does more damage than good. And you'll do better if you stick to facts. In the case of traumatic experiences, the facts are usually pretty well established and clear. Trauma causes a breakdown in three key brain regions: the prefrontal cortex, which is responsible for focusing attention; the brain's fear circuitry, which directs attention towards or away from the source of trauma; and the hippocampus, which is responsible for encoding experiences into short-term and long-term memories. Trauma destabilizes these functions and causes an unpredictable mix of vivid memories, fragmented memories, and gaps of either the assault or the peripheral details that surround an assault. It's this jumbled storage of sensations and experiences that causes victims to occasionally sound confused. That's important to know for how you structure your questioning."

Another hand went up in the back of the auditorium.

"So, is it safe to trust the details they do remember, or do they get those wrong too?" this agent asked. "I'm thinking of how this might create problems for profiling."

"I know it feels counterintuitive," I said. "But those details are the most reliable information you'll get. You have to understand that, at its most basic, the narrow, vivid sensory details that victims tend to recall—the sounds of a train, the feeling of a cold floor, the image of a gloved hand—are limited because that's just how the brain protects itself. It's defensive in nature. It's a way of blocking out trauma by masking the experience in fewer concrete details. But all those details are real. They've just been made bigger, in a sense, to block out the bad."

As the lecture went on, I could see that some agents were following the conversation while others were drifting off. In a way, I couldn't blame them. The psychology of violence wasn't exactly a crowd pleaser. It couldn't compare with the adrenaline rush of a successful raid or high-speed chase. It didn't have that type of instant gratification. And besides, agents weren't used to giving much thought to victims. Their mindset was more like that of a bloodhound, trained to home in on the killer's scent and focus solely on that one objective. But none of that made the psychological elements of a case any less important. Because when our methods did work—when the agents gathered in a room with only sketches of information and managed to shape them into a fully realized profile that was instrumental in breaking a case wide open—that was a pretty good feeling. We solved the cases that no one else could. And victimology was one of the best tools we had.

I tried to make this as clear as possible with the few minutes I had left.

"Look, eventually every single one of you will run into a case where focusing on the offender just isn't enough. They'll be too smart, too careful, or too whatever to get caught. You'll need to step back and take a different approach. That's when victimology can help. It explains *why* a victim was targeted. You'll look at things like a victim's physical and psychological characteristics, their possible connection to the offender, and their vulnerability at the time of the attack, and you'll start to see why the killer chose them instead of anyone else.

"Pauline was targeted during a busy time, as people were changing trains. Everyone in that station was focused on their next train. The offender knew what would happen and planned his crime *because* of how busy it would be. Chaos created his cover. His motive was sexual. His risk was high. Her risk was low. He started his crime with plenty of witnesses, but the bystander effect worked.

"These are the pieces of victimology that will shed light on the offender's motive. And by analyzing both the victim and the motive, as well as all the other files you've collected on the crime, you'll start to narrow in on the defining characteristics of the offender. You'll reduce the pool of suspects to its smallest possible list. You'll chip away at the rogues' gallery of options until you're left with the one choice that's clear and obvious. Because ultimately, that's what victimology does— it holds a mirror to the perpetrator of the crime."

———◦—◦—◦———

There was more to the Suburban Station case that I didn't share with the agents that day. I had to be careful not to overwhelm them, not to desensitize them to the realities of sexual violence. And yet, at the same time, I knew how important it was to prepare them for the specific horrors they were sure to see throughout the years ahead. Lecturing was a balancing act in that sense. And in terms of victimology, I felt that Pauline's story had illustrated my point well enough. Besides, what happened next in the Suburban Station case was difficult enough for me to think about. I wasn't sure how the agents would react.

Months after the original assault, Pauline's lawyer, Henry Fitzpatrick, had descended into the train station's catacombs accompanied by a photographer to shoot pictures of the crime scene for the upcoming trial. The catacombs were a dark and secluded underground subsystem of the area's commuter line. They were hot and poorly lit. The air was chalky, and it took Fitzpatrick a moment to realize that the lump he was squinting at in the darkness was the body of a woman lying barefoot right in front of him. He stood still. His eyes adjusted until he could just make out the woman's chest rising and sinking in shallow swells. She looked young, maybe mid-thirties, was well dressed in a two-piece navy suit, and had a scuffed-up brown leather briefcase just to her right. The photographer placed a lens on his camera and clicked a button to shine a light on the scene. Fitzpatrick saw a bag from Wanamaker's department store. He saw the woman's awkward positioning. And he saw puddles of blood around her face and arms. Footsteps echoed against the platform above. The photographer then took a picture, and for a moment the tunnel became brightly lit, a stark flash of absolute light.

This second victim was barely alive. Fitzpatrick called 911, and an ambulance quickly transported her to the intensive care unit at Jefferson Hospital. This attack had all the marks of a serial offense, though it was far more brutal than the one suffered by Pauline. The victim, Joan—a lawyer and Upper Darby resident with a ten-year-old daughter—had been beaten and raped, and her head had been smashed repeatedly against the station's pavement floor. She was in a coma and needed multiple surgeries. Nurses kept watch, and after weeks without improvement, they made a recording of Joan's daughter talking and singing, then played it daily until Joan began to respond. Joan awoke after forty-five days, but the attack had left her with permanent brain damage and partial paralysis. She kept asking when her mother would visit. And each time nurses reminded her that her mother had passed away several years ago, Joan would break down and cry.

Unlike Pauline, who was haunted by the details of her assault, Joan's brain injury left her with no memories of the events whatsoever. She struggled to find answers. And she was further denied resolution when, because of the irreversible nature of her memory loss, she was unable to testify at court. But Pauline could testify. She could take back a small piece of what had been stolen from her. And as far as I was concerned, the grit she showed in confronting her attacker— while at the same time being deeply affected by the complicated aftermath of rape trauma syndrome—was absolutely critical to her story, even more so than the victimology lessons that new agents could take away from her case.

Despite the fact that all signs pointed to both Pauline's and Joan's cases being connected, Fitzpatrick brought them to trial separately. Investigators found no witnesses to Pauline's attack—the station didn't have cameras, and security guards claimed they hadn't seen anyone suspicious at the time noted in Pauline's claim. So Fitzpatrick brought a trespassing action against Consolidated Rail Corporation, the owner of Suburban Station, to advance Pauline's case to the legal system. The company responded with a small settlement offer, which was quickly denied, and the case eventually proceeded to court.

On the day of the trial, Pauline took the stand and testified in a very quiet, staccato voice about what she'd experienced during the attack and how isolated she'd felt. She was articulate throughout. She offered the rawest and most vulnerable details of her life to a room full of corporate lawyers, strangers, and media personnel. Then came the defense's turn. They started right off with a familiar cross-examination technique—one particularly common in rape trials—that was intended to call into question Pauline's credibility. They asked her about the offender's clothes, about visual details within the station, and about the day's weather and other peripheral details. Pauline was confused at some points and recalled some details inaccurately. After each mistake, the defense corrected her in front of the jury, using the opportunity to describe Pauline as unreliable and disingenuous. But what the defense didn't explain was that Pauline's answers had nothing to do with her credibility; they were just a reflection of how the human brain processes traumatic situations. The defense knew this. They knew that ignorance of how memory works plays a major part in why rape is one of the most commonly acquitted crimes in the world. But they didn't let on. I suppose you could say they were just doing their job. Soon enough, however, I'd get a chance to do mine.

When it was my turn to take the stand as an expert witness, I made sure to clarify the psychological reasoning behind memory storage and recall of victims of sexual assault. I explained how gaps or partial memories are common for anyone who experiences a traumatic situation, whether they're a soldier, a survivor of an accident, or a victim of a sexual assault. It's how the brain works. With or without the details, the experience never goes away. For Pauline, as is the case with many others, the attack completely changed her life. She couldn't go back to work, take public transportation, take care of her children, or leave the house alone. It's unreasonable to expect someone to have full recall of their trauma. The impact is what matters most.

The jury awarded Pauline $250,000 in compensatory and $500,000 in punitive damages. That verdict was subsequently molded by the trial court to include delay damages of $115,208.29, which accounted for annual interest on the total award of $750,000 from October 16, 1979, to April 29, 1981. Consolidated Rail appealed to the Superior Court, which ordered a remittitur (reduction) of the delay damages, but this was overturned by Pauline's subsequent appeal.

The success of Pauline's case allowed Fitzpatrick to turn his attention to the second victim, Joan. Police had identified a suspect in the case, a repeat offender known to authorities for raping a woman in a subway concourse in 1977. The man had served a short prison sentence for his crime. But within the past few months, he'd again been convicted of rape, this time targeting a nineteen-year-old Temple student in an attack that took place underneath a platform in Suburban Station.

The prosecutor was able to bring Joan's case to trial with the help of a female witness who described seeing the suspect take a woman down a ladder into Suburban Station's catacombs on the day Joan went missing.

"For some reason or instinct, I started looking around," the witness said. "I saw a man and a woman standing near the escalator doors. They were very close together, and I was wondering what they were doing there." The witness described seeing this after getting off an incoming train. "I saw them go down the ladder. I didn't know what to do. I was scared to death." She tried to get help but couldn't find anyone. "I started to walk back to the ladder. I stooped over and I saw this face that was staring at me. I was so scared and frightened I froze. He didn't expect to see me. He went to the right side and I saw his profile. I saw the girl's feet laying there. There were no shoes on. That's all I saw. Her feet and legs are all I saw."

The witness was asked if the man she saw was in the room that day.

"The man right there, the defendant," she said, pointing at the defense table.

But despite this testimony, the suspect was acquitted. Those who followed the case were shocked. Several people audibly gasped. The prosecutor hurried from the courtroom, ignoring requests by the press for comment. Only the defendant and his defense attorney smiled.

Sadly, the outcome wasn't surprising. It followed a pattern common to many rape trials around the country at that time. Victims had the deck stacked against them. Part of this was because rape kits were still uncommon and DNA profiling wouldn't exist for several more years. And part of it was the secluded nature of sexual assault, which tended to preclude dependable witnesses. But the bigger truth was that rape was often a man's word versus a woman's word. And women, in the late 1970s, were viewed as unreliable, emotional, and untrustworthy, meaning that in cases like these, juries rarely took the side of victims.

CHAPTER 8

Beneath the Mask

Following my lecture on victimology, Hazelwood found me at my desk in the bomb shelter and asked if I had a minute to talk about a new case out of Baton Rouge he'd been asked to profile. Local police were investigating a sexual predator linked to dozens of crimes across multiple states, and Hazelwood wanted my input on some of the offender's unusual behaviors.

"This guy's an odd one," Hazelwood said. "He only enters homes between eight p.m. and one a.m., and only homes with unlocked doors or windows. Now maybe that's not so strange, but the really weird part is how he toys with his victims. He starts off by trying to comfort them, then rapes them while forcing whoever else is in the house to watch—the sick bastard." He paused, collecting himself. "Sorry about that. What I mean is . . . I'm just trying to get a better understanding of the typology we're dealing with so I can build out the case."

Hazelwood always tried his best to treat me like any other colleague. But the graphic nature of our work, and the raw emotions that came along with it, sometimes caused him to slip up and say things pretty bluntly. Then he'd get flustered and self-conscious about having spoken crudely in front of a woman. It was just his nature. He tried to walk some imaginary line of social decorum while talking to me about extreme acts of violence, regardless of how many times I told him to knock it off. And it wasn't just him either. I got this same treatment from nearly all the agents at the FBI. Even Ressler and Douglas showed this subtlety of caution toward me from time to time. But Hazelwood, his discretion was different. It seemed to be protective in a way—maybe because he was the one who'd brought me into the group. And as he laid out a set of files and began listing the relevant facts of the case, he hesitated, just barely softening his voice, as he broke down some of the more graphic details.

"Newspapers are calling him the 'Ski Mask Rapist,'" Hazelwood continued. "I'm sure you can figure out why. He's over six feet tall, has a slender frame, and dark hair. He's usually armed with a knife or a gun. He ties up his victims and rapes them in full view of any males in the house, sometimes taunting the men as he does it. Then he leaves the victims tied up while calmly robbing the house of televisions, stereos, or other valuables."

"Back up a second." I stopped him. "Have all his victims included a male witness?"

"No. That's more recent," Hazelwood said. "This guy's changed his method quite a bit since this started. He's unlike anyone I've ever seen before. He's the same guy, but it's like he's become a whole different offender. That's why I need your help. I'm hoping we can fill in a few trigger points on the timeline before I bring this back to the team."

Hazelwood's request for my insight was fairly common among agents within the BSU. Every person on the team brought unique knowledge and experience about a specific area of the field. I was no exception. And in the case of the Ski Mask Rapist, my combined background studying both victims of rape and violent offenders made me a good fit. Hazelwood saw me as the most qualified person to ask.

"This guy's linked to dozens of crimes," Hazelwood said. "But I think it's enough to look at his first five, middle five, and last five. That shows his progression. Make sense?"

I concentrated on a photo of a middle-aged woman with black-and-blue marks covering her breasts.

"The cases get pretty graphic. He savagely punched that woman in the breasts over and over again," Hazelwood muttered, reaching out to grab the picture from my hands.

I waved him off. "Stop apologizing, Roy. I don't need you to insulate me from the details. That only slows down the work. It's data. Now let's figure this one out."

Hazelwood nodded. "Okay. Here's what we know. Starting with his first five victims, the guy's just a run-of-the-mill rapist. He surprises single women alone in their house, promises them they won't get hurt, then binds them with their own clothing and vaginally rapes them. Fast-forward to the middle five victims, he starts using handcuffs and becoming more aggressive, forcing anal and oral penetration, sometimes in front of family members, and sometimes raping more than one woman during the same attack. Fast-forward again, and the latest five rapes show a transition to a much higher level of aggression. Like that picture you were looking at." Hazelwood motioned to where I'd placed the photo on the table. "He punched her in the breasts repeatedly, taunting her husband the whole time. Strange, right? What do you think?"

"I think he's chasing the thrill he got from his earliest victims," I said. "That much is clear. And he's having to go further towards violence to get there. But his motive hasn't changed. It's still the sense of control he gets from rape."

"That makes sense," Hazelwood agreed. "But the part I don't get is all the violence in front of the male partner. What's that about?"

"It's power: control as well as humiliation," I explained. "The need for an audience and to make someone else watch speaks to psychological factors in the rapist's life. It suggests that he's had his own history of trauma, and that this ritualistic behavior is rooted in a childhood experience of viewing, watching, or experiencing abuse."

"Do you think he's building up to murder or would that be at odds with the ritual?" Hazelwood asked. "That's what the police are worried about."

"Ritual can change to accommodate an offender's growing disconnect with reality," I said. "So, yes, I think murder's likely, but it's important to distinguish that that's not the primary motivation here. This guy's reliving an experience from his past. He's just flipped it. Now he's the one in control, and he wants to make sure others witness it."

In the days that followed, Unit Chief Depue arranged for me to travel to Louisiana to meet with the task force dedicated to the Ski Mask Rapist case. The plan was that I'd speak with victims and the local police to collect as much information as possible so that we could hurry up and catch this creep. The community was on edge, the frequency of attacks was increasing, and the media was making things worse by writing stories about the Ski Mask Rapist's ability to evade and outsmart the authorities. Hazelwood was particularly interested in a quick resolution as he was the FBI agent representing the case.

My phone rang as soon as I arrived at the hotel.

"Hey, Ann. How's it going?" Hazelwood asked.

"Fine. I just got in. I'm looking to—"

"That's great," he interrupted. "Listen. I need you to get the following information from the victims about the unsub's behavior during the assault. It'll be important when we start profiling this one."

"What do you mean? Are you thinking profiling is different between rape cases and sexual homicide?"

Hazelwood was so focused on what he wanted to tell me that he ignored my question and just kept talking. He could be that way sometimes—hyperfocused to the point of getting lost in his own thoughts. But I knew he'd come back to the question eventually. So I just kept listening.

"There are three basic steps I think we need to take with this one," he said. "The first is to get a specific set of information from the victim about the rapist's behavior. The second is to analyze that behavior to determine an underlying motive for the assault. And the third is to characterize the person who committed the crime, given the motivational factors indicated by their behavior."

"Hold on." I stopped him. "I'm going to need a pen."

Hazelwood then had me write down a series of questions he wanted me to ask. Some were questions about the unsub's behavior, such as: How did he manage to get to the victim? What was his method of control? How did he react to the victim's distress? Others were questions about the victim's interactions: Was the victim forced to talk? What sexual acts were they forced to perform? Did anything they do change the offender's attitude? And some questions aimed to learn more about the unsub's character, like: Did he have any sexual dysfunction? Did he use any precautionary methods to avoid detection? Did he take anything or leave anything at the scene of the attack?

It was clear that Hazelwood had a very specific approach in mind for this case. He seemed to be placing a larger value on the opinions of the surviving witnesses rather than on crime scene analysis and police reports. But why he'd made that decision and how he thought it would affect the profiling process, I wasn't yet sure. All I could think about was that he'd overheard me say something in my victimology lecture, that it interested him, and that he wanted to test out the theory to see it in action for himself.

I ended up meeting with five victims during the trip. They were all fearful and distressed—especially the two who'd been raped in front of family members—but they each made an effort to talk about their experiences as best they could. I found that all of them were showing clear signs of rape trauma syndrome. They described feeling numb or dead inside. They opened up about having constant stomach problems, having nightmares about their assailant raping them again, and being terrified that they might have AIDS. They panicked when in small spaces, were frightened by dark clothing, and constantly worried that the assailant would come back. All five of them were concerned about their relationships with their friends and family.

As I was thinking over the unsub's unusual behaviors while writing them into my report, I got a phone call from Unit Chief Depue.

"Ann. It's Depue. How'd the trip go?"

I thought carefully before answering. Depue never called about a trip unless something was up. "We have some good information from the victims," I said after a long pause. "Did you hear anything?"

"I sure did. I got an urgent call from the police department that there was a woman impersonating an FBI agent. I had to reassure them it was an official visit from the BSU and that you're one of us."

"Thanks," I said, not really sure what to make of the whole thing.

But Depue just laughed. "Louisiana isn't exactly DC. I probably should've been clearer that I was sending a woman. I'll remember that for next time. Now hurry up with that report. I don't want to read any more news coverage about how smart this one is."

A week or so later, Hazelwood led a group of agents in developing a formal profile of the Ski Mask Rapist, making sure I could attend. We stuck to our now-standard process of studying police reports, looking at crime scene photographs, and talking through the offender's motives and patterns. Hazelwood made sure to include notes from the conversation we'd had earlier as well as analysis from my trip to Louisiana. He also asked that I provide context for the validity of certain victim statements, because even seasoned agents had their own biases to overcome. Afterward, however, instead of taking all the information and writing up the profile on his own, Hazelwood asked the group to write the profile as a team. And he specifically wanted us to split this assessment into two distinct parts.

The first part was informed by our traditional profiling approach, which characterized unsubs in terms of likely demographics, background, and personality. We were well practiced in this process by now, and it didn't take long to write down our ideas. For the Ski Mask Rapist, based on how long he'd been active without getting caught, we classified him as a man in his late twenties or early thirties who'd never been married. His domineering behavior showed that he was confident and saw himself as an alpha male. He was also meticulous about the details—he made sure to discreetly cut telephone wires before breaking into a house—and he was a perfectionist, and this knowledge helped us characterize him as someone who kept in good physical shape, watched and/or played sports, kept a cleanly manicured appearance, and likely had a tendency to project this masculinity in the way he dressed and the flashiness of his car. His evasiveness and the frequency with which he moved to different states—a rover, as we called unsubs with this habit—showed that he was educated and had served in the military, most likely abroad.

For the second part of the report, we made a point of clarifying the Ski Mask Rapist's psychological makeup. This part was much trickier. We struggled to fit the facts of the case to a known classification of offender, largely because of the evolving nature of his crimes. So we referenced previous cases, mostly from the serial killer study, to define the offender as someone who was undergoing a progression from a power-assertive type—the Ski Mask Rapist's early crimes showed his need to project an image of potent masculinity—to the anger and escalated violence common to vindictive rapists. Violence was becoming an important part of the offender's ritual. Not violence as a tool to overcome a victim's resistance, but violence as pleasure. Ultimately, the Ski Mask Rapist was showing signs of increased aggression in his attacks. He was becoming more dangerous, more sadistic, and more confident. He was improving his MO (modus operandi—the way an offender carries out a crime), inching closer to some ideal he was trying to re-create. And he was clearly giving in to his murderous temptations.

Hazelwood submitted the behavioral profile to a large number of police departments in areas where the unsub had committed crimes, warning them to keep an eye out for anyone who matched this description. In October of that year, a Louisiana policeman based out of Gonzales (just southeast of Baton Rouge) noticed a suspicious car parked in a residential area as he was driving along on neighborhood patrol—a lipstick-red Pontiac Trans Am. That same night and in that same general area, police received a call about a ski-masked gunman confronting three women in one of the women's homes. One at a time, the women had each been bound and raped while the others were forced to watch. The unsub then robbed them of their personal items before stealing one of their vehicles and speeding off into the dark. The Gonzales-based

Ann Burgess teaching at Boston College, 1978.

Ann Burgess and Lynda Lytle Holmstrom collaborating on their rape victim counseling program, 1978. *Photo courtesy of Boston College*

Psychologist Nick Groth and Ann Burgess.

Boston College interdisciplinary conference on victims of violence, 1978. Left to right: research assistant Anna Laszlo, Nick Groth, Ann Burgess, and Detective Paul Rufo.

UNITED STATES DEPARTMENT OF JUSTICE

FEDERAL BUREAU OF INVESTIGATION

FBI Academy
Quantico, Virginia   22135
February 20, 1980

Dr. Ann Burgess
School of Nursing
Boston University
635 Commonwealth Avenue
Boston, Massachusetts   02215

Dear Dr. Burgess:

I would like to take this opportunity to invite you to the
FBI Academy on February 22, 1980, to consult with members of
the Behavioral Science Unit regarding future research in the area
of the criminal personality.

We deeply appreciate your past assistance to the
Training Division of the FBI and look forward to continued cooperation in the future.

Special Agent Robert K. Ressler of the Behavioral
Science Unit will coordinate your travel plans.

Sincerely yours,

James D. McKenzie
Acting Assistant Director

FBI welcome letter to Ann Burgess, 1980. *Photo courtesy of Ann Burgess*

PART 3
OFFENSE DATA

	A	B	C	D	E

3.J. The following pages have columns on the right, in order to collect data on both the current offense and previous sexual offenses on which information is available. If a total of more than five offenses occurred, use supplement sheets to enter data. Column A is for current offense; column B for the next most recent offense, etc.

1. Age of offender at time of offense: J.1
   List type of sexual offense:_____

   _____

2. Plea to charges of this offense: J.2

   0=no data available   3=changed from not-
   1=guilty   guilty to guilty
   2=Alford plea:unadmitted   4=not guilty
     but uncontested

 . Initial stance regarding offense: J.3.1

   0=no data available
   1=admits fully
   2=qualifies, minimizes guilt
   3=states he has no memory of offense
   4=denies committing offense

   3.2 current stance regarding offense   J.3.2

4. Sentence: Minimum (yrs.)   J.4.1
                      Maximum (yrs.)   J.4.2

   00=no data available
   99=none/does not apply

5. Premeditation of assault: J.5

   0=no data available
   1=intentional, premeditated
   2=opportunistic, impulsive
   3=unplanned, spontaneous

Sample page from the data assessment tool Ann Burgess designed for the FBI's Behavioral Science Unit. *Photo courtesy of Ann Burgess*

The original FBI profilers. *Courtesy of* Psychology Today, *1980*

Crime scene photo of victim in the Joubert case.

Attorney General William French Smith's 1984 task force on family violence. Left to right: Ann Burgess, AG Smith, and Assistant Attorney General Lois Haight Herrington. *Photo courtesy of Department of Justice*

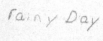

Opal Horton's drawing of her best friend being kidnapped, 1985. *Photo courtesy of Ann Burgess*

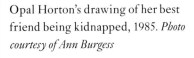

Opal Horton's drawing of hiding from her friend's abductor, 1985. *Photo courtesy of Ann Burgess*

The Men Who Murdered

Statistics from the FBI's Uniform Crime Reports document the alarming number of victims of sexually violent crimes. One of the disturbing patterns inherent in these statistics is that of the serial or repetitive criminal. Law enforcement officials have questioned whether a small percentage of criminals may be responsible for a large number of crimes, that is, a core group of habitual serious and violent offenders. This has been documented in one study on juvenile delinquents, [1] and other studies have reported similar results, [2] with average estimates of from 6 to 8 percent of delinquents comprising the core of the delinquency problem.

To address this problem, law enforcement is studying techniques to aid in apprehending serial offenders. These techniques require an indepth knowledge of the criminal personality, an area that, until recently, was researched primarily by forensic clinicians who interviewed criminals from a psychological framework or by criminologists who studied crime trends and statistics. Missing from the data base were critical aspects relevant to law enforcement investigation. Researchers have now begun to study the criminal from law enforcement perspectives, with a shift in focus to the investigative process of crime scene inquiry and victimology.

Our research is the first study of sexual homicide and crime scene patterns from a law enforcement per-

spective. It includes an initial appraisal of a profiling process and interviews of incarcerated murderers conducted by FBI Special Agents. The interviews contain specific questions answered from compiled sources plus lengthy, open-ended interviews with the murderers themselves. A subsample of 36 sexual murderers was selected for analysis to develop further information for profiling these murders. Here, we present what we learned about these 36 men. It is important to recognize that we are making general statements about these offenders. Not all statements are true for *all* offenders, although they may be true for *most* of the 36 men or for most of the offenders from whom we obtained data. Responses were not available from all offenders for all questions.

Feature article in a 1985 issue of the *FBI Law Enforcement Bulletin.*

Crime Scene and Profile Characteristics of Organized and Disorganized Murderers

". . . there were significant differences in the crime scenes of organized and disorganized offenders. . . ."

When requested by a law enforcement agency to assist in a violent crime investigation, the Agents at the Behavioral Science Unit (BSU) of the FBI Academy provide a behaviorally based suspect profile. Using information received from law enforcement about the crime and crime scene, the Agents have developed a technique for classifying murderers into one of two categories—organized or disorganized, a classification method evolving from years of experience and knowledge. In the service of advancing the art of profiling, the Agents were anxious to know if this classification system could be scientifically tested. This article describes the research study and statistical tests performed by a health services research staff on data collected.

Objectives of the Study

Thirty-six convicted sexual murderers were interviewed by FBI Agents for a study on sexual homicide crime scenes and patterns of criminal behavior. These study subjects represented 25 serial murderers (the murder of separate victims, with time breaks between victims ranging from 2 days to weeks or months) and 11 sexual murderers who had committed either a single homicide, double homicide, or spree murder.

The major objectives of this study were to test, using statistical inferential procedures, whether there are significant behavioral differences at the crime scenes between crimes committed by organized and disorganized murderers and to identify variables that may be useful in profiling orga-

Crime scene of an organized offender investigated by Pierce Brooks in 1958 while a homicide detective sergeant with the Los Angeles Police Department.

Feature article in a 1985 issue of the *FBI Law Enforcement Bulletin.*

The Split Reality of Murder

"... to many serial killers, ... fantasies of murder are as real as their acts of murder."

"Murder is very real. It's not something you see in a movie. You have to do all the practical things of surviving,"[1]

Murder is, indeed, very real. Yet to many serial killers, their fantasies of murder are as real as their acts of murder. To them, their existence is split into two realities: The social reality of the "normal" world where people do not murder, and the psychological vitality of the fantasy that is the impetus for the killer to commit his heinous crime. It is a split reality because the fantasy life is such a preoccupation. It becomes an additional reality, distinguishable from the "other" reality of the day-to-day social world.

Interviews with 36 convicted sexual murderers have provided insights into their attitudes, beliefs, and justifications for their crimes. In order to interpret the murderer's sense of

what is important, this article presents thoughts and beliefs articulated by the murderers themselves. First, we discuss the structure of conscious motives for murder, the killer's longstanding fantasy of violence and murder. Second, we look at what happens when the fantasy of murder is played out through its various phases. By presenting our interpretation of the fantasy's importance to the serial killer, we hope to suggest perspectives for law enforcement on the investigation of sexual homicide.

Motive and Fantasy

How does the motive for a murder evolve, and what triggers the murderer to act? Many murders puzzle law enforcement because they appear to lack the "usual" motives, such as robbery or revenge. Motives, however, need to be determined, since understanding the motive is criti-

cal to the subsequent apprehension of a suspect.

The 36 murderers in our study, replying to this fundamental question of what triggered their first murders, revealed that as a group, they were aware of their longstanding involvement and preference for a very active fantasy life and they were devoted to violent sexual fantasies. Most of these fantasies, prior to the first murder, focused on killing, while fantasies that evolved after the *first* murder often focused on perfecting various phases of the murder. The following illustrates an early fantasy of one of the serial murderers that developed following the move of his bedroom to a windowless basement room. This fantasy

Feature article in a 1985 issue of the *FBI Law Enforcement Bulletin*.

Special Agent Robert K. Ressler consults with the project staff of the Criminal Personality Research Program at Boston City Hospital. Pictured are Dr. Ann W. Burgess (at computer) and (standing from left) SA Ressler, Holly-Jean Chaplick, Marieanne Clark, and Peter Gaccione. *Courtesy of* FBI Law Enforcement Bulletin, *1986*

Left to right: Robert K. Ressler, Edmund Kemper, and John Douglas. *Photo courtesy of Ann Burgess*

Crime scene photo of victim by aqueduct. *FBI photo*

Title slide of sexual homicide study used to present behavioral characteristics and data to the FBI. *Photo courtesy of Ann Burgess*

Demographic slide of sexual homicide study used to present behavioral characteristics and data to the FBI. *Photo courtesy of Ann Burgess*

The FBI Serial Killer Blue Ribbon Panel. *Courtesy of Mark Prothero, author of* Defending Gary

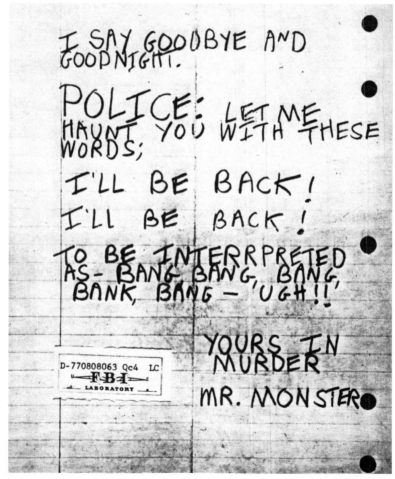

A Son of Sam letter left at a crime scene to taunt police. *FBI photo*

One of Henry Louis Wallace's drawings of killing his first victim. *Photo from private collection*

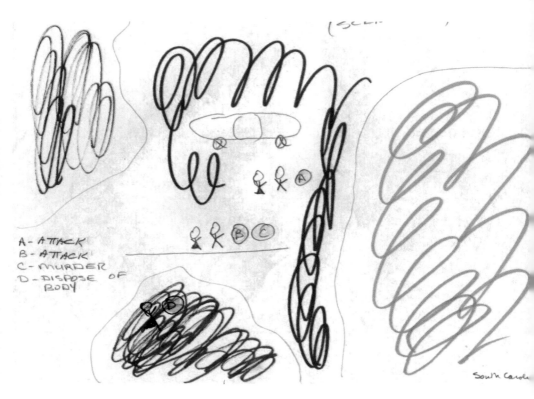

One of Henry Louis Wallace's drawings of phases of a crime. *Photo from private collection*

officer picked this up over his radio and, on a hunch, he returned to where he had seen the Trans Am earlier that day. The Trans Am was nowhere to be seen, but in its place was the victim's missing car. The officer also found a pair of men's gloves discarded just to the side of the vehicle. The gloves were an exact match to the victims' report.

The case progressed quickly. Investigators issued a regional BOLO (be on the lookout) for the Trans Am, and when police next saw the car, they ran the license plate and verified the car's owner: thirty-one-year-old Jon Barry Simonis. Simonis was arrested in Lake Charles, Louisiana, a week after Thanksgiving, as he walked out of a convenience store carrying a loaf of bread and two packs of cigarettes. His capture ended a three-year terror spree that included eighty-one crimes across twelve states, from Florida to Michigan, Louisiana to California.

The FBI profile we'd developed for the Ski Mask Rapist was categorically accurate in its detail and scope. Simonis was a former All-State Louisiana high school quarterback and had served in the Army from 1973 to 1977. He had a full-scale IQ of 128 (the average is 90–110) and maintained an athletic build. But Simonis also had an abusive upbringing in which it was believed that he witnessed his father committing sexual acts on his sister. He was clearly driven by a deep anger toward women, because his assaults intended to degrade, demean, and humiliate his victims—defining behaviors of a vindictive rapist. And though his conviction was clearly important for its own sake, it also presented us with a unique opportunity to better understand the motives and evolving patterns of violent sexual offenders simply on the basis of the sheer volume of his crimes. Simonis was ideal for this because of his confidence, his desire to take ownership of his crimes,[*] and his habit of bragging about what he'd

---

[*] When Simonis was told that another man was serving a prison sentence after confessing to a rape Simonis had also confessed to, he became upset and reportedly said: "What the hell did he do that for? I did that rape."

done as a way of defining who he was. His desire to impress others by violent means was deeply disturbing, of course, but it also came with an upside for our criminal personality study as a whole. Simonis wanted to talk. He wanted others to step inside his head so he could relive his most violent episodes—and share them with an audience. Voyeurism, forcing others to witness the rawness of the details, was a fundamental part of how Simonis's mind worked. But it also gave us an advantage. We could use his obsession with control and his sense of grandiosity to gain a more deeply nuanced understanding of serial offenders than we'd ever collected before. Simonis would be a case study in how a serial killer's patterns and behaviors progressed.

To understand the full scope of Simonis's case, we decided to follow up on both the profiling aspect and victimology. Hazelwood and Lanning would conduct a recorded interview of Simonis, and I'd meet with his victims to corroborate their accounts. Essentially, we wanted to compare the offender's account to the victims' experiences. By understanding both perspectives, we could learn how a serial offender's patterns could change and evolve over time, and we could start to track the rate of escalation from rape to violence, and from violence to murder. But we needed both sides of the story to fully understand what triggered each step of a serial offender's escalating behaviors.

As agents, Hazelwood and Lanning had no trouble setting up prison interviews to speak with convicted criminals. Their only challenge was establishing how to conduct the interview itself. The Bureau made a point of training each agent in a wide variety of interviewing styles and philosophies: the Reid technique, in which basic tricks of psychology are used to help the interviewee feel comfortable talking about their crime; the cognitive approach, which uses open-ended narration and follow-up questions to guide an interviewee through their continuous memories of a crime; and the kinesic method, which relies on creating an atmosphere of pressure and stress for the interviewee to see how they react. But this situation was different. Simonis *wanted* to talk. So Hazelwood and Lanning decided to use a straightforward, deliberately investigative tone. This would help minimize emotion and keep the conversation as unembellished as possible. Also, they decided to throw in a few deliberately misleading questions that they already knew the answers to—as a sort of control variable. Conversation was data. The agents needed to keep it truthful and authentic, or risk skewing the results and rendering the whole meeting null and void.

"One last thing," I warned them. "You can challenge Simonis's memories and interpretations of the attacks, but never challenge his belief system. If you do, all he'll have left is denial. He's a house of cards just waiting to collapse."

———————————————

In the winter of 1985, Hazelwood and Lanning met with Simonis at Angola Prison in Louisiana, the largest maximum-security prison in the United States. They were brought to a large, brightly lit interrogation space, with fake wood paneling adorning the walls and a lacquered wooden table sitting squarely in the middle of the room. Simonis—dressed in a white T-shirt, his hair cropped short, and donning a neatly trimmed mustache—took a seat at the end of the table, while the agents, both dressed in gray suits and plaid ties, sat on either side. The agents had brought a video camera in case Simonis agreed to be filmed. And in his typically self-indulgent fashion, Simonis quickly consented to having part of the session recorded.

The interview started with the basics. Simonis admitted that he first began window-peeping when he was fifteen years old, and that this turned into a habit in which he would sneak through his neighborhood in the middle of the night, break into nearby homes, and snoop around undetected without committing any significant crimes. These escapades were like training for his future sex crimes.

Simonis then explained that his first sexual transgression took place when he exposed himself to women during his Army days while he was stationed in Europe. He never attacked anyone at that time, but he thought about it on many occasions. Once he returned to the States, he started robbing women, with the sole intention of theft. He liked the sense of power this gave him, but soon, theft wasn't enough to scratch the itch. He started considering rape as a way of expanding on that feeling of power.

"So, what led up to your first assault?" Hazelwood asked Simonis directly. "Was there a particular incident or because it was a particular day of the week? Did you wake up that morning knowing you wanted to rape someone?"

"There was nothing like that," Simonis insisted. "The first one just started out as a burglary. I entered a house and was confronted by a lady who lived there—who I'd followed from a shopping center earlier that day. After confronting the woman, I kinda let her know that I was in control. After I got money from her, then I kinda bound her hands and took her into a bedroom and had her perform masturbation on me. But I couldn't get an erection. I was too nervous."

"All right," Hazelwood pressed on. "So you start off doing that kind of thing. But then you get a job at a hospital as a lab technician and seem to be doing okay. Did you ever do anything sexual to the patients?"

"Yeah, sometimes." Simonis nodded. "I was the one who'd sedate them, so sometimes I'd play with their breasts or whatever. I mean, the opportunity was there. It was all so easy. I used to go through surgery schedules so I could take a patient's key while they were still in surgery and get copies made. Then I'd go to their home to commit a robbery or a burglary or a rape whenever I wanted." Simonis added that he sometimes copied surgeons' keys and would enter their homes to rape and rob their wives, then make a game of observing whether or not the surgeons showed signs of knowing their wives had been raped.

"What about the men?" Hazelwood prodded, intentionally provoking Simonis to see if he could get a reaction. "Would you make them give you a blow job?"

"No. I've never had any sexual contact with a man."

"No? Because just now when we were talking, you were talking kind of fast and it sounded like you said you raped a man tied up on the floor . . ."

"No, and I don't know why you keep asking me."

"Okay. . . . The way I understood it—let me just clear the air here—is that you were bisexual and like to have sex with men."

"I don't know where you got that idea from," Simonis said, maintaining his calm. "I suppose I might have bisexual tendencies to a certain extent, like most men probably do, but as far as actually coming into contact with them goes, no."

"That's fine," Hazelwood said, switching the subject. "What about your transition to assault and violence? How'd that happen?"

"Near the end of my criminal activities, it got to be a much more violent thing, a form of degradation toward the women, making them feel completely dominated," Simonis said. "My intentions were to inflict fear into them, to force them to do things they wouldn't normally do."

"What do you think motivated that?"

"It's pretty complex. I think there was a multitude of things involved. Money was a motive. Sex was a factor. Urges just came on to me to the point that I was uncontrollable near the end. The effects on me when I saw women had more of a hold on me than I had on them."

Simonis went on to describe the adrenaline rush he felt when breaking into a home, noting that the turn-on was amplified by the risk of being caught. He called it a cat-and-mouse game he was playing with the police. He staggered his crimes by going to different states, changing his clothing, and throwing the old clothing away to avoid leaving behind evidence.

"It got me high just going into a place that belonged to somebody else," Simonis continued. "Any kind of illegal activity, knowing there was a risk of being caught, created stimulation. It was a turn-on, so to speak. But it was a different high than the sexual aspect. They kind of coincided with one another."

"Did you ever feel guilty about what you were doing?"

"I always felt guilty, especially after ejaculation. I felt sorrow."

"All right. But then why get so violent?" Lanning asked. "You choked women, punched them, deliberately caused pain."

"Yeah, but I still felt sorry for them. My intention was, see . . ." Simonis paused. "That's what's really strange about the whole situation. I was in there doing so much harm, but yet there were times I would do stuff to alleviate the discomfort or the pain because I didn't want to hurt them. It's so contradictory, because I was in there to cause pain and yet I did what I could to alleviate it."

"Did you ever apologize for what you were doing?"

"Yes, but that doesn't make sense either. I'd turn around and beat one, and then apologize for raping the other one. Sometimes I'd be nice and talk to them, but it's complex, there's so much involved that I don't understand. I don't know why I did certain things, why I raped some, why I beat some, why I burned some, and why I was nice to one but not another—I don't know. But I know it doesn't make sense."

While the agents interviewed Simonis, I met with his victims. Like most serial offenders, it was clear that Simonis had a "type." The victims were all in their early thirties or younger, most could be described as attractive, and the majority were wealthy and lived in well-to-do neighborhoods. Some were married, some were in committed relationships, and some were housemates who'd all been attacked together as a group. Those who spoke with me were relieved that Simonis was in prison. But they still had their scars.

One victim told me that she, her husband, and her daughter had been busy packing up for a vacation. They'd been going back and forth between the house and the garage as they loaded suitcases into the car. Suddenly, the mother realized her husband and daughter had stopped helping, so she went back in the house to see where they were. As soon as she stepped into the kitchen, a hand grabbed her around the neck and she felt the cold muzzle of a gun pressed up against her temple. She turned to see a man with a dark mask that had frayed slits for the eyes, nose, and mouth. A deep voice instructed her to strip. Naked and shivering, she was picked up by her breasts and forced to commit multiple sexual acts on her offender in front of her husband and daughter. Then she was raped on the cold tiles of the kitchen floor.

In another case, the Ski Mask Rapist broke into a home and surprised a thirteen-year-old babysitter, forcing her to perform oral sex on him. Afterward, she warned him that he was in a police officer's home, thinking that would scare him away. It only antagonized him further. He smiled and told her he would wait. An hour or so later, when the husband and wife returned, the rapist forced them to hand-cuff each other, and then vaginally raped the wife. The husband, at one point, asked his wife if she was all right. She responded, "Yes, he's being a gentleman," hoping this would make everyone calm. Suddenly filled with great rage, the ski-masked rapist began brutally punching the woman's breasts. The injuries were so extensive that she later had to have a double mastectomy.

Speaking with Simonis's victims reinforced some of the takeaways I'd learned from my original study on sexual violence—namely, that these acts weren't about sex, they were about control. But now, given the additional context of understanding offenders through my work on the serial killer study, I was able to carry that knowledge one step further. I realized that an offender perpetrates their acts to achieve two goals: physical control and sexual control. Listening to the victims' stories—as horrifying and traumatic as they were—helped clarify how this worked. Some offenders (like Simonis) gained control by using a direct physical confrontation, such as launching a sudden surprise attack or employing overwhelming strength. Others used the verbal ploys of a confidence gamer, such as threats or intimidation. In both scenarios, the offender took sexual control of the victim by force, not by consent. They were two different approaches, but they ultimately ended with the same outcome.

I classified the first of these two approaches as a blitz-style rape. This type occurred "out of the blue" and without much, if any, prior interaction between assailant and victim. The victim would be having a normal day when suddenly, in a split second, their life was shattered without warning. As one thirty-one-year-old victim confided, "He came from behind. There was no way to get away. It happened so fast—like a shock of lightning going through you."

From the victim's point of view, there was no cause or explanation for their assailant's presence. He would suddenly appear, his presence would feel strange and inappropriate, and he'd force himself into the situation. There was a great degree of anonymity on both sides. The victim would be selected anonymously, and the assailant would make efforts to remain anonymous himself. Often, the assailant would wear a mask or gloves, or else cover the victim's face during the attack. In many cases, victims of a blitz-style rapist just happened to be at the wrong place at the wrong time.

The second, more-verbal approach I classified as that of the confidence-style rapist. It could be distinguished by its subtlety. The confidence-style assailant would use false pretenses—deceit, betrayal, and violence—to force unwanted sexual interactions. There was commonly some sort of interaction, however minor, between the victim and assailant prior to the assault. Sometimes the assailant knew the victim, and at times, they might have even had a formal relationship prior to the attack. Confidence-style rapists tended to strike up a conversation with their victim and try to earn their trust before ultimately betraying them. For example, they might offer or request assistance or the victim's company, or promise their intended target information, material items, social activities, employment, social pleasantries, or niceties.

At a first glance, Simonis appeared to have some of the tendencies of a confidence-style rapist. But after listening to Hazelwood and Lanning's interview with him, I realized that Simonis's style veered increasingly toward blitz attacks over time. The thrill of surprise, or the "cat-and-mouse game," as he called it, was an important ritualistic element of the way Simonis structured his attacks.

That was the key to Simonis—the element of ritual. Douglas helped us clarify what we were seeing by describing this element of a criminal's behavior as his "signature." He saw it as a counterpart to MO. But whereas a serial offender's MO could change as they refined their process of committing a crime, signature was a reoccurring feature that went beyond just the standard process of criminal activity. Signature was permanent.

"You're right to think of it like a ritual," Douglas said. "It's something that's not a necessary part of successfully committing a particular crime. It's only necessary for the unsub's fulfillment."

"Let me get this straight," Hazelwood cut in. "If MO shows an offender's dynamic behavior, signature shows—what—the fantasies behind those behaviors?"

"It sounds like personation," I said.

"Try again in English, Ann," Douglas joked.

"What I'm saying is that, as an offender broods and daydreams, they feel increasingly compelled to express their violent fantasies in the real world. And when they finally do act out everything they've been building in their head, some aspect of that fantasy gets left at the crime scene—signs of excessive force, trails of blood showing that a victim was dragged around the area, or something like that. That's personation. The more crimes an offender commits, the more this personation gets repeated as a signature."

"Now you're talking," Douglas said.

"And to take it one step further, the elements that comprise signature are deeply tied to an offender's fantasies. They're full of meaning."

"Okay. So that's what we need," Hazelwood said. "Once we identify a serial offender's signature, we've got a reliable way of linking him to his crimes."

We'd seen the process of signature play out with Simonis. In one of his earliest rapes, he broke into the home of a young couple, ordered the husband to lie face down in the hallway, then placed a porcelain teacup and saucer on the man's back and said, "If I hear that cup move or hit the floor, your wife dies." Then he shoved the wife into the bedroom and raped her. Several assaults later, Simonis's behavior escalated when he entered a house and ordered the woman to call her husband to say there was an emergency and to come home as soon as possible. When the husband arrived, Simonis was waiting. He tied the man to a chair and forced him to watch the rape of his wife.

The pattern was clear. In the earlier rape, Simonis had used the cup and saucer as an effective way of controlling the husband. On a later rape, he went one step beyond this by not only raping the wife but also staging a scenario where he could humiliate and dominate the husband as a means of fully satisfying his fantasies. In the first rape, Simonis dealt with the husband because he was there. In the later rape, he *needed* the husband to be there and to witness the rape. His personal needs compelled him to perform this signature aspect of crime.

Simonis received twenty-one life sentences on rape convictions, with extra years for armed robbery, burglary, and auto theft. He was an organized criminal—one who not only planned his rapes and robberies but also thoughtfully designed ways to avoid detection by law enforcement. He was also a power-assertive type who was, by his own admission, becoming bored with rape and starting to have murderous fantasies. At his trial, Simonis claimed he was sorry about everything but that he couldn't help himself. "I am guilty of these crimes. I knew extremely well what I was doing beforehand, while I was doing it, and I know now." But I never bought into this. He was always trying to control the larger narrative around him. He knew he'd been exposed. And he didn't like it. This was his way of trying to wrestle back a small semblance of control by hiding behind another mask.

At the same time, Simonis's admission that he "couldn't help himself" was not uncommon. Over the course of our casework, we quickly realized that most of the time, offenders couldn't stop their own criminal behavior—and many of them didn't want to. Their crimes only stopped when they were apprehended and put behind bars. Some criminals even said that they were glad they were stopped. For them, violence had become an addiction they couldn't control. This idea impressed upon us how critical it was to find serial offenders, particularly sexual offenders, as early as possible—before the violence escalated further. Sometimes, local law enforcement officials would shrug us off, saying "he committed only one rape." But I knew that was a myth. One rape would never be the end of it. Once the behavior was set in motion, the rape fantasies became more frequent and the urge intensified. It was like a disease. Once the offender became infected with the obsession, they had no choice but to act.

CHAPTER 9

"There's No Cookbook"

During lunch one afternoon in the Quantico cafeteria—a brief moment of downtime in which the agents and I raced through our trays of mashed potatoes and Salisbury steak so we could get back to a particularly frustrating case—Hazelwood said something that stopped me in my tracks. "Anytime you're working with human behavior, you're going to find atypical situations and variables you haven't encountered before. There's no cookbook, and there never will be a cookbook."

Hazelwood didn't say this to be dismissive in any sense. It's just what he believed. He felt that behavior wasn't always rational, that there were times it couldn't be understood, and that, because of this, profiling could never be a fully standardized technique that we could teach to new agents coming on board. And to a degree, I knew he was right. The best profilers had a "knack" for the job. Douglas, for example, while helping a local police department solve a brutal case in which an elderly woman had been beaten and sexually assaulted, was interrupted by a confused detective, who asked, "Are you a psychic, Douglas?"

Douglas didn't miss a beat. "No, but my job would be a lot easier if I was. Exactly how this happens, I'm not sure," he continued. "If there's a psychic component, I won't run from it."

To some, this admission was startling. But despite our work in developing a step-by-step process for criminal profiling based on behavioral psychology, case data, and an evidence-based process of rigorous analysis, there was still an ineffable quality that set the best profilers apart. Those agents brought an element of the unexplained to the process, a water dowsing–like quality that resulted in perfectly inexplicable predictions. Things like Brussel's insight into the Mad Bomber ("He'll be wearing a double-breasted suit. Buttoned") and Douglas's later profile of the Trailside Killer ("The killer will have a speech impediment") were undeniably accurate. And yet, it wasn't always clear why.

Still, those minutely specific assertions, though incredibly helpful, were more often the exception than the rule. Our intention with criminal profiling was to design an evidence-based system that could be universally applied by law enforcement across the country, regardless of whether they had a knack for the technique itself. We wanted to shift the approach away from the older methods of relying on gut instinct and biased assumptions and turn toward a deliberate design, backed by evidence, data, and documented patterns. We saw standardization as a strength. Our technique guided agents methodologically, step by step, through the process of reconstructing the physical, behavioral, and sociological nature of the killer. This information then became the basis for a multipage, deep analysis of an individual unsub—the profile itself. Through clarity, detail, and totality, the profile guided each investigation toward a small list of the most likely suspects capable of committing a specific crime. The process worked. And over time—through experience gained and practice—we refined it to work even better, streamlining our approach to profiling by breaking it down into four stages, all of which built to the single goal of apprehending the offender as quickly as possible.

We called stage one "profiling inputs." This was when the lead profiler collected and studied all available background information, evidence, and investigative reports to put together the most comprehensive overview of forensics, the victim, and the context of the crime. It was also, by far, the most time-consuming part of the process. Many of the BSU's cases came in from remote areas where law enforcement was ill equipped to handle the bizarre nature of our unique brand of crimes, and, as a result, the original case files were often incomplete. This meant that the lead profiler had to dig back through the records to piece together weather conditions, the political/social environment, and crime statistics from the area at the time of the offense, as well as full background information about the victim and any unwritten observations or impressions that they could squeeze out of the shell-shocked police.

Throughout the profiling inputs stage, the lead profiler collected enough data to see the overall structure of the crime: the core elements. These were things like offender classification (organized vs. disorganized), the level of criminal sophistication, and the basic victim–offender dynamics that played out during the offense. But there were inherent pitfalls within this stage, too. Human nature made a habit of looking for answers as quickly as possible. Our process acknowledged this and accounted for it by warning lead agents to keep their guard up so that no outside influences could compromise their objectivity within the case. Bias was a shortcut to failure.

We called stage two "decision process models." Here, the lead profiler sifted through the collected data from stage one and began organizing it into recognized patterns and known classifications. The purpose was to create a baseline of understanding that helped speed up collaboration in the later stages of the process. This was done by identifying and naming seven key elements of the case, including homicide type and style, primary intent of the murderer (criminal, emotional, or sexual), victim risk, offender risk, escalation (changes to the pattern of a serial killer's crimes), time factors (length of time with the victim, postmortem acts, body disposal), and location. This step was how we standardized the way profilers talked about unsubs. Just as clinicians used standardized language to make a diagnosis based on symptoms, patient history, and trained observation, profilers needed a similar methodology. The seven decision points of stage two were our way of doing that. We standardized the language of these seven points to help give profilers greater clarity and understanding of the case at hand, which in turn helped speed up the whole process.

Stage three was "crime assessment." This was when the lead profiler reconstructed a step-by-step chronological timeline of the crime, from both the victim's and the offender's perspectives. This included the planning of the attack, victim risk, the confrontation, and post-offense actions and behaviors. The primary focus was on causality of the offender's behavior throughout the duration of the crime. This stage helped us narrow in on the classification of the crime—especially for cases originally labeled as "mixed-offense" be-cause of a lack of information. This was also the point in the process when, in the case of serial offenders, familiar patterns became clear and obvious. In these instances—or if there were no familiar patterns but a serial offender was still suspected—the lead profiler would reference the BSU's extensive catalog of criminal files to find similar unsolved cases that matched the current crime. Our catalog was an invaluable resource, essentially taking the experience and talents of one profiler and amplifying them within the collective knowledge of all the profilers who'd come before them.

Another core element of stage three and its meticulous process of re-creating the attack was the light it shed on an offender's motivation.

In the case of disorganized offenders, for example, re-creation often showed the offender's motivation to be spontaneous—the result of an emotional trigger, mental illness, drugs, or a deep sense of panic. With these offenders, pinpointing the exact motivation was challenging because of their irrational behaviors and thoughts. Organized offenders, by contrast, left a much clearer picture of their motivation. They displayed their motivation in the logical, often premeditated nature of their attacks.

Stage three culminated in description of crime scene dynamics—what changed and what stayed the same—throughout the timeline of the attack. These were details such as location of the wounds, staging of the victim's body, ritualistic markings or symbols, and any additional elements of chaos or overtly conspicuous order that indicated an item had gone missing—organized offenders had a habit of taking souvenirs from their victims to relive the thrill of the attack. If a killer had a signature, stage three was where it came to light.

Stage four was the creation of the criminal profile itself. This was when the lead profiler gathered a group of profilers together to present their findings on the first three stages of the process, as well as all the original materials connected to the case. The lead profiler then reviewed their findings in as objective a manner as possible, and they opened the session to questions and conversation. The key here was the collaborative nature of the process. Each profiler looked at the data through their own individual lens of understanding and expertise, but it was profilers' combined efforts that helped actualize the offender in the greatest possible detail: physical characteristics, background information, habits, beliefs, values, and rationale for their crimes.

This final criminal profiling stage, with all the insights it revealed about the offender's behavior and psychological characteristics, served a second purpose, too. It validated, or in some cases illustrated conflict with, the earlier stages of the profile-generating process. For example, if there was discord between how the body was treated and our description of the unsub's physical capabilities, we knew we had to go back and review all the data. A profile only worked when it reflected—wholly and unconditionally—the evidence it was built from.

In December of 1986, our official criminal profiling process was published in the *FBI Law Enforcement Bulletin*: volume 55, issue 12. It became standard issue for all agents at the BSU, bridging the divide between investigation and criminal psychology through a research-based methodology. And that was the key. Our work wasn't intended to replace an investigator's boots-on-the-ground instincts. Instead, it saw the value of these qualities and provided agents a structured process that enhanced their own merits and success.

It was funny. Almost every day throughout those first six years at the BSU, I heard the tired old cliché that profiling was "more art than science." But I'd never felt the need to choose between the two. Profiling was both art *and* science. It was a human attempt to understand and describe a fringe aspect of the human condition. It was two sides of the same coin. It just took longer for everyone else to see both sides.

CHAPTER 10

A Deeper Look

Payoff. After years of research and uncertainty, our publication in the *FBI Law Enforcement Bulletin* marked a turning point for our work. It was 1986, and the Bureau tasked Douglas with bringing profiling to the world through the recently funded NCAVC (National Center for the Analysis of Violent Crime) program. He was given resources, too: twelve full-time profilers, who, under his supervision, would use our methodologies as their blueprint for creating official analyses of unsubs in strange and difficult-to-solve cases. They quickly began seeing hundreds of cases a year. It was telling—the promotions, added resources, and increased case volume all spoke to how far profiling had come. But perhaps most telling of all was the team's new offices in their own fully dedicated aboveground space. Douglas was amazed.

"What do you know?" he joked. "The sun *does* shine on Quantico."

Around the same time, Ressler went on to oversee his own project under the canopy of NCAVC. He became the manager of the FBI's Violent Criminal Apprehension Program (ViCAP), which was a first-of-its-kind computer-based program unlike anything the Bureau had ever seen. Ressler described it as "a nationwide data information center designed to collect, collate, and analyze specific crimes of violence." ViCAP was a profiling tool for the modern era. It was a way of uploading and analyzing case information from law enforcement agencies across the United States. Inspired by our original idea of cataloging serial offenders for future reference, ViCAP looked for patterns and shared characteristics that existed among the vast number of individual cases being recorded and uploaded all across the country. By comparing such factors as victimology, motive, physical evidence, witness testimony, and criminal behavior, ViCAP could exponentially speed up the process of narrowing in on likely suspects based on the patterns of their crimes.

Having Douglas and Ressler in charge of profiling's future applications was a big deal. They brought unparalleled experience to their new roles. They knew the process inside and out. And their input in profiling's final design had been just as fundamental as my own. More importantly, they understood that the technique itself was an imperfect science. It benefited from constant research and revision. Crime was always changing. Criminals were becoming more advanced. And, in response, profiling needed to adapt if we wanted to keep our edge. I saw it as my responsibility to make sure that it did.

So, while Douglas and Ressler enjoyed their newfound glow in the spotlight—responding to interview requests and getting write-ups in the *New York Times* with articles headlined "The FBI's New Psyche Squad"—I stuck to the shadows of research. Of course, this didn't go unnoticed by my colleagues at the BSU, all of whom had built their careers by paying attention to details. Ressler was especially quick to notice my disappearing act. And once, after I turned down his offer to join him on an interview talking about the early days of profiling, he joked, "You're like a mad scientist hiding out in that office. You should come up for fresh air every once in a while."

I laughed at how accurate this assessment was. "You might be right. But who knows a monster better than a mad scientist? And I'm telling you, Bob, I'm closer than ever to figuring them out. We've made so much progress since our earliest findings of predisposition and categories of type. We've drilled into the core of their psychology and behavior, and so much of it is almost textbook. If it weren't for a few outliers, I could build killers by design."

"Who are the outliers?" Ressler asked.

"Rissell and Kemper," I said.

"Lucky for you we've got plenty of tape on those two. Why don't you revisit them? I must have interviewed the both of them at least a half a dozen times myself. Not that you'll hear much of me on the tapes. I could hardly get them to shut up."

By this point in 1986, my work at the BSU had grown beyond just the criminal personality study and profiling of serial killers. I was working on multiple projects with multiple agents, including a behavioral analysis of child molesters with Lanning* that was a follow-up to the first project we'd worked on together. And at the same time, I also started to receive requests to provide courtroom testimony on strange and unusual murder cases slated for trial—apparently, no one else shared my background of expertise in criminal psychology, forensic nursing, and years of research to understand the makeup of serial killers' minds. But despite these new opportunities, I wasn't done with profiling just yet—the process remained unfinished. My goal from the start had been to use every available resource to refine profiling into the most effective tool possible. And there were still a few resources I hadn't fully exhausted yet.

---

* The project was a collaboration between the FBI and the National Center for Missing and Exploited Children. It aimed to understand child sexual exploitation in terms of an offender's behaviors, patterns, and type.

The first of these resources was the data from new agents. I looked at the feedback we were getting from young agents just starting off in the field, and I interviewed them for possible insights after cases in which they utilized our technique. The second resource was the BSU's catalog of older cases—outliers, especially—that the team had never fully figured out. These were the cases that had the potential to make the greatest impact. Because regardless of everything we'd done over the last six years, and regardless of our success in finding reason within the most bizarre elements of human behavior, there were still things we didn't know and criminals we didn't fully understand. Montie Rissell and Edmund Kemper were the two that haunted me most. They stood out within a small group of the most unique killers I'd analyzed. They were also two of the most successful in terms of the number of lives they took. That alone made them worthy of further attention.

Quite a few of the original subjects from our serial killer study had been disorganized killers. They were a type that, as Ressler put it, "has no idea of, or interest in, the personalities of his victims. He does not want to know who they are, and many times takes steps to obliterate their personalities by quickly knocking them unconscious or covering their faces or otherwise disfiguring them."

Rissell and Kemper, however, were the polar opposite of this. Both were exceptionally bright. Both showed an unusual quality of being empathetic—almost sensitive even—in how they thought about their victims. And both had a strange and deeply personal fantasy-based view of the world. Of course, these two killers had their differences as well. Individually, their earliest expressions of violence couldn't have been more dissimilar. And the way they murdered, their behaviors throughout the four distinct phases of murder (the antecedent behavior and planning, the murder itself, the disposal of a body, and the post-crime behavior) were starkly unique. But tucked within their discrepancies, so much of the underlying psychology was the same: their antisocial nature, their sudden bouts of anger, and their confused blending of fantasy and reality.

They were like two unique expressions of the same psychological mind, held together by a common fantasy. Whereas most killers saw murder as a means to a sexual end, Rissell and Kemper used murder as a means of bringing life to their deranged fantasies. They saw their victims as opportunities to help them tear down the walls that separated external reality from the reality that lived in their heads. And yet, despite all these levels of complex awareness, they were still calculating killers who stole the lives of young women without any remorse. That's what stood out to me. And deep down, I believed that by understanding the way these two individuals thought, I could better answer the fundamental question connecting everything we did: What drives someone to kill?

Montie Rissell, the youngest of three children, was born in Wellington, Kansas, in 1959. Seven years later, his parents divorced and his mother separated the siblings from their father, uprooting the family to Sacramento, California, with Rissell crying throughout the whole car ride. He wanted to stay with his father. He felt that his mother didn't truly want him. And when he arrived at his new home, he began lashing out in increasingly violent ways. It wasn't long before he got into trouble.

It would be easy to write off Rissell as a problematic adolescent, but that doesn't give him the consideration he deserves. Ultimately, Rissell was a paradox. He earned good grades at school and tested above average for intelligence. He was athletically inclined and showed an aptitude for baseball. He was outgoing, often attended social events, and was well liked by a close circle of male and female friends. He saw himself as a leader, not a follower. And he lacked the typical antisocial nature shared by many known rapist-murderers active at that time. Still, as Rissell grew older, his violent tendencies peeked out from behind his positive reputation, and before long, his suppressed aggression began to dominate his personality.

Even back in my original analysis of Rissell's case file and his interview series with Douglas and Ressler, I'd been struck by how grounded he was. He stood out from the thirty-five other subjects in our serial killer study. He spoke clearly, well grounded in reality. And unlike most killers—who tended to dissolve into fantasy when remembering their crimes—Rissell had an unusually controlled manner of describing his upbringing and the memories of his earliest attraction toward violence. He wasn't shaped by the nature of his fantasies; rather, he shaped his fantasies to better fit his nature. He seemed to define himself by his own sense of control. Rissell's early crimes tended to occur whenever he saw this control being challenged, and that was how he justified his increasingly violent reactions.

The first indication of trouble occurred when Rissell was only nine years old. The school principal caught Rissell and three other boys writing swear words on the sidewalk. All things considered, this was a small infraction, something that might be dismissed as common in children of that age, but in Rissell's case, it marked the beginning of his escalating anger. A year later, Rissell's aggression bubbled to the surface again. He shot his cousin with a BB gun and was promptly reprimanded with a fierce beating from his ex-military stepfather. According to Rissell, this type of punishment was common at home. Rissell's mother would mysteriously leave for long stretches at a time and task the children with taking care of each other. She never told her anxious children where she was going or when she'd return. This separation added more stress to the already tenuous parent–child dynamic within the household.

171

Rissell's stepfather's approach to parenting was similarly problematic. He was a violent and unpredictable man who sometimes
bought gifts for his new stepchildren and sometimes punished them
arbitrarily, lashing out at them with a military-informed approach to
discipline. But the conflict with his stepfather was short-lived. When
Rissell was twelve, his mother filed for her second divorce in five years
and uprooted the family once again, this time to settle in Virginia.
Rissell pointed to his troubled relationship with his stepfather—and
the lack of positive male role models—as a key stressor in his life. As
he explained it, "That divorce has always been a problem, and that
was always in my head. Because my older brother had never been
around, because he was always out on dates and joining the Army and
going overseas and everything from the time I was nine or ten until I
was sixteen. I hardly had any male supervision."

In Virginia, Rissell started stealing cars, using drugs, and breaking
into houses. At age thirteen, he was arrested for driving without a
license. A year later, he was charged with the rape and robbery of his
upstairs neighbor in the apartment complex where he lived with his
mother. He'd returned from a party around midnight, after several
hours of drinking, smoking marijuana, and taking black beauty pills.[*]
He tried to sleep but was feeling "horny as hell" as he fantasized
about raping his twenty-five-year-old neighbor upstairs. In the end,
the thought became an urge too powerful to ignore, and so he put on
a stocking mask, scaled the apartment wall, and broke into her living
room through her patio door. He then raped her at knifepoint. The
next morning, his mother woke him up around seven a.m., saying
there'd been a rape in the apartment upstairs. Like many serial offenders, Rissell quickly inserted himself into the investigation. He talked

---

[*] In the 1960s and 1970s, "black beauty" was the standard street slang for pills of
pharmaceutical amphetamine. It was the name most commonly used for tablets
of Biphetamine.

to the police and gave a phony description of how he'd gotten into a fight with an unknown prowler the night before, suggesting that this could be the same individual they were looking for. The unnecessary lie, though inconsequential, was one more example of Rissell's deep attraction to fantasy. It also exposed him to a certain degree of risk— and through risk, he flaunted his own sense of control.

But investigators saw through it. Rissell became a suspect once investigators learned that his alibi wasn't true, and they arrested him three weeks later when his fingerprints and hair samples were found to match evidence left at the crime scene. After his juvenile hearing, Rissell raged about the judge—a woman—who he felt unjustifiably found him guilty because of how his face turned red when the victim described being attacked. He complained, "That goddamn bitch put me into this thing without good reason."

Far from deterring his criminal activity, Rissell's punishment acted as a catalyst for future violent outbreaks. In his own words: "That woman judge sent me to a diagnostic center. That's what started me off resenting authority. . . . Nobody could tell me what to do or when to do it or how to do it."

This deflective response was part of Rissell's recurring pattern of blaming others for his actions. And because the verdict itself had come from a female judge, Rissell felt justified in seeking his revenge through further acts of violence. He saw himself as a victim. In his mind, violence against women was a way of restoring order. It was his way of setting things right.

After Rissell was convicted, he was sent to an out-of-state Florida psychiatric residential facility and diagnosed with "adjustment reaction of adolescence"—a once-common informal type of diagnosis that was used when mental health clinicians couldn't clearly nail down what specifically was wrong in the case of a child's abnormal behavior. He spent eighteen months receiving individual insight-oriented psychotherapy and was later discharged with the recommendations that he live at home, attend public school, and continue psychotherapy on a weekly outpatient basis with his mother actively involved in his treatment.

One probation officer noted that "psychiatric and psychological evaluations of Montie indicated he was a disturbed youth who was desperately in need of intensive therapy in a closed setting." But despite receiving therapy, none of the treatments worked. Instead, Rissell intentionally fooled doctors into believing he was making steady progress, while in reality he managed to rape five women undetected during the period of supposed treatment. One of the attacks even happened in the psychiatric facility's parking lot. This seemed to embolden Rissell. It was during this time that his escalation of violent tendencies pushed him to make the leap from rape to murder.

Rissell's second rape victim was another woman in his apartment building. He was sixteen at the time and on leave from the residential facility for Christmas vacation. On his last night home, he approached a woman in the elevator, threatened her with a knife, and took her to a nearby wooded area before raping her. His third attack was three months later, when he approached a woman in the parking lot of a local school he attended. He again used a knife, forced the woman to drive to her apartment, and raped her in her own home.

The next two attacks included co-assailants. This shift in his criminal style was unexpected but grounded in logic. Whether at home, in school, or residing in a detention facility, Rissell was popular and made relationships easily. It fed into his narcissism to include co-assailants in his sexual assaults. So one night, while on a weekend pass, Rissell and two other patients stole a car, traveled out of state, broke into a house, and each took turns raping a seventeen-year-old girl. Three months later, he and another patient broke into the women's locker room at a local swimming pool, covered a young woman's head with a towel, and raped her repeatedly. The gang-type behavior added an element of voyeurism to the rapes. It was a thrill at first, but Rissell's paranoia quickly set in—additional assailants meant additional variables, which could increase his chances of getting caught. He soon went back to his solo ways.

The sixth attack was his last before progressing to rape-murder. As before, the victim was a woman he'd seen in his apartment building. He approached her with an air pistol, took her to a storage room, and covered her face with her jacket before raping her twice. And although the attack was horrific in its own right, to Rissell, it was just another iteration of the same old crime. He needed a new thrill.

<hr>

On a late August evening in 1976, when Rissell was an eighteen-year-old high school student on probation, everything changed. It started when he realized his girlfriend was cheating on him with another guy. Earlier that day, he had driven to her college to surprise her. But instead, through a window, he saw her being romantic with another guy. This event became Rissell's homicidal "stressor"—a term used to catalog triggering moments that reoccur throughout a serial killer's active phase—that predicated his transition from a rapist to a fully realized murderer.

Furious, Rissell sped back to his apartment in Alexandria. His mind raced with murderous fantasies as he pulled into the parking lot, sitting there for several hours, getting drunk and high and fueling his unmoored rage. Rissell's planning and thinking about murder showed that the design process—the first phase of sexually motivated murder—had begun. At two a.m., when a young woman pulled her car into the lot, Rissell, aware that no one else was around, saw this as an opportunity to nurse his bruised ego by reclaiming the pride and control that had been stolen from him. He approached the woman at gunpoint, forced her to drive to a secluded area, and raped her outside the car. Rissell didn't know it at the time, but his victim turned tricks as a massage parlor worker in Maryland. He became suspicious when she, in Rissell's words, "tried to control the situation" by faking orgasms and asking "which way I wanted it." This validated all the vitriol he was feeling toward women at the moment, confirming that they were liars and whores. And although he hadn't planned on murdering her after the rape, the dynamic between them shifted when she tried to escape.

According to Rissell, "She took off running down the Ravine. That's when I grabbed her. I had her in an arm lock. She was bigger than me. I started choking her . . . she stumbled . . . we rolled down the hill and into the water. I banged her head against the side of a rock and held her head under water."

As the woman's lungs filled with water, Rissell entered the second phase of murder, the point where fantasy became reality.

"Why'd you take her there?" Ressler had asked.

"I used to go down there as a small kid and play in the water— play Army and stuff . . . but I wasn't thinking other little kids go down there, and there were two little kids who found her. I never went back after that."

Rissell's decision to leave the body in the open without covering it or disposing of it marked the third phase of murder. By leaving it out in the open, he was conveying that he was in control. It was flagrant. He was no longer hiding from who he was. He was exposing it for the world to see.

Rissell's post-crime behavior, also called the fourth phase of murder, wouldn't take shape until he claimed his next victim and started collecting small souvenirs: jewelry, a watch, sunglasses. But his patterns and behaviors had already been set. Over the next five months—a time in which he was on probation and undergoing mandated psychiatric counseling—Rissell proceeded to commit four more murders, nearly escaping detection entirely. He was only caught when police searched his car on an unrelated assault charge and found souvenirs from his most recent victim, including her keys, wallet, and comb. At trial, he was given five life sentences for the five rape-murders he committed. After two years of incarceration, he confessed to an additional six rapes, none of which ever resulted in a formal charge due to insufficient forensic evidence and the fact that, during the 1970s, sexual violence against women was still considered a low-priority crime in the United States.

Rissell was a willing participant in the FBI serial killer study. He was thoughtful in his interviews, often seemed sincere, and was unique in that he had become active at a surprisingly young age. He also liked to talk. This wasn't always the case with serial killers, so the agents took advantage of his openness to record multiple interviews that retraced even the smallest details of his murders, his behaviors, and his thoughts.

But patterns stay hidden if no one bothers to look for them. And Rissell's tapes hadn't been touched in years. By analyzing their content now, in this moment, aided by the context of everything I'd learned over the past six years, I hoped to better understand the obsessive nature of offenders. Rissell's files presented me with the opportunity to do just that. His methods of sexual violence were chronic and repetitive, building in severity the longer they went unchecked. And his particular capacity for manipulation helped broaden his ability of control. Rissell wasn't just an obsessive type; obsession was his signature. It's what motivated everything he did. It was the root of all of his fantasies. This became clear to me as soon as I clicked play on that first tape.

"I'm too slick for them," Rissell said, laughing and explaining why the local police didn't consider him a suspect. "And none of the girls were saying anything. It was a real turn-on to realize [they] weren't reporting or identifying me."

"Where did this all start? How far from where you lived to where you found your victims?" Ressler asked.

"It's only about two, three blocks," Rissell answered. "Let me draw you a map to show you. This is all my area. All the murders were taken place in the area where I came from."

"Did you ever think of jumping in a car, cutting to Maryland or something like that?" Douglas prodded. "There'd be less heat on you if you took your victims somewhere else."

"Yeah, yeah," Rissell said, arrogantly dismissing the idea. "But I figured knowing the area was in my benefit. And going somewhere that I didn't know or where the cops patrolled might get me caught. That's why I committed as many murders as I did and stayed out there as long as I did, because I knew the area and I knew what time the cops came by in the morning because I'd be sitting out there. You see, even the newspaper article said that the reason I hadn't been caught was because they were looking for strangers, right? The police were looking for strangers and suspicious characters, but me being a young teenager and living around that area, I was seen every day."

Chillingly enough, he was right. One of the main reasons Rissell wasn't caught until after the fifth murder was that the police were looking for older strangers—especially "suspicious strangers," according to their reports—not a teenager living in the area. But while the police chased false leads, Rissell continued his spree unimpeded, despite his past criminal record and the fact that he lived in the same building where the majority of these crimes had been committed. He was hiding in plain sight.

Location, however, was the investigative thread that should have linked these cases together. Most of the victims were approached at knifepoint as they entered the elevator in their apartment building. All of the rape-murder victims were abducted from the same place, killed in different areas, and found fully clothed anytime from one day to six weeks later. For the most part, Rissell chose his five rape-murder victims at random, by watching cars drive into his apartment complex. In one case, however, the pattern was reversed. Rissell hitch-hiked a ride home from a woman going to a party in his apartment complex. She let him off at his building, then went to park her car. He waited, entered the elevator with her, and abducted her there.

Rissell's MO was eerily consistent. First, he signaled his intent to victims by approaching them with a gun, promising that he wouldn't hurt them if they had sex with him. Then he let the victim's reaction dictate what happened next. The ones that complied received no additional orders or threats. The ones who screamed received verbal threats. And the ones who refused to cooperate were punched and beaten into submission. In almost all cases, Rissell would maintain his control by forcing his victims to drive them to a nearby wooded area. Still, there were variables that he couldn't always account for. And these unpredictable interactions often marked significant turning points that either neutralized or escalated his urge to kill. As Rissell explained, "The more I got to know about the women, the softer I got."

When Rissell secured his third victim, things really changed. At first, he ordered her to be quiet, then turned on the radio. "I was thinking . . . I've killed two. I might as well kill this one, too. . . . Something in me was wanting to kill. . . . I tied her up with her stockings and I started to walk away . . . then I heard her through the woods kind of rolling around and making muffled sounds. And I turned back and said, 'No, I have to kill her. I've got to do this to preserve and protect myself.'" Her body was later discovered abandoned in the woods, with twenty-one stab wounds scattered across the left side of her thorax and upper abdomen.

Rissell's fourth murder victim marked another crucial moment in his progression as a serial sexual killer. He was now choosing victims knowing full well that he'd end up killing them. There were no more inhibitions. And with this new clarity of mind, Rissell's fantasies became more intentional, more violent, and more deliberate. In describing this fourth attack, he recalled that "she scratched me across the face. I got mad. She started to run. I got up from falling down and chased her. She ran into a tree. I caught her. We wrestled, rolled over the embankment into the water. . . . She was fighting and she was strong, but I put her head under the water and just sat there with my hands on her neck."

The most brutal of all was his fifth and final murder. The woman, who lived near his apartment complex, recognized who he was. This both escalated his fears of being caught by the police and made him feel less in control of the situation. He tried to overcome his anxiety by dominating his victim with fear. He told her about his four previous murders and about the joy he felt while killing them and then informed her that she was next and there was nothing that could stop him. But he couldn't shake his paranoia. It bothered him to be seen so clearly and distinctly by someone whose life he was about to steal. As the two were walking through the large culverts beneath a nearby highway, his paranoia overwhelmed him and he attacked—savagely. "That's when I pulled out the knife and without even saying anything, I stabbed her," Rissell said. "Maybe fifty, a hundred times."

The more Rissell talked, the more vividly I saw him come into focus. His nuanced way of understanding his crimes, and the carefulness with which he described his victims, revealed a strange paradox. Rissell wasn't as one-dimensional as the agents' initial reports described him. He couldn't simply be dismissed as a monster or psycho or freak. He was more complex than that. In fact, Rissell was more complex than any other offender I'd analyzed up to this point in that his goal wasn't to dominate and control his victims. He was trying to control the world around him. He was trying to bridge the gap between the perfectly constructed fantasies in his head and the imperfect realties of his own corrupt existence. By acting out his fantasies—Rissell believed—he could correct the past by taking from others what had been taken from him. He saw violence as a tool for making himself whole. But at the same time, he understood that violence was a deeply flawed solution to an impossible problem. No one can change the past.

"How would you feel afterwards?" Ressler asked. "What was it like once you were all finished and got rid of the body?"

"After I got home and cleaned up and thought about what I did, I'd get scared again. I was nervous. I was ashamed of myself. I didn't know what was happening, why I was doing this."

"Why ashamed?"

"It was complicated," Rissell explained. "I remember one night, when I was watching the news coverage with my mother about one of them, the victim's father got on and says, 'Whoever did this, please turn yourself in. We don't want to get back at you for what you did. We know you're sick.' That started affecting me. I had to walk outside and then got my keys and drove to the store. My mother didn't associate these two things. But it messed me up when he said all that."

"And your mother had no idea?"

"She was just worried for my safety. She kept telling me there were people out there killing while I was walking around at night going to parties and such. She told me to watch it." Rissell paused, then added: "I tried to put it out of my mind, because I knew how wrong it was."

"Do you think you would have turned yourself in if you felt you would get some treatment?" Douglas asked.

"No." Rissell didn't hesitate. "I'd been through that whole role. I didn't believe nothing was going to stop me until they caught me. And when they did, they were going to have to kill me. I did think about joining the Marines. I felt some stern hand would straighten me out. I needed some type of self-discipline to restrain myself from these violent actions that were going on in my mind."

"What about the last victim you let escape?" Ressler asked. "You were already killing at that point. What made her different?"

"She told me her father was dying of cancer. I thought of my own brother who was back from overseas and had just gone through a cancer operation. Twenty-five years old and got cancer . . . that was on my mind. I couldn't kill her. She had it bad already."

I paused the tape, rewound it, and listened again to that last exchange.

"She had it bad already."

This was the key. In that instant, as the woman relayed her troubles to Rissell, his whole delicate framework of fantasy collapsed. He no longer saw the woman as a depersonalized representation of her gender. She was a real person, a unique individual. She'd managed to connect to Rissell by representing the same emotional instabilities at the root of his obsessive need for control—like his parents' divorce, his absent father, his rejections by women, his brother's cancer. This woman's world was just as flawed and messed up as his was, and as soon as he realized that, he empathized with her. It was also why he told her to pull over and toss her car keys out the window before he leapt out of the car and ran off into the woods.

The Rissell tapes gave me a rare chance to observe the step-by-step progression of how a killer came to be. They chronicled how his patterned way of thinking—his need to relive and revise past experiences by playing them over and over in his head—fueled his obsessive fantasies in a way that set him apart from typical individuals. And they showed what triggered his evolution from anger, to petty theft, to rape, to murder. But what was most compelling was the constant self-awareness Rissell displayed. He knew exactly what he was doing. He saw the effect it had. And he continued regardless.

"On the surface, I think I'm normal just like anybody," he said. "But deep inside, there's something down there I feel has become my downfall. It's a fierceness of how I feel and how I want to react sometimes."

"But you've deviated from the most basic rule of society," Ressler said. "You've taken human life. That's what makes you different."

"Yes," Rissell acknowledged.

———◆———

What struck me most about Rissell was the fact that he committed most of his crimes while under psychiatric supervision. This exposed certain flaws and limitations in common psychiatric interviewing techniques. Most notable was the practice of self-reporting. The technique was predicated on the idea that patients wanted to get better, that they were willing participants in their treatment, and that they were truthful in the reports they gave on themselves. But it didn't account for offenders who outright lied to their psychiatrists or purposefully manipulated those around them into believing false improvement.

Rissell acknowledged similar feelings of surprise about being able to get away with his crimes while under psychiatric supervision. He explained that his psychiatrists never went back to talk about his crimes. They just wanted to talk about how he was feeling in the moment, which made it easy for him to lie and say he'd learned from past mistakes. They never asked about the crimes themselves or his relationship with his parents or his drinking or the breakup with his girlfriend.

It would have been "gut-wrenching to go through it again," Rissell admitted. But at the same time, he felt like his psychiatrists missed an opportunity by not asking the right questions. If they had, maybe they would have found a reason for his crimes. "In the long run, it helps to talk."

This was rare, this level of awareness that Rissell showed for who he was and the nature of his actions. But he wasn't the only one. Kemper showed this same characteristic, too. Only, it affected him differently.

CHAPTER 11

Fantasy or Reality, You Can't Have Both

Douglas once said of serial killer Edmund Kemper, "I would be less than honest if I didn't admit that I liked the guy." And though it's a strange admission, I could certainly understand where he was coming from. Kemper didn't have the typical arrogance of other serial killers. He was calm and articulate. He liked to joke around and was friendly, open, and sensitive. But over the course of less than a decade, he also coldly butchered three of his family members and seven defenseless women. Unlike Douglas, I couldn't separate the criminal from the crime. I saw the value in the data Kemper offered—that was it. To me, he was just a means to an end.

But in the context of data, what fascinated me about Kemper was that he was incredibly self-aware. This trait was something I'd only ever noticed before in Rissell—and I'd assumed Rissell was simply an outlier. Now, with Kemper, I had a second point of reference. I could analyze the patterns, behaviors, and criminal psychology of the two and apply what I learned to both the act of profiling and the criminal personality study. It was somewhat rare to find these types of outliers at the later stages of a research project. I was excited. So, I dove right in.

Despite several immediate differences between Kemper and Rissell, there were important underlying similarities as well. For example, they were both serial killers and rapists whose sexually deviant behavior showed complete disregard for the value of individual life. They both fantasized about having power and control in the most absolute sense. And they both saw their acts of violence as a form of connection. The notable difference was the point at which they established that connection with their victim. Rissell raped and attempted to connect with his victims while they were still alive. Kemper didn't think that was possible. He fundamentally believed that connection—true connection, without fear of resistance or rejection—could only happen after his victims were already dead. That was when he'd rape their bodies to feel the most elevated sense of control.

It took some unraveling to separate Kemper from the larger-than-life myth he'd developed in the years after his crimes. It seemed like every newspaper printed its own embellished version of the Kemper story, and every psychologist crafted their own analysis based on hearsay and rumors. Even Kemper himself contributed to the confusion. He had a habit of tailoring each retelling of his crimes to the expectations of the person who interviewed him, testing what they knew about him, and adding in new wrinkles where he could. It was a game he played, satisfying his need to always be in control. But for me, it just meant more work to uncover the truth.

Born in Burbank, California, on December 18, 1948, Edmund Kemper III was the middle child and only son of Clarnell and Edmund Kemper II. His sisters, Allyn and Susan, were five years older and two years younger, respectively. As the only male child, Kemper was seen as special from the moment he took his first breath.

He was even named in honor of his father and grandfather, signifying their legacy and family pride.

In spite of this, his childhood was defined by instability, conflict, and the eventual divorce of his parents, after which his mother moved the family to Montana. Kemper was devastated. Worse still, without his father around, he felt that his mother was taking out her anger on him. "I wanted the whole world to kick off when I was about nine or ten. I didn't want my family to break up. I loved them both. There was a lot of fighting and that had me crying watching it at night. They divorced. I've got two sisters, and my mother treated me like I was a third daughter, telling me what a rotten father I have. I'm supposed to be identifying with my dad and I never did. I got an older sister that beats up on me a lot—five years older. I got a younger sister that lies on both of us and gets us punished. I had the instinct to feel like I'm getting a rotten deal."

Kemper's growing resentment toward his family manifested in bizarre "games" and role-playing that often involved his sisters. Kemper's younger sister—the agents had recorded interviews with her, too—volunteered an example of one of her brother's odd favorites, which involved having his sister blindfold him, lead him to a chair, and then pull an imaginary lever. Kemper would then writhe about and convulse on the floor as if he were dying in a gas chamber. Kemper later added to this routine by constructing a pretend "coffin box" to lie in after being "gassed."

From here, Kemper's childhood was marked by many of the same unfortunate circumstances as his fellow offenders within the FBI's original serial killer study. He was made fun of at school, sat alone on the bus, was picked on by his sisters, and became a constant target of his mother's alcohol-fueled abuse. Kemper internalized much of this humiliation, but, occasionally, he acted out cruelly toward animals or his sisters. After one particular incident with his younger sister—very personal in nature—Clarnell decided the two shouldn't share a bed-room anymore and separated her son from the rest of the family by moving him to the basement. Kemper, who, like Rissell, was another chatty and willing participant in the FBI's serial killer study, recalled the basement with haunting precision:

> It was a walk-in basement, a long flight of wooden steps down to the basement floor . . . native granite walls, rattling pipes overhead. It was great for a kid with an imag-ination . . . unfortunately, I was terrified of monsters—all the scary negative aspects of things. After a fashion, during the six months or so I was in that basement, I was making a bargain with demonic forces that I was convinced were going to consume me, somehow do me in. There was a converted furnace in the basement that had been a coal-burner in years earlier. . . . To me that was the fires of hell. When my parents separated at my age of seven, in 1956, I spent some months, like I said, in familiar surroundings—sharing a bedroom with my younger sister, younger by two years. And then when I was put in that basement, the rest of the family went upstairs to retire for the evening and I went to the basement, so we had an entire floor of the house between us, and it was very scary. My mother wouldn't allow me any negotiated settlement of light. I couldn't have a nightlight, it was too expensive. For an eight-year-old boy—seven and eight years old—I was terrified.

Shortly after this, when Clarnell married for the third time, Kemper—at his own request—went to live with his father and step-mother. But he was unwanted in their home as well. His stepmother found his "strangeness" unsettling. She would often catch him staring at her, which gave her the creeps, and she told her husband to send him off. This situation came to a head when the family gathered at the family farm in North Fork, California, for Christmas in 1963. At the end of the holidays, with no explanation to fifteen-year-old Kemper, he was abandoned by his father and left behind to stay with his grandparents. He stood and watched as the car pulled away from the farmhouse's dirt driveway, then got smaller and smaller as it sped off down the road without him.

At first, it appeared that Kemper was adjusting well enough to his new home on the farm. He had a .22 caliber rifle that he used to shoot gophers and rabbits, and he seemed to do well in school. But by the end of that first summer, his grandmother became worried that he'd regressed. She, too, felt increasingly uneasy with his "strangeness." And by his own admission, Kemper was becoming further and further obsessed with murderous fantasies. He'd killed plenty of animals. Now he wanted to see what it was like to kill a person.

"How did that develop into fantasies?" Ressler asked.

"I was being called 'stupid' pretty frequently, and unfortunately that was sinking in. . . . That's when I went into the morbid fantasy, and that's when the death trip started. The devil was sharing my bedroom with me, he was living in the furnace. . . . I built up a lot of hostility unconsciously, and then it gets off into the fantasy bullshit. So this festered. They should have noticed it in school, so excessive was my daydreaming in school, it was always on my report cards."

"What'd you daydream about?"

Kemper explained that his daydreams consisted of "fantasies that slowly became more advanced, along the lines of wiping out the whole school. That was bad. But they thought I was off watching tulips flying by the window and the birds upside down—like any normal daydreamer would do."

It didn't help that Kemper, who was fifteen at the time, was six-foot-seven and weighed 173 pounds. His classmates constantly made fun of him, and he was an introvert who was too big to hide from his tormentors. He was also incredibly lonely. He had no friends, was separated from his parents, and was kept isolated on a rural farm away from everything he knew. All he had were his fantasies. His only outlet was to play them over and over again in his head, perfecting them until they became something sacred—a place where he made the rules.

On August 27, 1964, Kemper was watching his grandmother proof-read a children's book in the kitchen when she abruptly yelled at him to stop staring at her. Kemper got up, grabbed his .22 rifle, and said he was going outside to shoot gophers. His grandmother warned him not to shoot birds and then turned back to her work. As she did, Kemper shot her once in the back of her head and several more times between her shoulder blades. He then stabbed her and covered her head in a towel. When his grandfather returned home, Kemper shot and killed him, too. He then called his mother and confessed, and she told him to call the police, which he did. After years of enduring so many small triggers and rejections, his grandmother's harsh rebuke was all it took to tip him over the edge. With his murderous fantasies fully realized, he could now kill with impunity.

Kemper's reaction of calling the police after committing his first murders, however, was fairly uncommon. Unlike most of our subjects in the serial killer study, killers who did everything they could to avoid detection, Kemper's instinct was to acknowledge what he'd done. This indicated that he hadn't thought through what to do afterward—or what consequences he might face. But what struck me as even odder still was what Kemper actually told the police once he called them.

"I just wondered how it would feel to shoot Grandma," he said, adding that he then killed his grandfather so he wouldn't have to find out his wife was dead.

There was so much to unpack from these statements. Clearly, they illustrated the very low, if any, attachment Kemper had for family relationships. But at the same time, he rationalized killing his grandfather as a way of protecting him from emotional pain. And he immediately called his mother to explain what he'd done. It was a contradiction that spoke to Kemper's early attachments, rejections, and isolation. And it gave me a glimpse into how he perceived the world around him. Fantasy was Kemper's dominant lens. He knew this and tried to stay grounded through an attachment to his mother. But their relationship was antagonistic and could be incredibly volatile. His mother proved to be his primary stressor, and yet, in his mind, his mother was his salvation as well.

Like Rissell, Kemper was also a juvenile when he was first convicted. He spent four years at the Atascadero State Hospital for the criminally insane before he was eventually released back into his mother's care. Several doctors disagreed with the release agreement, considering the well-documented hostile relationship Kemper had with his mother, but the Juvenile Authority Board disregarded the clinical reports. Now, at 280 pounds and a massive six-foot-nine, Kemper returned home with a chance at a new beginning. He attended community college and tried to go into law enforcement, but he was rejected from the academy for being too tall and so took a job with the State of California Highway Department instead.

By all accounts, it looked like Kemper was on track to live a normal life. He had a job, occasionally dated, and gave the impression of being an intelligent young man. But inside his head, a quiet world of dormant fantasies was stretching out like a disease. Kemper found his old temptations hard to resist. He spent the next two years picking up female hitchhikers to test whether he could control his impulses to harm them. But despite these experiments, he was fully aware of what would happen next. "I knew long before I started killing that

I was going to be killing, that it was going to end up like that," he admitted. "The fantasies were too strong. They were going on for too long and were too elaborate."

Kemper finally acted on these fantasies in May of 1972. One evening, as he was driving around Berkeley, he stopped to pick up two female college hitchhikers, Mary Ann Pesce and Anita Luchessa. He originally intended only to rape them, but instead, he panicked, killed them, stuffed them in his trunk, and drove to his house, where he repeatedly raped the bodies and later dismembered them. This signaled a new phase in Kemper's murderous course, and he soon embarked on a deadly spree, attacking college co-eds (this would later lead to his nickname as "the Co-ed Killer"). He would murder them, decapitate them, have sex with their corpses, and butcher them to dispose of their remains—dumping hands, torsos, and other body parts in different locations. In some cases, he also held on to their dismembered heads to repeatedly violate them, only getting rid of them when they started to smell.

When asked if he could justify the reasoning behind his violent actions, Kemper's answer was very matter-of-fact. "Yeah, originally the decapitations, I think part of it was kind of a weird thing I had in my head. It was a fantasy I had in childhood." Kemper added that "there was the satisfaction gained in the removal of the head. In fact, the first head I removed was that of Miss Luchessa in the trunk of the car with the knife that killed Miss Pesce and I remember it was very exciting, removing Miss Luchessa's head. There was actually a sexual thrill, and, in fact, there was almost a climax to it. It was kind of an exalted, triumphant-type thing, like taking the head of a deer or elk or something would be to a hunter. I was the hunter and they were my victims."

Kemper's self-identification as a hunter collecting trophies is central to understanding the nature of his mind, and it partially explained why he turned to dismemberment as a tool for disposing of the bodies afterward. He became fascinated by the dismemberment process, studying it and improving his efficiency with each kill, such as when he started severing his victims' Achilles tendons before rigor mortis set in to make it easier to manipulate their bodies. But it was the act of decapitation itself that was most essential to Kemper's violent fantasies. Heads were his favorite keepsakes.

This fascination with heads started in early childhood, when Kemper decapitated his sister's dolls in a game of sexual rituals. "I would sit there looking at the heads on an overstuffed chair, tripping on them on my bed, looking at them [when] one of them somehow becomes unsettled, comes rolling down the chair, very grisly. Tumbling down the chair, rolls across the cushion and hits the rug— 'bonk.'" This idea grew throughout childhood until it became central to the fantasy, where a dead female corpse essentially transformed into what Kemper considered a real-life doll. As Kemper described it, "If I killed them, you know, they couldn't reject me as a man. It was more or less making a doll out of a human being, carrying out my fantasies with a doll, a living human."

Kemper came closest to enacting this idealized crime with the murder of his last co-ed victim, Cynthia Schall, whom he shot, stuffed in the trunk of his car, and then brought back to his mother's apartment. He kept the body in the closet overnight so he could dissect it in the bathtub the next day while his mother was at work. He then buried the decapitated head in the backyard with its face turned toward his bedroom window. Kemper added, "Sometimes at night, I talked to her, saying love things, the way you do to a girlfriend or wife."

With each new murder, Kemper's confidence and competency grew. He began to admire his approach, romanticizing both his victims and the process itself. "It was like seeing gorgeous butterflies going by and you just want one to check it out closer because it goes by so fast, and I reached out knowing that when I grabbed it, the butterfly would be crushed and not alive anymore. It would not be beautiful, but it would be still. That's why I got past that God-awful thing that comes from people saying you can't mess around with the dead. It's awful. It's icky and all that."

In the spring of 1973, after a two-month hiatus, Kemper's spree culminated with the murder of his mother and one of her friends, Sally Hallett. That Friday, Clarnell had gone to a party, got drunk, and woke Kemper up by making a racket when she arrived home. When Kemper went to check on her, she said, "Oh, I suppose you're going to want to sit up all night and talk now?" Kemper looked at her and said, "No, goodnight," while fully knowing what would happen next. Once his mother fell asleep, he crept into her bedroom and bludgeoned her to death with a claw hammer. He then severed her head and spent the next several hours violating her body, using it for oral sex, then screaming at it before using it as a target for darts.

I could hear him crying into the tape recorder as he recounted the details. But I wasn't moved. Like usual, Kemper made everything about himself: "I came from my mother," he said. "And in a rage, I went right back in."

———◆———

As disturbing as they were to listen to, acts of dismemberment and necrophilia were fairly standard among serial killers. I'd heard many of the same details before, but with Kemper, it was different. He mutilated his victims with ease. And he spoke about it as if it were a sacred act. "There's only one [kind of] guy more casual around a body and that's a mortician or a pathologist who's done it for years. Because I've seen some icky shit, but some of those fantasies were so bizarre that it would probably turn the stomach of a frigging pathologist. It wasn't a sadistic trip. It was just a development. In other words, getting tired of a certain level of fantasy and then going even farther and even more bizarre and deeper off into it. Year after year after year, and finally it got off in such deep ends that I'm still not exposed to the worst of the fantasies that I had."

The implication was clear. For Kemper, killing wasn't the point. Dismemberment was. He satisfied a crude form of connecting to his fellow humans by tearing their bodies apart. And as disturbing as this was, as flawed as its logic seems, the process made perfect sense to a sociopath like Kemper. It reflected his lack of empathy, his need for dominance, and his inability to sustain emotional bonds with others. This was most notable in how obsessive he was when it came to pre-serving his victims' heads, which he used both ritualistically and in the service of prolonging his fantasies. Kemper explained his thinking in the FBI's recording of his trial testimony with DA Pete Chang and Detective Mickey Aluffi of the Sheriff's Office.

"I wanted [her body] to decompose quickly because there was a bullet in her head and I didn't want there to be anything visual," Kemper explained. "I didn't want there to be too much problem with odor or what you call it, decomposition. I skinned her head, removed the hair, scalp, facial and neck tissue, and any meat I could from her head."

"Did you bury that with her head?" Detective Aluffi asked.

"Yes, right underneath," Kemper replied. "I knew it would go first but I didn't want it to be still attached to the skull area. I wanted the skull area to decompose quickly, anything left on it or in it. But hair and scalp I did not put in it. Just the facial areas of the head."

"What did you do with the hair and scalp?"

"I cut the hair off the scalp, deposited it in the garbage of a service station in a sack, and cut the scalp up in pieces and flushed it down the toilet, figuring it would not be discovered."

This pragmatic, unemotional retelling of horrifically gruesome events—similar in tone to how a mechanic would describe dismantling a car piece by piece—showed Kemper's transactional approach to violence. His victims were merely blank canvases to be painted with the tremendous fantasies that escaped from his head. But it was Kemper's sister, Allyn, who offered the deepest insight of the trial. She recalled wondering if her brother had anything to do with the co-ed killings before he turned himself in. "A childhood incident flashed in front of my face," she testified, quickly describing how her brother had killed and beheaded the family cat, then hid the remains in his closet until his mother noticed the stench. Allyn also mentioned asking Kemper if he had anything to do with the killings. He denied it but told her not to mention it to their mother because "she'll start wondering and things could get heavy."

At the core, the way in which Kemper carried out these murders reflected the adversity he'd experienced in his early childhood experiences, including the abandonment by his absent father and his unavailable mother. He killed both as an expression of this inability to connect with others and as a punishment for his parents' stubborn refusal to show him comfort. Violence was Kemper's attempt to prove his self-worth amid constant attacks and verbal emasculations, to reclaim the emotional bonds with other people that were being withheld from him. If Freud were to design a serial killer, Kemper would surely be the archetype. It was classic: he was desperate for his parents' uncompromising favoritism, and when they failed to provide him with the positive attention he craved, he lashed out— with merciless brutality.

Both Kemper and Rissell epitomized—and, in turn, complicated— an aspect of serial killer development that I hadn't fully understood before. The dominant approach to analyzing these types of criminals had always focused on nature versus nurture, implying that either biological or environmental factors predetermined someone's potential for becoming a murderer. But Kemper and Rissell complicated those clear-cut divisions. They showed that serial killers weren't necessarily born to be violent but that they were susceptible to violent behavior and that they developed a stronger likelihood to kill through exposure to specific triggers. Still, even with the right conditions, the urge to kill was something they developed over time. It was complex and slow forming. And, more often than not, it all traced back to an inability to connect—both with others and with themselves. In the mind of a serial killer, violence could be a form of self-medication. It calmed their obsessions, confusions, and overwhelming fantasies. It gave them a sense of control. But, like all self-medication, the effects were only temporary. Kemper knew this all too well, admitting that "reality never lived up to the fantasy."

No matter how self-aware a serial killer was, or how many new rituals they added to their violent crimes, it would never be enough. The line between fantasy and reality was impermeable. Their primitive urge to kill—that relentless, unyielding thirst—was insatiable. No amount of violence could tame or extinguish that underlying desire. Rissell and Kemper understood this better than anyone else. It was why they couldn't stop talking about their crimes. The memories were all they had left.

CHAPTER 12

Patterns of Dismemberment

Lecturing could be a polarizing part of the job at the BSU. Some agents enjoyed it, some used it as a social outlet, and some considered it a burden to their already thinly stretched resources. But I looked at it differently. To me, it was a unique opportunity to test out new ideas on a live audience and then fine-tune my work on the basis of their collective response. I saw it as equal parts an opportunity to teach and an opportunity to learn. There was value in the process—in the questions new agents asked, the excitement they showed when something clicked, or their silent looks of confusion when I failed to make any sense. Lecturing motivated me. It made my work more comprehensive. It brought out my best.

In the spring of 1986, shortly after publishing a paper on murderers who rape and mutilate their victims, I had an aha moment for a new lecture idea. I'd just spent the better part of three months comparing sexual murderers who themselves have a history of sex abuse to murderers with no such history. The findings surprised me. The data revealed that murderers with a history of childhood sexual abuse were more likely to mutilate their victims. This type of vindictive behavior—overcompensating for the trauma of the past by mirroring it in ways that were more extreme, more sadistic—spoke to the singular nature of serial killers in ways that I was anxious to explore further. It had to do with patterns of thought. And it was exactly the type of idea that would benefit from the contextual experiences of others outside the team.

The motivation behind this particular inquiry came from an interview with Edmund Kemper. Robert Ressler asked Kemper about his choice of victims and why he killed. Kemper's response was surprising.

"I had a real bad problem depriving people of their lives," he said. "It wasn't the aspect of killing them, it was the aspect of possessing their bodies afterwards."

The moment clicked. What Kemper said—not his words, necessarily, but the sentiment of tension and moral principle behind them—made perfect sense. It suggested a whole new dimension to these serial killers that we hadn't considered before. Up to that point, we'd been studying serial killers and developing offender profiles based on what we knew of their upbringing, their planning, and a crime scene's record of the acts of rape and murder. But we hadn't given serious consideration to the ritualistic elements that went into how offenders interacted with a victim's body after death. Not really, anyway. We'd only focused on that element of the crime in practical terms: how the body was disposed of, whether it had been posthumously raped, and how it could be used to collect forensics. But Kemper's case suggested that offenders could also be very intentional, even particular, about their post-offense behavior, that it had meaning, and that analyzing it further could lead to a better understanding of how serial killers' minds worked. It seemed obvious in retrospect: ritual was a serial killer's third act.

This realization also broadened the scope of our work. It showed that, for certain individuals, the satisfaction of committing a crime didn't come from killing but rather from the ritualistic acts that followed: butchering human bodies, collecting souvenirs, and successfully displaying or disposing of a victim's corpse. This type of disposal and then post-offense behavior hadn't been well studied before in this regard. And although it was disturbing to think about, part of my job at the BSU was to understand the more extreme fringes of serial violence and use it to predict how offenders might evolve. As John Douglas liked to say:

> Behavior reflects personality. The best indicator of future violence is past violence. To understand the "artist," you must study his "art." The crime must be evaluated in its totality.

"There are two reasons why someone mutilates or dismembers a human body," I said, diving right into the start of my lecture from the familiar podium of a Quantico auditorium. "The first is practical—dissecting a body to conceal the victim's identity or to more easily dispose of the remains. But for some individuals, post-offense acts serve to gratify a primary fantasy of sadism, which is ceremonial in nature and includes carving symbolic patterns and markings on a body or amputation or dismemberment of sexual parts."

I clicked on the projector to show an image of investigators standing around a disembodied head in the mountains near Santa Cruz. The features were all clear and wholly intact. There was no decay, just visible shriveling. You could tell that the victim was a young girl still in her teens.

"In both cases, dismemberment presents a huge challenge for investigators. A mutilated corpse makes it far more difficult to perform basic acts of forensics. And the scattering of various body parts across multiple locations helps conceal the identity of both the victim and the offender."

I clicked forward to a close-up of just the victim's head.

"It's not easy to look at or think about," I told them. "Trust me, I know. But by investigating the planning of these acts—the decisions involved in mutilating, displaying, and/or preserving a victim's body—we have an opportunity to collect valuable information about who an offender is and how they think. There's a signature element to each of these cases. There are patterns. And if you can look at it in that light, you'll be one step closer to piecing together an understanding of an individual offender before they act again."

I noticed looks of confusion among the agents, so I paused to take questions.

"Isn't this type of thing an example of what you'd call an irrational behavior—something unpredictable and unexplainable?" an agent near the front asked. "I mean, this seems pretty far out there."

"Not really," I said. "Postmortem rituals were common in religious traditions for most of human history. It's only recently that the practice has become rarer without those types of cultural supports. But every single modern case I've looked at shows clear examples of offenders acting deliberately, meticulously, and with a narcissistic interest in their own sadistic self-gratification. They show intent, not insanity. Just look at the examples of Edmund Kemper, Ted Bundy, Carlton Gary. They all acted within reason."

"I understand what you're saying," the same agent pushed back. "But doesn't it get to a point where the unsub's reasoning is so convoluted, so crazy—to be honest—that it's no longer helpful to use it for clues?"

"The point isn't whether it's crazy or not," I said. "The point is that the *offender* sees some sort of logic in their actions, that *they* follow a pattern of reasoning, and that it makes sense to *them*. Let me explain. When I first started working at the BSU, one of the fundamental questions I asked the thirty-six sexual murderers in the original study was 'what triggered your first murder?' Without exception, every single offender's answer followed the same pattern of logic. First, they explained being fully aware of their long-standing obsession with an active fantasy life—often describing it as a 'dominant presence' from as far back as they could remember. Second, they described how their fantasies evolved from vague ideas of violence into more complex obsessions with rape, murder, and the control of others. And third, their answers showed how their intricate fantasy worlds reached a tipping point, realizing a depth of authenticity that rivaled reality itself.

"It's that final component—that blurring of lines between reality and fantasy—that's most important to understand. That's the key. Because it's in that moment where the abstract fascination with killing finally escapes from an offender's head and takes on a life of its own, violently targeting real victims in the very real world.

"And here's why that should matter to all of you," I added, clicking one slide forward to a picture of Ed Kemper's mugshot, taken by the Santa Cruz Sheriff's Department. "In the offenders' minds, they understand their motivation for sexual violence as a symptom of sadistic fantasy. But they don't see this as any fault of their own or as a misunderstanding of reality. Instead, they believe that their perception of reality is clearer than the perceptions of others', that they're entitled to whatever they want, and that they live in an unjust world in which control is the ultimate reward. For them, fantasy *is* reality. It's a private and powerful existence that follows its own complex set of rules and rituals, a self-serving narrative that becomes the framework for their complete disregard of human lives. For them it has meaning. Once you can see that, it'll have meaning for you as well."

———————

Throughout our research, Douglas, Ressler, and I were fully aware of how layered the nature of offenders could be. There was never one overarching reason for their development. They weren't "destined" to pursue violence. They weren't simply conditioned to kill. It was far more complex than that. And though there were common themes to their stories, such as abuse or exposure to violence when they were young, their destructive acts weren't predicated on that past violence. Rather, violent sexual offenders were motivated by their own unique patterns of thinking. The offenders we studied were inclined to mentally repeat and reenact childhood trauma as a way of understanding their experience—not as a means of overcoming trauma but as a form of indulgence. For them, fantasy as repetition helped reinforce and encourage early traumatic events. It was a form of rehearsal. It was a rare pattern of thinking that shaped deep cognitive grooves and realigned traditional means of perception, all of which would later justify the conscious planning of their own violent acts.

Our major takeaway from this was what it meant for an offender's evolution. The patterned nature of their thoughts and intentions was obsessive in nature, meaning it demanded continuous refinement, continuous practice, so that the act of killing could mirror the perfection of the fantasy. In this way, an offender's dangerous thought patterns became more complex and more violent the longer they went unchecked. Their fantasies evolved with each murder. They advanced, focusing on greater control and possession, and expanding into ritualistic forms of rape, torture, and mutilation. And although most offenders were caught before their fantasies could ever reach this point, others were calculated and paranoid enough to avoid detection as this process continued to evolve. It was these offenders, the ones who were able to act out their fantasies most completely, that gave us our deepest insights into the unique nature of their minds. And it was these same offenders that committed some of the most horrific acts we'd ever seen.

I analyzed my fair share of dismemberment cases during my time at the BSU, examining each one carefully regardless of the rawness of the details. Of course, this didn't mean I ever got used to the horrors of such gruesome crimes. I just knew I couldn't look away. Data was data. Each case offered something useful. Each case brought new perspective. Each case added to my understanding of serial killers as a whole. Because really, that's the nature of research: it only works when you account for the full reality of a phenomenon—you can't simply ignore what makes you uncomfortable. I'd learned that with the rape study. And I knew the importance of applying that philosophy to the criminal personality study as well. To fully understand crime, I needed to fully understand the individuals involved in their crimes. Even the crimes that were more haunting than others.

Gerard John Schaefer Jr., for example, described having fantasies of bondage and sadomasochism starting around age twelve. "I'd tie myself to a tree, masturbate, and fantasize about hurting myself. I discovered women's underwear and would wear them. My father favored my sister, so I wanted to be a girl."

Schaefer's homicidal routine was to abduct teenage girls and bring them to a remote area of a Florida nature preserve, where he tied them up, gagged them, and had them balance on roots with nooses wrapped around their necks before murdering them. He'd then butcher the bodies to suppress evidence of his crimes. Once investigators identified Schaefer as a prime suspect, they searched the home where he lived with his mother and found a stash of trophies from his various victims: jewelry, weapons, graphic photos, reports of missing persons, and teeth and bones. They also found over a hundred pages of handwritten manuscripts and drawings that detailed violent fantasies about violating and mutilating young women. But the most graphic display of Schaefer's fantasies was a tribute of sorts hanging on his walls. There, in great detail, Schaefer had meticulously crafted a collage of soft-core pornographic posters that gave visual form to his savage thoughts. One showed a woman leaning against a tree with her hands hidden behind her back, upon which Schaefer had drawn bullet holes, bondage ties, and marks of defecation in her underwear. Another showed three naked women standing across from a single man, above which Schaefer had outlined a thought bubble and written: "These women will please me. If not, they will be taken to the plaza square and entertain the villagers as they dance on the end of my rope." On another section of the wall, several posters had been grouped together and depicted young women hanging from trees.

But Schaefer wasn't alone in his gruesome fantasies. There was also the Carmine Calabro case, in which the victim, Francine Elveson, a twenty-six-year-old special-education teacher, was found dead on the roof of her Bronx apartment building. This was a particularly brutal example of dismemberment. Elveson had been tortured before death and violated after—beaten beyond recognition, tied up with her stockings and belt, and posed in a spread-eagle position that mimicked the Hebrew letter *chai*, which she wore on her necklace. Her entire face had been fractured and was covered by her underwear. There were bite marks on the inside of her thighs and around her knees. She had been stabbed with a pen knife. But most noteworthy of all was the level of sexual frustration apparent in the offender's post-offense acts. He had cut off her nipples, mutilated her sexual organs, written obscenities across her abdomen, forced an umbrella into her vagina, masturbated on her, and then defecated next to the body and covered it with her clothes. On her leg, written in ballpoint pen, was the phrase "Fuck you. You can't stop me"—a direct challenge to the police.

The BSU's profile of the unsub included details that he'd be disheveled in appearance, unemployed, would live with his parents nearby (possibly in the same building where the attack took place), was a high school or college dropout, that he had a large collection of bondage pornography, and that he recently had spent time in a mental institution, where he'd been prescribed medication for depression. Investigators used this information to narrow in on Carmine Calabro, a high school dropout who lived with his father in the same apartment building as Elveson and who had a history of mental instability. The break in the case came when Calabro willingly allowed investigators to take a dental impression of his mouth, which three independent experts matched to the bite marks on the victim. Calabro was then arrested and the bite-mark testimony was a key piece of evidence in securing his murder conviction.

"Biting is often part of a violent sexual assault, whether it's rape or murder. It gets back to the issue of control and dominance," Douglas explained. "It's about anger, aggression, and power. To them, it's total domination. They're consuming that person in every possible way. Their teeth are tools. They're destroying with every weapon they've got."

Calabro was found guilty, but never admitted to his crimes. In fact, in early 1986 he'd written a letter to the BSU questioning our profile: "If the profile is supposed to be me, there are two minor faults. 1. I am a high school graduate, 2. I did not have a pornography collection." He then added, "How long did you believe, in your professional opinion, it took the murderer to commit each and every aspect of this crime? How long do you think he actually spent at the scene of the crime? There's nothing involved in these answers for you, but for me a great deal. If in fact your answer is what I expect it to be, then I will write you a second letter and lay the facts to you. You can then decide whether or not it was merely an error on someone's part or intentional neglect."

Douglas and Ressler went to visit Calabro in prison shortly after that. Right away they noticed Calabro was missing all his teeth. And when they asked him about this, Calabro said he'd pulled them himself because the bite marks were used against him at trial, and he wouldn't let that same thing happen at his appeal.

Calabro, it seemed, was even willing to use acts of dismemberment on himself.

But even Calabro's case seemed tame compared to some of the others that we saw. There was one in particular, a case from Ohio, that stood out for how disturbingly drawn out the acts of dismemberment were. It had taken place a few years back and had stumped the local police for months. Eventually, after a task force took over, an arrest was made, and the investigation was declared a success. But I had my doubts. Something about the case didn't sit right with me, and I felt like they'd arrested the wrong guy. I wanted to test out my theory as part of a lecture to see if any agents felt the same way I did.

———◆◆◆———

I prepared the case for lecture differently from how I normally would. I made this one as simple as possible—stripped down and bare bones, only including the local police's findings, none of the later insights that came from the FBI. I wanted to present it exactly the way local investigators would have seen things in the immediate aftermath of the crime. Typically, I presented each case in its entirety, including the BSU profile, so that young agents could see the full design of our process without having to guess how all the elements might connect. Here, though, I wanted the young agents to see this case with fresh eyes and instincts, not through the lens of the BSU's conclusions. I wanted these agents to reach a decision on their own.

"Good morning, everyone." I put down my files and got straight to the point. "We're going to review a case with multiple victims today: one male, Todd Schultz, and one female, Annette Cooper. There's some interesting interplay going on between different people here. So, I'll cover that first, then I'll go through the sequence of events from the day the victims went missing. Then we'll have a round of questions. Just remember, even if you've heard about this case before, it doesn't mean you know anything about it. Bias will only slow you down. Now let's get started."

I treated the lecture just like a real profiling session, starting with victimology and highlighting the individuals involved in the case. This wasn't just an exercise in investigative strategies. At least to me it wasn't. Real people had died. I needed to make that weight of the situation feel as authentic as possible, as urgent as possible. I needed the case to hit home.

Eighteen-year-old Annette Cooper and her nineteen-year-old fiancé, Todd Schultz, first met while attending high school in Logan, located in southeast Ohio. Cooper lived with her stepfather, Dale Johnston; her mother, Sarah Johnston; and her teenage stepbrother and step-sister. But on August 6, 1982—two months before the crime took place—Cooper left the Johnston residence and moved in with her fiancé's family. Her reasoning, according to friends, was that her step-father was abusive and nasty. But the situation may have been more complex. Cooper had a reputation for being ambitious and was cast as a bit of an outsider at school and within the small community as a whole. She had many acquaintances but few close friends. And yet, at the same time, she was a national honor student, exceptionally smart, and was seen as someone with a bright future. She had no known arrest record, no known involvement with drugs or alcohol.

Her dichotomy made her somewhat complex—a girl with two very different faces to two different groups within the community.

Schultz was easier to pin down, socially speaking. He was a clean-cut boy who worked as a volunteer firefighter. He spent his free time hunting and going to concerts, and he was a car restoration fanatic. There are reports of him occasionally using recreational marijuana, but he didn't have a known arrest record. He was a fairly straitlaced kid.

On October 4, 1982, Cooper and Schultz met with an attorney in the early afternoon to discuss the marriage process and then returned to the Schultz residence around four p.m. According to Schultz's mother, the couple began arguing on the second floor of their home, then came downstairs, at which point Cooper, visibly upset, ran from the house. A few minutes passed before Schultz eventually ran down the street after her, calmed his fiancée, and then turned and waved to his mother on the porch, signaling that everything was okay. Their conflict apparently resolved, the couple continued to walk down the road. That was the last time the mother saw them.

At eight a.m. the next morning, when the couple still hadn't returned from their stroll, Schultz's father called the Logan Police Department to report them missing. Ten days passed before a search team discovered the victims' torsos in the nearby Hocking River in West Logan. Two days after that, the victims' heads, arms, and legs were found buried in shallow graves beneath a cornfield adjacent to the river. Both victims had been shot several times.

While the forensics team was on the scene, police noticed a man watching the events unfold from a partially hidden position within the cornstalks. He was identified as Kenny Linscott, a town resident who lived three blocks away and frequently fished and hunted along the river. He explained that he was simply curious about why the police were there, and the investigation moved on without paying him further attention. But the case quickly stalled after that. And as the days continued to pass with no new leads or resolutions, rumors began to spread throughout the community. Church sermons warned that the devil had come to Logan, that the murders were some sort of satanic ritual, and that there was no telling who might be next.

The coroner's report revealed that the gun used to kill the victims was a .22 caliber firearm. Schultz was shot six times, Cooper twice. Both had been shot in the head. The report also indicated that Schultz had been castrated, postmortem, during the ten days he'd been missing. A sock located in one of the graves contained human tissue that was originally believed to be Schultz's scrotum but was later identified as a piece of Cooper's vaginal area. The report noted that both victims' gunshot wounds were full of pests and maggots, while their cutting wounds appeared to be fresher. This suggested that the bodies were buried first, then dug up afterward and dismembered. As for the cuts, the coroner described them as being made with deliberate surgeon-like precision, similar to how someone might field dress a deer or other large game.

Other witnesses stepped forward to help fill in the sequence of events for the evening of October 4. In addition to the mother seeing Cooper and Schultz leave their home at 4:00 p.m., a neighbor confirmed this version of events as well. A second neighbor saw Schultz and Cooper walking down the street, stopping for a moment to hug and kiss. A third witness saw them walking toward the nearby railroad tracks at 4:15 and watched as they passed an old depot. At 4:30, a railroad employee noticed them on the train trestle. Multiple witnesses attested to their walking together along the tracks from 4:40 to 6:30. Another witness reported them walking east between 6:30 and 7:00, but then stopping to talk with the drivers of a red truck and a Golden Eagle Jeep. Yet another witness watched as a vehicle carrying three people pulled up, a man got out, and Cooper and Schultz hopped into the car with the remaining passengers.

An additional witness was brought in to undergo hypnotic regression—a process whereby a hypnotist guides a witness back through time to recall particular events that would otherwise be inaccessible. During the session, this witness described observing the couple shortly before they drove off and claimed that Cooper's step-father, Dale Johnston, had angrily forced Cooper into the car while threatening to punch Schultz.

———————◆———————

"Here's a picture of the sock with the body parts in it," I said, running through a few final slides. "And here's the cornfield with blood on the ground. This last one shows the male victim. That was the boy. You can see the long incision across his mid-abdomen, exposing what's left of his internal organs after the bugs got to them. Now remember, the goal here is to come up with a motive by walking through the process. Who's got questions?"

"What was known about the relationship between the girl and the stepfather?"

"It wasn't the easiest. People said he was a drinker who punched his kids around sometimes. He was also strongly opposed to his stepdaughter's engagement to Schultz, that much is clear."

"And was he a hunter?" the same agent asked. "Because the coroner's description of 'surgeon-like precision' could be a key differentiator."

"I wouldn't get too hung up on that," I told him. "Local county coroners use that expression all the time. It's a red herring for these types of rural cases. You saw the pictures. There's nothing surgeon-like about them. They're chaotic and choppy and look like they were made with an unsharpened blade of some type."

"Well, did he have a .22?"

"Yes," I confirmed. "He'd had one up until recently. It was no longer around at the time of the investigation."

"I can see it being the stepfather," a second agent said. "But what throws me off is how the victims were buried, then excavated so they could be carved up in all sorts of sick ways. Why would the stepfather do that?"

The first agent cut in before I could respond. "Maybe he does it to get rid of the ballistic evidence. Maybe he was confronting the stepdaughter and her fiancé, they got in a fight, and he killed them in a fit of rage. Maybe he's drunk at the time and starts to feel guilty a little later on. Then he starts thinking about the evidence, starts to get worried, and so goes back to clean up the bodies and throw the torsos in the river. It's not that much of a stretch to see things playing out this way."

Several agents nodded. A third one raised his hand.

"What about the man they found in the cornfield, Linscott? Was there any follow-up on him?"

I was hoping someone would bring up Linscott. His potential role in the case had stuck out to me too. But I was careful not to lead the conversation. "Yes. More than a month into the case, two tipsters called investigators and said that, on the day the couple disappeared, Linscott had suffered a deep cut on his right arm. Investigators then followed up by obtaining Linscott's hospital records, but they stopped pursuing him as a viable lead after Linscott explained he'd been cut when his arm went through a window."

"I'm coming around to the stepfather idea," the second agent backtracked. "I think there's a certain amount of staging going on here. I think if the crime were sexual, the perpetrator would have done that right away and not gone back to hack up the bodies later. I think he just did that to throw the investigation off his track. He tried to make the attack look like some sort of ax murder. But really, there's only one possible motive here: anger towards these two kids. The primary motive is the stepdad's anger."

I waited a moment to see if anyone else would speak. But no one did. The room seemed to have reached a consensus.

"All right," I said, trying not to sound disappointed. "I'll bring you up to speed on what's happened with this case in the few years since it happened. See you next week."

The trainee agents in the Quantico auditorium that day followed the same line of logic as the original investigators on the case. They saw the stepfather as the only logical suspect, motivated by anger, allegedly because he didn't want the couple to marry. But this failed to take into consideration a possible sexual motive for the case. It didn't account for the element of post-offense ritual, which, I was beginning to see, was the clearest expression of an offender's patterns of thought.

In this case, the killer's removal of male and female genitalia demonstrated not only sexual involvement with the female—actual or fantasized—but also a resentment of the sexual relationship that existed between the victims. The stepfather had a history of violence, but none of it sexual in nature. At forty-nine years old, it would be unlikely for him to change up his MO at that point.

In addition to this, I kept coming back to the significance of the gravesite. It would be a place that had meaning to the killer. It would be part of the ritual. Much like Kemper would bury his victim's head in his yard so he could talk to it at night, this killer would want to sustain his relationship with his victims for an extended period of time. In this killer's case, I saw two possible reasons for the gravesite's significance. On the one hand, the location might be easily accessible to the killer and so aided in their desire to revisit and relive the fantasy for repeated pleasure. On the other, its location might enable the killer to keep tabs on the investigation and see what was happening at the scene. Either way, both of these scenarios pointed away from the stepfather, given his lack of familiarity with the field itself.

The level of control required to subdue multiple young, active victims was also important. Especially when you took into consideration all the physical components involved: transporting the bodies to the field, digging their graves, cutting up their limbs and sexual organs, carrying their torsos to the river. This was time-consuming and labor-intensive work that suggested the possibility of two mid-twenties to early thirties unsubs being involved, not a solo forty-nine-year-old man.

And finally, the fact that all signs pointed toward this being a spontaneous and unplanned act meant something as well. The step-father had lived with Cooper for years without attacking her. And the nature of their relationship meant he'd have further opportunities to plan and execute an attack, if that was what he wanted to do. He'd also been interrogated for more than eight hours in the immediate aftermath of the bodies being found, and he consistently denied any involvement whatsoever. Spontaneous killers tend to be extremely anxious and uncertain, which is something that can be exploited during the interrogation process. I'd always felt that Johnston, although a good surface-level fit for the crime, lacked the depth of connection that a suspect needs to meaningfully be paired with a BSU profile. Investigators saw Johnston as the easy solution, but I still felt that there was a puzzle piece missing—something that would end up proving who the real perpetrator was, once and for all.

———◆———

I'd been following this case ever since Johnston was charged with murder on January 31, 1984, and sentenced to death several months later. This conviction made no sense to me. The prosecution's case was built around testimony from the hypnotized witness and backed up by an anthropologist's testimony that a muddy impression in the field where the victims' limbs were found was a match for the heel of Johnston's cowboy boot.

But it wasn't until August of 1986, several months after lecturing on the case, that Ressler gave me an update that helped to validate my nagging sense of uncertainty.

"Hey, Ann. Did you see this?" He was holding up a copy of the *Chicago Tribune*. "They're overturning the conviction in the Johnston case. Apparently, they've decided that the testimony from the hypnotized witness was unreliable and shouldn't have been allowed."

"Let me see." I quickly scanned the article for myself. "How about that? And the prosecution withheld evidence about another suspect, too—a butcher that was infatuated with the girl."

"There you go. Your instinct was right."

I paused for a long moment, mulling over what I'd just read. "But we profiled this one. If the investigators relied on our work, then this outcome is on us."

"I know," Ressler said. "It happens."

"But doesn't that sit uneasy with you? I mean, the wrong guy ended up going to jail."

"Our job was to make the profile. We did that, and we did it the best way we know how. At that point, it's out of our hands. If the police chose the easy answer and not someone who fit the profile, that's on them. All we can do is learn from it, apply it to the next one, and move on."

Ressler was right. I knew that. But knowing didn't bring comfort.

"So that's it? That's how we leave it?"

"That's how we leave it," Ressler said.

I nodded. But this case would stick with me for years to come. It pointed to one of the remaining challenges with the profiling process.

Our job at the BSU was to use every bit of case information at our fingertips to reconstruct unsubs into their most essential and defining characteristics. Once we did this, it was up to investigators to use the fully realized profile in its entirety. In other words, our work wasn't just a hodgepodge of character traits for investigators to pick and choose from to make any suspect fit a crime. It was a meticulous reflection—a carefully developed understanding through which each piece synthesized into a comprehensive whole. Of course, the individual details were important, but only as part of the larger picture. After all, serial killers operated within the same nuanced framework of psychology as everyone else. They were complex. And it made no sense to try to understand them by reducing them to one or two simple characteristics. Profiling only worked because it brought the unsub to light through a collection of patterns, behaviors, and finely crafted narrative. It was this totality that mattered most.

The Johnston case failed because investigators got lost in the details. Once I understood this, it made me realize that profiling needed to be more than just a "here you go, good luck" type of process. We needed to stay involved in the cases longer. And it made sense. Because, by the very act of going through the profiling process, we already understood the psychology of the unsub. Now we just needed to turn this understanding into investigative strategies to help solve cases more quickly. We needed to use the unsub's own patterns and behaviors against them.

CHAPTER 13

Reading Between the Lines

The BSU was always up for a challenge. But in the mid-eighties, as we saw the need to stick with cases longer and offer more prescriptive advice to investigators in the field, we were forced to come face-to-face with a complication we'd long tried to avoid.

From the start, the BSU had a somewhat uneasy relationship with the media. Some days we were praised for our innovative, groundbreaking work, and other days we were described as charlatans, pseudo-investigators, or hacks. None of this really mattered to the agents or me, but it mattered immensely to the FBI as an institution. In fact, J. Edgar Hoover, from the very beginning of his tenure as the Bureau's director, saw public relations as a core element of his job. He put immense effort into managing how the Bureau was portrayed in the news and in popular culture—promoting a heroic narrative of selfless G-men who skillfully brought justice to the nation's most dangerous criminals. In fact, the term *G-man* itself, which stands for "government man," was a riff on the idea of superheroes like Batman and Superman. Hoover's ingenuity transformed the men of the Bureau into American icons.

Regardless of these motivations,* there was something to be said for this endeavor. Having a positive public image helped with the quality of recruiting, secured the Bureau's ever-increasing budget, and made it easy to engage public cooperation as a tool for fighting crime. This lasted even well after Hoover was gone—perpetuated by idealistic portrayals in books, movies, radio, and TV, including *The Silence of the Lambs*, *The X-Files*, and *America's Most Wanted*.

Within the BSU, though, we realized that we could use the media as a tool for connecting not only with the public but also with many of the offenders themselves. Serial killers often took pride in what they did. It mattered to them how the newspapers and TV covered their crimes. And in cases like the Lonely Hearts Killer and the Mad Bomber, the act of engaging with media was intrinsic to the crime itself. Most serial killers were cautious, reluctant to come out of the shadows and expose themselves in even the smallest possible way. At the same time, if they wanted to continue their crime sprees uninterrupted, they needed to know how far along the police were in their investigations. And one way of gauging that distance from afar was to tune in to the media's reporting.

If we could figure out how to manipulate the media to our advantage, it could be used as an invaluable weapon in our arsenal as we tracked down these killers.

At the BSU, one of the most important meetings we had each day was referred to as the "Morning Report." This was when we regularly gathered as a unit to go over any profiling work being done and to review new cases coming in from external agencies or various task

---

* Hoover's main goal in controlling the FBI's public image was to imbue the Bureau with enough goodwill and trust so that reputation alone kept it from having to deal with any unwanted oversight behind the scenes.

force groups. I made sure to attend these as often as I could. Even in the mid-to-late eighties, as my focus shifted more and more toward courtroom testimony and other specialized work, I would either pop in or get a recap from Douglas or Ressler. After all, profiling was still incredibly important to me. And when unusual or uniquely challenging cases came in, I wanted to analyze what set them apart so I could help find the right fix. That was the situation in which I found myself in the winter of 1987.

That morning, Unit Chief Depue began the meeting with his standard introduction—the same one he gave every day—of how important the BSU was and how far we'd come in such a short time. He talked about how it was our job to help investigators do their job better. And he stressed the importance of staying ever vigilant. But it's what he said next that caught my attention. Depue began briefing us on a new trend the Bureau was seeing. There'd been a recent uptick in the number of criminals starting to seek out communication with media and law enforcement about their ongoing crimes. They did it for attention, for the thrill, for the sake of further savoring violence. And their motivation was often clearly visible in the messages themselves, which could be taunting, threatening, confessional, or angry rants about the coverage they were receiving in the news. Whatever the reason, police departments had never seen anything like it before. They were unsure of how to respond.

"It's our assignment now," Depue announced. "The Director wants a full report on the meaning of this behavior: an analysis, and a framework for how best to respond. Some of these are high profile, including BTK, who's turned up again with two more victims, so the turnaround's got to be quick. Who's got an initial thought?"

The room was silent for a moment. Someone slowly tapped the eraser side of their pencil against a desk, until Ressler finally spoke up.

"Do any of you remember the 1945 murder of Frances Brown?" Ressler asked.

A few agents nodded.

"I was only ten at the time. But I remember it got a lot of coverage in the papers. There was one description of the killer using the victim's bright red lipstick to write a message on her mirror. It said: 'For heavens sake catch me before I kill more. I cannot control myself,'" Ressler recalled. "Anyway, that case always stuck with me. It's what got me interested in serial killers. Me and three of my buddies from the neighborhood formed our own detective agency after that. And we spent the next couple weeks at school passing notes back and forth about how we'd catch the criminals we were reading about."

Douglas grinned at Ressler and said, "That's great, Bob. We'll tell the police to put the neighborhood kids on the case. They'll have this thing buttoned up in no time. Problem solved."

Even Ressler laughed at that one. "You didn't let me finish," he protested. "My point is this: if these guys are passing notes to the media, we should use the media to pass notes back to them."

———— ◆ ————

In typical BSU fashion, we got down to work right away. Our first step was to look through old case files for previous examples of offenders who'd shown this same kind of engagement. Most of what we found consisted of direct threats coming into police departments. But Hazelwood was able to find clues in the case of Harvey Glatman, the case that had originally inspired his interest in serial violence in the first place. He pointed out that Glatman—also known as the Lonely Hearts Killer—was an example in which media interaction wasn't about sending threats. It was about using newspapers to reach out to potential victims directly, which Glatman did by advertising for models that he then sexually assaulted and killed.

"The message isn't what matters," Hazelwood said. "It's merely context. Our focus should be on what the message can tell us about the message sender. That needs to be the focus of our approach."

Douglas took Hazelwood's idea and ran with it. The BSU had done previous research on psycholinguistics—the study of the psychological aspects of language—and Douglas saw the value in applying this to these new types of media cases. Analyzing an offender's messaging is really no different from any other aspect of profiling. By breaking down the key elements of how, when, and why an offender communicated with others, we could gain deep insights into the offender's thinking. Douglas explained this using the famous Lindberg Baby case, citing a note that was discovered on the windowsill of the abducted baby's nursery. It read:

Dear Sir

Have 50000$ ready 25000$ in 20$ bills 15000$ in 10$ bills and 10000$ in 5$ bills. After 2–4 days we will inform you were to deliver the money. We warn you for making anyding public or for notify the police. The child is in gut care. Instruction for the letters are singnature.

Douglas broke down the importance of language analysis in the case. He showed how spelling and syntax, as well as word choice and stilted phrasing, suggested that the author had been born in Germany and probably retained a heavy German accent. In this note, the author used the German word *gut* for the English word *good*. And in subsequent notes, the author wrote phonetically as a native German speaker would, with words like "mony" and "shuld." The clues were all there for investigators who knew how to see them.

"They caught the guy by tracking serial numbers off the ransom money," Douglas said. "But they could've easily used language analysis instead. We just need to develop a set of techniques for the analysis."

I remember the breakthrough moment I had helping Douglas work out the kinks of this new technique—psycholinguistic analysis, as it came to be known. We were sitting in his office when a call came in. It was a case out of Chicago. Police had received an untraceable letter that threatened to blow up a bank with a bomb.

Douglas brought several of the agents together and gave us a rundown of the call. "It's a city bank that's been laying people off, and they've been doing it by letter, not in person. What's interesting is that the letter police got doesn't mention any employees by name. It just threatens the bank. So, what's the victimology in this case?"

"It has to be the bank," I said.

"Why's that?" Douglas asked.

"Because that's the focus of the attack," I explained.

The agents looked confused, so I added, "Don't get hung up on the fact that a bank isn't a person. That's not the point. What matters is how the victim and the offender are connected. The unsub sees the bank as the overall problem."

"Okay. Then why even bother sending police a letter?" Douglas wondered.

Hazelwood jumped in. "This feels like an empty threat to me. We're looking at a guy who lost his job and has no one to complain to. He's trying to make himself feel big."

"Just be careful not to give the investigators a reason to take this lightly," I added. "It might be an empty threat now, but the longer he stews on it, the more real it becomes in his head. Something could trigger him pretty quick."

Douglas nodded and dismissed everyone from his office. He then followed up with the Chicago police and suggested they look for a longtime employee who'd recently been fired, most likely a white male with a history of complaining to his fellow employees about how unhappy he was with the bank. They weren't looking for a tough guy—just someone who would crack after a few hard questions. That's all it would take.

Later that week, Douglas got a call from Chicago PD saying they'd identified the author of the letter. He was a white male, middle aged, and one of the employees that was recently let go. He had a history of complaining about the bank and how poorly it was managed.

Like that, psycholinguistic analysis became a viable tool in profiling.

And it made sense. Because although psycholinguistics might have seemed overly technical at a first glance, it was completely rooted in human behavior. This was the kind of innovative research that fascinated me most about the BSU. While the rest of the investigative world was getting swept up in a technological arms race—especially our counterparts at the CIA, who were increasingly relying on computers, databases, and a whole new paradigm of advanced surveillance systems in the Cold War with the Soviet Union—we stayed focused on the human aspect. It was people who committed crimes and threatened security. We never lost sight of that fact.

Of course, we weren't complete Luddites. There were times when we saw the value of using new technologies to help the BSU improve as a unit. Once, for example, when seven of us were on our way to a conference in Baltimore to present a profiling case study, the two cars we were driving in got separated. We were supposed to meet at the Holiday Inn, but there were multiple locations in the city and we hadn't coordinated where specifically to meet. It was getting later and later in the evening when finally both cars called in to the Academy using pay phones. We managed to coordinate meeting under a bridge in Baltimore and figured it out from there. Afterward, Nick Groth—a psychologist who worked in correctional settings and lectured on rapists at the FBI Academy—turned to me and said, "These are FBI agents. How do they solve crimes if they can't even find each other?"

The BSU was quick to adopt pagers after that.

For the next few months—the better part of fall and early winter of 1986—I worked my way through the BSU's six filing cabinets of records to put together a list of past cases involving notes or other types of communication that could have benefited from investigative psycholinguistics. There weren't many, but that didn't surprise me— most serial killers had enough common sense to avoid any type of interactions that could lead to their arrest. Of course, we had notes and letters from classic cases as part of our records, including Jack the Ripper ("I shant quit ripping till I do get buckled. Grand work the last job was. I gave the lady no time to squeal"), David Berkowitz ("Hello from the gutters of N.Y.C. which are filled with dog manure, vomit, stale wine, urine, and blood"), and a high-profile, still-at-large killer out of Wichita, Kansas ("When this monster enter my brain, I will never know. But, it here to stay"). Even so, despite those bigger names, I kept coming back to a small-town extortion case out of Ohio. It caught my attention for how intricate the unsub's messages were. Communication started the day after a teenage girl went missing. Her parents received a call stating, "We have your daughter. We want $80,000 or you'll never see her again." Police then raced to where the call was traced to—a small residence on the outskirts of town— but all they found were a few items of the missing girl's clothes and a map.

The map directed investigators to a second location—a grassy area along the Sandusky River—where they found a second map covered in indecipherable drawings and the remainder of the missing girl's clothes. A closer inspection of this second location revealed that something, possibly a body, had been dragged from a vehicle and thrown into the river. But in the days that followed, the parents received additional calls describing how the ransom exchange needed to work if the family ever wanted to see their daughter again.

I was curious about the maps, so I popped into Douglas's office to see if he remembered anything about the case.

"Yeah, I know the one," he said. "Demanding $80,000 seemed extremely low to me. At first I figured the unsub wasn't particularly bright, but the extortion notes he wrote, those were fairly well designed."

"What do you mean?" I asked.

"Well, for starters, he used a stencil for the words. And he'd write things like, 'go to a phone booth at this location and look underneath for a message that will be taped to the bottom of the phone.' He was leading people on goose chases, trying to distract the investigation from the fact he'd committed murder. But he slipped up because he kept doing the same thing. We ended up placing surveillance in all the local phone booths and got pictures of him taping a note underneath a phone."

"I got it," I said. "So, he was making it easy for the police, leaving a trail like the crumbs in Hansel and Gretel. Let me guess: he'd never intended to murder her. It was a rape gone wrong. Something triggered him. Then he mixed everything up in his head and staged extortion as a way of covering up the murder. He was trying to separate himself from the case, but as an antisocial type, he got caught up in the risk-taking part of it and couldn't just walk away. Does that about sum up his game?"

"Bingo." Douglas nodded. "But what's with the sudden interest?"

"I've been going through some old cases like this one to see if psycholinguistics would've helped. I figured it'd be a good resource for the newer profilers on the team. I thought this one isn't much of an example though."

"Not really. There was no need for him to keep it going to the point of getting caught in a phone booth. He was being too elaborate. It's the same thing that happened to Berkowitz or the Zodiac killer, these guys are elated. They're on a high. Bundy, Williams—all of them. They get lost in the risk-taking aspect of the crime. It fits with the risk-taking personality."

"Wait a minute," I interjected. "Then that's the takeaway. For the ones that want to interact with us—the ones taunting the police or newspapers or whoever—they're basically screaming for attention. If they're after a thrill, then we'll give them one. We'll play to their ego by picking up their breadcrumbs and telling them how clever they are. The more we engage with them, the more they'll try to impress us. It's basically approval-seeking behavior 101. Their desperate need for attention is the bait we'll use for our traps."

CHAPTER 14

Bind Them, Torture Them, Kill Them

In 1987, when the FBI tasked the BSU with figuring out why serial killers were seeking media attention, it was clearly a response to one unsub in particular. The self-named BTK Killer (Bind them, Torture them, Kill them) was active again. He'd taken seven victims between January 1974 and December 1977, before going silent for nearly a decade. Then, starting in the spring of 1985, he'd killed two new victims. He also resumed his familiar habit of sending communications to both the media and local police in Wichita, Kansas. It was odd. The fact that he'd suddenly gone dormant without getting caught was strange enough for a serial killer—although there were some cases where unsubs went to jail for an unrelated crime and later confessed to their murders. But for a killer like BTK, someone who clearly sought out recognition and attention as a fundamental component of his criminal acts, this prolonged period of inactivity was unlike anything we'd ever seen before.

"These people don't just stop for years at a time," Ressler said.

To make matters more complicated, the BSU had been involved

in the case on multiple occasions over the years, but with no success. The killer was in total control. At times, he taunted the investigation with elaborate word searches or collages that hinted at his obsession with fantasy. At other times, he practically begged to be caught. He sent one message to the *Wichita Eagle* that gave a graphic retelling of how he broke into a house and killed four family members during the middle of the day. Later, he followed up with an apologetic rambling full of grammatical mistakes and misspelled words: "I'm sorry this happen to the society . . . I can't stop it so, the monster goes on, and hurt me as wall as society. Maybe you can stop him. I can't. Good luck hunting."

In a way, BTK haunted the BSU. He was vague and fleeting and unknowable, a pervasive threat that hung heavily over our obligations to the Midwest. We never knew when he'd appear again, only that he would. And despite the BSU's best efforts, he'd already slipped away twice before: once in 1979, and again when we tried to lure him out in 1984. But now, with this new assignment from the FBI director William Webster himself, the team had one more chance to learn from past mistakes. We could finally make things right—and put this dangerous criminal behind bars.

Our original involvement began when a homicide detective with the Wichita Police Department reached out to ask us a few questions. His department had never experienced anything as severe as BTK's killings before, and they didn't have any suspects. All they had were the crime scene photos and two letters that threatened future attacks. The detective said he'd heard about our serial killer research and the success we'd had with cases like this. He was wondering if we could help. The team was interested, and one week later, a lieutenant from the Wichita Police Department flew out to Quantico to get us up to speed.

From the news coverage alone, I already knew we were dealing with a killer who craved recognition. He was someone who felt important but overlooked, ignored and self-assertive—disaffected to the point of seeing crime as an opportunity to command the attention he felt he deserved. But this was just the surface. BTK was more complex than the reductive news coverage could ever show. And as we read his letters and examined stacks of crime scene photos showing victims posed like abandoned dolls, I got my first glimpse of how clever and obsessed this killer was. He used murder as an attempt to be acknowledged, as a way of finding acceptance, as a tool for stepping outside societal confinements to express his truest ideas of self. And this was only the start. It was clear that BTK would kill again—unless we could get inside his head and figure out how to get one step ahead of him.

But there was a challenge. Since BTK was an active offender, Douglas, Ressler, and I had to be careful to keep his influence separate from the serial killer study we were working on at the time. We'd set parameters that limited us to known offenders who were already convicted and had gone through appeals, and we knew the importance of maintaining the integrity of our results. Still, the case fascinated me. Ressler, Hazelwood, and Douglas took a deep interest in it, too, and they were eager to talk about how strange it was compared to the more typical requests coming into the Bureau. They were especially intrigued that an unsub would communicate with both the media and the police. Unlike most serial killers, who shied away from activities that might expose who they were, BTK displayed an intense, almost reckless desire for public attention. Even his writing seemed authentic and unmasked. It all spoke to a new type of killer that needed to be thought about differently, in terms of both psychology and the criminal investigative approach.

Despite all that was novel about the case, BTK did incorporate elements of other serial killers into the construction of his persona. This made sense to me, given BTK's obsession with following the media's coverage of his own crimes. It confirmed his alienated nature, sense of arrogance, and self-inadequacies. He was the type that wanted to compare himself to other killers, to measure himself through the eyes of others, and to control the public narrative in any way he could. This made him most similar to the Son of Sam, David Berkowitz, a serial killer who terrorized New York during the summer of 1976 by shooting unsuspecting victims and leaving notes at the scene of his crimes. Both killers referred to their murderous side as "the monster," both suggested their own nicknames to the media, and both challenged police by leaving clues about who they'd murder next. This helped inform the BSU's original analysis of the case in 1979. And it became an integral piece within the strategy we suggested to the Wichita Police.

Our main advice? "Keep him talking and don't show any hostility." Our report explained that the killer felt entitled to some sort of public acknowledgment of the relevance of his crimes. He got off on feeding his exaggerated sense of self—therefore, he *craved* connection. And that's where the opportunity was. Our suggestion was to use a proactive media strategy in which law enforcement would work together with local papers to bait the killer into exposing himself. They could do this by creating an open channel of communication for ongoing dialogue between the killer and the police. He'd reveal himself through his pride.

That was the extent of the BSU's original role in the case. Still, we continued to monitor it, especially during the initial period of back and forth between BTK and local police. But there were no further requests for our help, and we were too involved in other cases for our serial killer study to offer any unsolicited advice. Like the rest of the public, we could only watch to see events unfold, letter by letter, victim by victim, over the course of the next few years.

Five years after their original call, the Wichita Police followed up with a second request for the BSU's help. They were in the early stages of forming a BTK task force—later known as the "Ghostbusters"—and they wanted to bring in an outside perspective for the behavioral elements of the case. So far, they'd amassed stacks of new case files, including police reports, witness testimonies, sketch artist depictions, extensive crime scene photos, autopsy reports, and nearly a dozen new letters and collages from the killer himself. But they weren't quite sure what to make of all the materials on their own. They needed help to develop a cohesive profile. And in October of 1984, two task force detectives arrived at Quantico for a daylong briefing, ready to give a detailed presentation on everything that had happened in the case since we last spoke.

Douglas, who was the lead on the case, brought the task force detectives to the subterranean conference room and introduced them to the team. He waited for everyone to get settled before speaking. "Before you get started, I have one question. Why go after BTK now? As far as anyone can tell, he hasn't been active for several years. And your briefing says he stopped communicating with Wichita Police some time ago too. So, why now?"

"That's fair," the taller of the two detectives acknowledged. "Truth is, WPD's longtime chief is retiring. This case has always haunted him. He's trying to shake off the ghost before he goes."

"So this is about smoking BTK out," Douglas said.

"Yes, sir."

"All right. I just want to make sure we're clear on what you're proposing. You're provoking a serial killer. And if this goes sideways, that's on you and the chief."

Later that week, after combing through the task force's new

data and comparing it to other cases from our study, we set to work refining BTK's profile. But it was slow going. Truthfully, there was no real precedent for this type of offender, no matching case to draw from. Despite patterning himself off of known killers and committing psychologically familiar acts that we could categorize and understand, the whole scope of his crimes was different. It was more complex and chaotic. The viciousness he showed to his victims' bodies, the ritualistic binding elements involved, their sexual nature, and the level of planning that went into each attack—these all spoke of violence to a higher degree. The number of psychiatric diagnoses was off the charts, too. BTK showed signs of seven paraphilic disorders[*] and numerous personality disorders. The average serial killer had two or three disorders at most—narcissism and psychopathy being two particularly common ones. In the case of BTK, we were dealing with a type of intricately layered criminal psychology like nothing we'd ever dealt with.

"The list goes on and on," Hazelwood said. "The guy's got an exaggerated sense of self, a lack of empathy for others, no feelings of guilt, remorse, or fear. You name it, he's got it."

The other challenge was how to make sense of the unusually long periods of inactivity between BTK's crimes, which was very strange behavior for a serial killer. Offenders tended to increase the frequency of their attacks as they fell further and further into fantasy and chased an ideal expression of the rage that played out in their heads. We knew BTK was taking personal items from his victims, and I wondered if this played a role in sustaining such long periods of inactivity. On one level, I knew that killers habitually used the souvenirs they took from their victim as a prop to help replay their

---

[*] Paraphilic disorders are recurrent, intensely persistent sexual fantasies or behaviors that involve atypical objects, situations, and/or targets, such as children, corpses, animals, or nonconsenting adults. Their key characteristic is their focus on distress, suffering, or humiliation and their potential to cause harm.

murders over and over in their head. But that was more of a stopgap, a temporary fix of diminishing rewards.

There was also another possibility for the unusually long stretches of inactivity to consider. From forensic photos, we knew that the killer took the time—and the inherent risk—of carefully posing his victims in sexually explicit positions. This suggested he was taking pictures of their bodies. It also fit into the idea of the killer using souvenirs as a way of prolonging the fantasy and reliving his acts of violence. Pictures would make it that much easier to relive the act. This made sense. And it worked with BTK's apparent knowledge and habit of imitating other serial killers. It was a nod to Harvey Glatman and his modus operandi of using photography in his crimes—Glatman bound his victims, raped them, and took photos of their terrified faces to savor the experience long afterward.

By the end of the session, the team had put together a three-page profile of BTK. We also offered advice about how to engage the killer without antagonizing him to further bloodshed. We suggested appealing to the killer's ego by treating him as an equal and building up a sense of mutual trust and respect. That strategy had worked to solve a previous case out of California in the early eighties, where Douglas used what was referred to as a "super-cop" to speak directly to the killer at press conferences. He stressed the importance of not making statements about the killer's mental condition, advising that the super-cop make a point of aligning himself with the killer rather than the media or psychiatric experts. If BTK wanted to feel important, the investigators should make him feel important. He'd eventually get so caught up in the attention that he'd give himself away.

The profile itself categorized BTK as a sexual sadist with a vivid fantasy life. We took all the evidence available (which, at the time, wasn't much) and broke it down into sections. Based on the deliberate, doll-like posing of bodies at the crime scene, we deduced that

BTK's murders were the result of a murderous fantasy that he was acting out in the real world. Committing murder was the first time in the killer's life that he felt himself to be in a position of importance and dominance. All of this pointed to a long-standing fascination with violence, one that had likely started as early childhood fantasies. Based on his actions and the area in which he was active, we believed the subject was raised in an overtly strict and religious fashion, likely by an overbearing mother who used harsh discipline to enforce household rules. His father—as was the case with many unsubs— probably left home when the unsub was still young.

The way the unsub brutalized and defiled his victims' bodies was particularly significant to the profile. "It shows that he's studied these types of crimes, and that he's not bothered by the violence," Hazel-wood said. "He's had violent thoughts as far back as he can remember. He probably tortured animals as a kid, became an outdoorsman later on, and took up an interest in psychology and criminology to learn more about himself and others like him. And the way he poses his victims—that's something he's seen before. I bet he's known to who-ever runs the nearest adult book shop. He gravitates to fantasy."

Victimology was important too. The unsub's early killings had been all over the place—male, female, younger, older—while his more recent killings focused on single women who were middle aged. This showed that the unsub was getting older himself, and that his targets were victims he could easily control since his killings were opportunities to exercise absolute dominance. He would hunt his victims by selecting familiar neighborhoods where he wouldn't easily be detected. He'd choose familiar areas, would surveil his targets to learn their schedules and routines, and would devise easy escape routes in case anything went wrong.

From the formality of his letters, combined with the stilted manner in which he wrote—"Where this monster enter my brain I will never know. But, it here to stay. How does one cure himself? If you ask for help, that you have killed four people, they will laugh or hit the panic button and call the cops"—we believed that he had some military experience and/or was a police buff. He'd have past breaking and entering charges, where the items he took were insignificant, more for fetish or the thrill of committing the crime than anything else.

The profile also stressed that it wasn't uncommon for subjects such as BTK to identify with investigators, even to the point of frequenting police hangouts to listen in on officers discussing the case (as Ed Kemper had often done). In this case, especially because of the unsub's prideful and bold nature, we knew he would revisit the crime scene shortly after its discovery and try to blend in as part of the initial wave of voyeuristic neighbors and passersby. This would allow him to both fulfill his ego and gain a feeling of superiority. It would also give investigators an advantage because the subject couldn't get out of his own way. He would slip up. But before he did, he was likely to kill again.

After the profiling session, I pulled Douglas aside to bounce an idea off him. I wanted his opinion on BTK's tendency to mimic or include elements of other serial killers. It seemed significant that BTK was borrowing habits from some of the most notorious serial killers and tailoring them to fit his own routines. It certainly confirmed the type of ego we were dealing with, and it spoke to his desire to obtain the same level of notoriety. But if BTK was a student of this type of violence, then he must know how other killers were caught. It was important to keep that in mind as we built out the strategy for the case. We had to be especially mindful of the Son of Sam case, David Berkowitz, which BTK seemed explicitly familiar with.

"What do you make of the symbol he uses in his communications?"

I asked Douglas. "It's a lot like what Son of Sam did. But this one's not satanic, it's erotic."

"This guy's so far in his own head that he sees it as part of his artistry," Douglas mused. "He thinks it adds to his importance. Why? Do you think there's something more to it?"

"I'm not sure. I think he partly does it for effect. But turning his initials into a sexualized drawing of a female torso, it's so explicit. It's kind of desperate in a way. It's like he has a compulsive need to constantly develop and maintain his own myth."

"When Ressler and I interviewed Berkowitz, we asked him about BTK," Douglas said. "That's how we got him to talk. We took the approach of: 'There's this new killer out of Kansas who idolizes you and is copying some of what you did.'"

"Did you tell him about the symbol?"

"We didn't get a chance to. As soon as we mentioned BTK, Son of Sam spent the next five hours going on and on about every detail of his crimes. We couldn't shut him up. He was angry that someone else was riding his coattails and stealing his fame. And he was angry about all the things the media got wrong about his case."

"I remember that." I nodded. "He was fine with being called a monster but was 'deeply hurt' about being called a woman-hater."

"Yeah. God forbid anyone hurt a serial killer's feelings." Douglas rolled his eyes. "What about the symbol, though? What were you thinking?"

"It just represents how badly he wants the credit for his killings—just like Berkowitz," I said. "But it has to be done the right way. These guys want the media to see and portray them in the same way they see themselves. For BTK, that symbol's part of the image he's trying to create. He wants to be known for sex and control."

It would take several more years to prove it, but we were right that pride would be BTK's Achilles' heel. The wheels were set in motion in the leadup to January 15, 2004, the thirtieth anniversary of BTK's gruesome Otero family murder, with the public showing renewed interest in the case. And on January 17, when the *Wichita Eagle* ran an article speculating that BTK was either dead or in prison for an unrelated crime, the killer himself took notice. It had been over a decade since he last committed a murder and years since he last communicated with the police. But BTK quickly responded to the *Wichita Eagle*, taking credit for his crimes. He mockingly wrote the name "Bill Thomas Killman"—BTK (Bind them, Torture them, Kill them)—as the return address. And within the envelope, he included photographs of a lifeless woman posed in sexual positions, as well as a photocopy of the woman's driver's license. The victim's name was Vicki Wegerle, a woman who had been murdered in 1986, but not officially linked to BTK. That letter was only the beginning.

As investigators dove back into their files to prepare for another go at the case, they realized everything BTK was doing and revealing about himself all fit with the BSU's original profile from the mid-eighties. It even anticipated his desire to identify with investigators, which BTK did in one letter where he called himself a fellow law enforcement officer. That's when the task force reached back out to the FBI for help. They wanted to use the BSU's original "super-cop" strategy to lure BTK out. But they were nervous about antagonizing the killer any further.

The BSU's strategy was simple. If BTK wanted to identify as a law enforcement officer, we'd help make that happen. The plan was to set up press conferences so that one specific officer would speak directly to BTK every time. In a sense, this officer would become a reflection for BTK, a devoted counterpart whose dedication to the case—in BTK's mind—was a form of camaraderie and understanding. The super-cop strategy would play to BTK's constant need for validation, comforting his ego, his sense of self-importance, and his need to feel accepted by authority figures on a personal level. In essence, the super-cop was a mirror. And in the convoluted fantasy world of BTK's mind, he'd eventually start to see himself in the super-cop. He'd look to him as a friend.

Over the course of the next eleven months, Wichita homicide detective Ken Landwehr—a clean-cut, no-nonsense detective who worked long hours fueled by coffee and cigarettes—took on the role of super-cop for the case. He became the face of the investigation, holding regular press conferences to speak directly to BTK, stroking the killer's ego, knowing that he'd be watching.

BTK played right into the strategy as planned. He quickly became hooked on the newfound attention he was receiving. And for the months that followed, he taunted investigators through a series of ten additional communications, which consisted of letters, puzzles, and disturbing packages of tied-up dolls that were made to mimic the crime scenes of his earlier murders.

In January 2005, BTK left a printed message in a cereal box for police to find. "Can I communicate with Floppy [disk] and not be traced to a computer. Be honest," it said. It went on to explain that, if the answer was yes, Landwehr should place a classified ad in the *Wichita Eagle* with the response, "Rex, it will be OK."

Investigators took out the ad as requested. Then they waited. After what felt like an interminable two weeks, they received a package containing a floppy disk that, unknown to BTK, stored traceable metadata showing that the disk had been used at a nearby Christ Lutheran Church and was last saved by a user named "Dennis." The church website identified Dennis Rader as president of the congregation. Police had their suspect. Now they needed to build their case.

They knew that if they asked Rader for a DNA sample, he'd simply refuse. But they were able to use a tissue sample collected from Rader's daughter, who had recently gone to a health clinic for some lab work. The forensic results came back twenty-four hours later. Kerri Rader was a familial match to BTK. From there, police quickly secured a warrant and arrested Wichita compliance officer Dennis Rader on February 25 during his lunch break, while he was stopped at a traffic light a short distance from his home.

The super-cop strategy worked so absolutely that Rader was genuinely shocked to learn that Landwehr had been involved in his arrest. He seemed almost heartbroken about what he saw as a betrayal of his trust. He even asked Landwehr: "How come you lied to me? How come you lied to me?"

"Because I was trying to catch you," Landwehr answered.

This was the moment Rader broke.

Afterward, he gave a thirty-two-hour confession—a chronologically scattered but exhaustively detailed retelling of how he tortured and murdered ten people, including a nine-year-old boy and an eleven-year-old girl.

He talked about his childhood: "I used to make sketches then. Annette Funicello was my favorite fantasy hit target when she was on *Mouseketeers.* I had imaginary stories of how I was going to kidnap her and do sexual things to her. I also liked mummies since they bound people up."

He talked about his stages of murder: "First, I watch—that's the trolling stage. Then came the stalking phase. You basically troll, stalk, and then lock in. And you just keep working that pattern. . . . Then comes the fantasy. See, you start dreaming of how you're going to do it or where to do it. Somehow it clicks, and then you gather your stuff, set a date, and try."

And he talked about the act of killing itself: "Strangling a person is hard. Your hands go numb after a while unless you have [them] in shape. It might take two or three minutes. You have to put pressure, wrap around their neck. If you let up for even a second, they get a gulp of air and they'll come right back . . . kicking and squirming."

Rader relayed an incredible amount of details over the course of his multiday confession. However, he never once showed signs of remorse.

"It was all about him," Landwehr said. "It always has been and it always will be."

CHAPTER 15

Ego Will Be Your Downfall

In 1978, the year after BTK's first spree of murders, a new serial killer showed up on the scene and caught the media by surprise. His parallels to BTK were striking. And yet, at the same time, both killers stood out as wholly unique from the bulk of their peers. It was a curious anomaly. Like BTK, this new unsub incorporated cryptic symbols and messaging into his methodology—a form of communication that would later evolve into an incessant need to be in direct contact with major media outlets around the United States. And like BTK, this killer was evasive, exercising a meticulous level of control over his crimes that left few clues behind for investigators to follow up on. But he wasn't a copycat—these two killers' MOs couldn't have been more different. Whereas BTK took a perverse satisfaction in direct physical contact and slowly strangling the life out of his victims' bodies, this new killer kept his distance. He was a bomber. His satisfaction came from the mass hysteria and terror he was able to inflict. He wanted to reshape the world to fit an idealized construct of how the world *should* be, an elusive fantasy that played over and over again in his own mind.

Despite rising concerns about his attacks, standard protocol was that the BSU didn't help with a case until we were explicitly asked to do so. So, from May 1978 to June 1980, we had no choice but to watch from the sidelines as news of the bombings played out repeatedly on the front pages of major national papers. We were bystanders just like everyone else.

The first attack took place on May 25, 1978. An abandoned package had been discovered in a parking lot and brought back to a Northwestern University professor named Buckley Crist, whose name was on the return address. Although the box bore his name, Crist insisted that he'd never even seen it before, let alone sent the package in the first place. The professor contacted a campus security officer, Officer Terry Marker, who opened the package and inadvertently detonated the homemade bomb inside. The explosion resulted in minor injuries to the officer's left hand, fortunately causing no other damage than that. The second attack also took place on the Northwestern University campus. And again, it resulted in the same (comparatively) fortunate outcome of minor cuts and burns—this time injuring an unsuspecting graduate student named John Harris.

The next two attacks were remarkably different in their modus operandi. Instead of targeting individuals, the bomber raised the stakes by targeting airline companies—showing a new layer of complexity that spoke to the unsub's growing sense of self-confidence. First, in November of 1979, a bomb detonated on American Airlines flight 444, filling the plane with thick smoke and forcing the pilot to land prematurely. The following year, the president of United Airlines, Percy Wood, received a package at his home address that was rigged to blow up when he opened it. This explosion resulted in severe burns over the victim's body and face, but he managed to escape with his life. Even so, for the physical damage it did, it was the bomber's most successful attack yet.

The case had initially been under the jurisdiction of the US Postal Service and the Bureau of Alcohol, Tobacco, and Firearms. But the airline attacks, which were clear indicators of the rapidly evolving criminal mind just learning to express itself, led to the BSU getting involved. That's when forensic investigators analyzed the explosive devices side by side and found a consistency in the bits of lamp cord, fasteners, and dowel-type switches that had been recovered at the crime scenes. The design was completely unique. Almost every piece had been meticulously crafted from wood, all the way down to the hand-made screws. It made the materials completely untraceable but also singular in their construction. This was the work of a serial bomber.

The BSU was charged with analyzing the behavioral elements of the attacks in order to deliver a preliminary profile. However, besides the scraps of bombs themselves and the people being targeted, there was very little information available for us. Even the code name for the case reflected how little we knew. We were calling it UNABOM, an acronym which stood for University (UN) and Airline Bombing (ABOM). It wasn't until the seventh bombing—July 2, 1982—that there was enough information to begin formally profiling the unsub in the case, the Unabomber, as he'd come to be known. Douglas, for the first time in his career, was assigned as the lead profiler on the case.

"This is a really tough one to profile," Douglas admitted. "We've got the bombs and the victims, but no interactions and no typical crime scenes. There's just not much we can work with."

"Let's start with the bombs," I suggested. "They're his tool, and we know that he makes them, so there must be some sort of meaning there. What are the specifics we've learned about them so far?"

"We've learned that they're untraceable," Douglas replied. "The first two were simple pipe bombs constructed from match heads, batteries, and some wooden elements. The third bomb, the one in the cargo hold of the American Airlines flight, featured a detonator controlled by an altimeter. It didn't explode, but the design of the detonation system indicated a new level of complexity in the Unabomber's MO."

"I'm most interested in the sixth bomb, the one with smokeless powder that he sent to Vanderbilt University. What'd you think about that one?" Ressler interjected, looking over at arson expert Dave Icove, who'd joined the meeting as a specialist for the case.

"I think he's improving at what he does," Icove said. "We're clearly dealing with a man of above-average intelligence. The chemicals he's mixing and the triggering devices he's starting to build—this isn't high-school-level chemistry. Most people would have blown themselves up by now."

"Ann, what about victimology. What are you seeing there?" Douglas asked.

"It's either been universities or airlines so far," I said. "But there's nothing consistent about the individuals being targeted. That makes me think that the message itself is more important than the actual victims. My current thinking is that we're dealing with an ideological killer. So, what's the message he's trying to send? Or what's the message he's trying to attack?"

"We'd have to know more about the ritualistic elements." Douglas paused to think. "He's building his own wooden components instead of buying cheap electrical components he could pick up at any hardware store. And he's started housing the bombs in elaborate wooden structures he's building. His victims also have links to wood, either as part of their name or address."

"We need to go back to the prototype for bombing cases," Ressler said. "If you look at the George Metesky case,* that one showed the

---

* The infamous New York City serial killer known as the Mad Bomber spent years terrorizing New York with strategically placed bombs because of a personal vendetta he held against his former employer, Consolidated Edison.

importance of signature for these types of crimes, the aspect of a calling card. Metesky did this by placing letters on his bombs and by writing angry letters to the paper that blamed Consolidated Edison for his development of tuberculosis. Those letters helped investigators figure out he was a disgruntled employee. That's what led to the arrest."

"But this guy's not writing any letters," Icove pushed back. "And his method of making bombs shows he's taking every effort to stay as hidden as possible. I mean, he made his own adhesive by melting down deer hooves, for crying out loud. There's no way he starts telling us who he is."

"I'm not so sure about that," I said. "There's a reason the unsub's doing this. He's trying to make a point. Behavior-wise, the only thing that separates him from all the rest is how cautious he's being. He's getting closer to making some sort of grand gesture to rationalize his attacks—that's just the nature of serial offenders. But this one's trying to make sure there's a big enough spotlight on him first."

"I'm with Ann on this," Douglas agreed. "This guy's building towards something. And I bet he's feeling pretty good about himself right now."

"Right." Ressler nodded. "So we use that against him. We feed the media whatever we can in terms of photos, analysis, and the types of details that will keep this guy in the news. We play to his ego. And when he lets down his guard to take credit for his work, we'll be ready for him."

———◈———

In May 1985, after a three-year silence, the Unabomber unleashed a new flurry of activity. And by December of that year, our worst fears were realized when computer store owner Hugh Scrutton was killed outside of his shop in Sacramento, California. This was the first fatality in the case, and it signaled a deeply disturbing turning point. The Unabomber had now moved from what we called a technician-type bomber—an offender whose satisfaction comes from the design, construction, and successful detonation of their devices—to a power-motivated bomber—an offender fixated on self-gratification through destruction and terror. In other words, the Unabomber was no longer satisfied with creating functional weapons. His intent was now to kill.

The death of Scrutton gave the Unabomber exactly what he wanted. It set the whole nation on edge and dominated the news cycle for weeks. It had become a power game, and the Unabomber was just starting to realize how fully in control he could be. In response, the FBI—which up to that point had taken more of a consulting role in the case—was now assigned to take charge of the investigation. But despite committing hundreds of agents and considerable resources, the Bureau saw little progress. The Unabomber had a grand plan— and he was terrifyingly skilled at concealing it.

"Look," Douglas said, after gathering us all in the subterranean conference room in late December of that year. "Headquarters is overseeing this one now. They didn't ask for our opinion, and they sure as hell don't seem interested in it, but they will be. They're going to need us on this case at some point, and we'll be ready when they do."

"What's the intel we're getting?" Ressler asked.

"At the moment, not much," Douglas said. "They're keeping a pretty tight lid on things over there. They see that as an advantage."

"How does that make sense?" Ressler looked around the table at each of us in turn, as if someone might have an answer.

"It doesn't." Douglas said. "They're doing the exact opposite of what we suggested three years ago. They need to share as much information as possible to play up this guy's ego and bring in the public's help."

"I heard they're worried about copycats," Hazelwood said.

"So, what then? That justifies hanging back and letting this guy blow up whatever he wants?"

"I'm just saying it's not happening," Hazelwood told him. "Not with the type of attention the Bureau's getting from this one. They'll stay behind the scenes and take the analytical approach as long as possible."

Both Douglas and Ressler were about to speak, but I interjected. "I'm not sure we'll see many more attacks in this round. The unsub stopped before, and I think that indicates a paranoiac personality. He'll want things to cool down for a little bit right now."

"I thought we all agreed that this guy's attracted to the attention he's getting. That he's going to do something to justify the attacks and then claim them as his," Ressler said.

"I do think that's the case. But this is also emotionally charging for him," I explained. "Part of the reason he's committing these attacks is because he's still piecing together whatever his underlying ideology is. That's the part we don't know yet—the why of the attacks. What we *do* know is that the attacks help him bring his motive into focus, and that they also make him paranoid. That's the reason for the long lapses between flurries of attacks—it's his way of trying to resolve the very different types of inputs he's getting."

"I'm with Ann on this one," Douglas said. "And I also think this plays into the fact we didn't catch him early enough. He's planning his next steps, and we'll have to adjust the profile accordingly."

"All right," Hazelwood agreed. "So, what's our advice when head-quarters calls?"

"The strategy hasn't changed," Douglas answered. "We tell them the same thing we told them last time—release all the details and relevant information we have on the case. We stress this guy into responding. We break this guy's sense of control and force him into making a mistake."

In the weeks that followed, the team stayed busy with an unusually high number of cases. There was the Beauty Queen Killer stalking women across the South, the Longview Serial Killer murdering teenagers in Washington State, and the Green River Killer, one of the most prolific killers ever, strangling women and underage girls throughout the Pacific Northwest. We were all working late when someone said: "Looks like Douglas has gone missing again."

I paused. The phrase was shorthand, and I knew exactly what it meant. The BSU was a constant hum of commotion: phones ringing off their hooks, copiers shuffling with paper, and fax machines *beep, beep, beep*ing in a chorus of high-pitched tones that was difficult to ignore. Douglas sometimes needed a break from it all to calm his nerves and collect his thoughts. He never told anyone where he was going, but I always knew where to find him. So, I took the Academy's elevator up to the library on the top floor and made my way to the northwest corner. Douglas was sitting at his usual table, partially hidden behind a stack of books and folders full of official documents. He didn't see me as I approached.

"They're asking about you downstairs," I told him.

Douglas didn't look up.

"I just needed a break." He sighed. "It can all start to feel a little crazy down there, you know?"

I nodded. "Hard to believe we signed up for this."

Douglas, usually quick to pounce on a joke, didn't laugh. "I like the perspective I get up here. Everything on the ground looks so small and far away. It's like it doesn't matter. Well, not that it doesn't matter, exactly, but it makes the cases feel a little less overwhelming."

"Which one are you thinking about?" I asked.

"The bomber. They should have caught him by now. If they'd just taken our advice . . ."

"You can't take it personally. Profiling is so much further than anyone expected it to get. It works. The trouble is, the second we proved that, it became the Bureau's tool to control. They'll decide when to use it and what advice they want to take."

"I get it," Douglas said. "We're not the off-the-record project we used to be. I'm just saying I sometimes wish we still were. It was a whole lot easier to get things done in those days. There was no one to answer to. We just did what we knew was right."

"That's the price of success. You end up becoming part of the system you were trying to fix."

"Boy, that's a depressing thought."

"Don't worry about it too much, John. I'm sure you'll find some new trouble to get into soon enough."

That one got him. Douglas laughed. "We better get back to see how the team's doing."

For the Unabomber, his ultimate misstep was trying to leverage the spotlight of his crimes for his own personal gain. That happened in June of 1995—less than two months after sending a powerful bomb to California Forestry Association president Gilbert P. Murray, killing him at his Sacramento office. In a surprise move, the Unabomber sent a thirty-five-thousand-word manifesto, "Industrial Society and Its Future," to the *New York Times* and the *Washington Post*. He'd been tentatively communicating with media and a potential victim since 1993 through letters. But it wasn't until the manifesto that he finally stated the reason for his attacks. He wanted the "destruction of the worldwide industrial system." He tried to justify this, as well as his violent actions, by explaining why he believed technology was evil. He saw himself as a prophet of sorts—a savior. And he felt it was his responsibility to convince the rest of society to tear down the technological system and go back to the ways of agrarian tribes. He also made a point of calling the FBI "a joke," which—not surprisingly—ruffled some feathers up the ladder.

The Unabomber's message didn't matter to me, but the fact that he'd proactively reached out presented us with a unique opportunity. It was the public cry for attention that I'd been waiting for. This was exactly what the profile had predicted early on, and it could lead to the types of additional information and details we needed to hopefully crack the case. The letters and manifesto gave the Bureau's psycholinguists a chance to analyze the Unabomber's writing style to learn about the author's education, psyche, background, demographics, and motive. And we could use our findings as a tool to engage the public's help. But there was a catch. The Unabomber would only stop killing, he wrote in his letters, if his manifesto was published in national newspapers. They'd have three months to make their decision.

This was a direct challenge. Calling the FBI a joke was bad enough, but an ultimatum like this ruffled the whole damn bird. It put the Bureau in a position of weakness. Nevertheless, after a heated internal debate—stoked in part by the fact that certain investigators felt that it set a bad precedent to give a violent criminal such a public forum—we reached a consensus. The manifesto was published on September 19, 1995, as an eight-page pullout supplement in the *Washington Post*. To satisfy the Unabomber's demand of wanting both papers to publish the treatise, the *Post* and the *New York Times* put out a joint statement, saying that they had decided to publish the document "for public safety reasons." They added that "we will split the costs of publishing. It is being printed in *The Post*, which has the mechanical ability to distribute a separate section in all copies of its daily paper."

Immediately, thousands of people responded, writing in to suggest possible suspects. One stood out. It was from a man named David Kaczynski, who recognized the familiar phrasing of his brother's writing style and some of the rambling manifesto's ideologies.* The Bureau asked David to provide whatever other written documents he could. And when he sent them a twenty-three-page document from his brother that read like an early draft of the published manifesto, linguistics determined the author of both documents to be a likely match.

Three months later, on April 3, 1996, investigators arrested Ted Kaczynski at his self-constructed cabin near Lincoln, Montana. The search uncovered one completed bomb, numerous bomb parts, and about forty thousand handwritten pages of journals that detailed his bomb-making process and described each of his crimes.

One of the main goals at the BSU was to develop techniques to help identify and apprehend violent serial offenders earlier than ever thought possible. But this didn't always mean we captured them within days or weeks. Sometimes it took years. This was the case with both BTK and the Unabomber. It took decades to bring these two killers to justice. But in both cases, our initial inclinations and profiles served as a road map, guiding the investigations as they inched closer and closer to identifying both perpetrators by homing in on their behavioral psychology and deeply self-interested flaws.

By the time of Kaczynski's arrest, I'd moved on from my behavioral science work to focus more on the trial side of serial violence. After

---

* It took David three weeks of rereading the manifesto online at a local library, then comparing it with the angry letters his brother had sent to his home over the years. He made the difficult decision while watching his wife eat cornflakes one morning. He looked at her and said, "Hon, you know, I think there might be a fifty-fifty chance that Ted wrote the manifesto."

decades of working directly with investigators to help them better understand these types of crimes, I wanted to do something similar in courtrooms. Still, for one spring evening in 1996, I was glued to my TV set just like everyone else, watching the first few images of Kaczynski flicker across the news. He was older than our original profile had anticipated, and he looked exhausted. But despite having very few details to work with, we got many other pieces correct: he was raised in the Chicago area, had isolated himself from society and was living like a hermit in Montana, and would eventually cave to his ego's need for recognition. More importantly, our suggestion of a proactive media strategy had worked. It took investigators sixteen bombs, twenty-three injuries, and three deaths to finally listen—the strategy had been avoided for years out of fear that it would some-how tip the investigation's hand or inspire copycat bombers, none of which happened—but enlisting the public's help proved to be key in breaking the case. And it set a precedent for how law enforcement and media could work together in the future.

Still, there was one thing that worried me about these types of media cases and their overall portrayal of serial killers: they came with a conditioning effect. The public was beginning to accept them as archetypal stories of classic Americana. Somewhere along the line, the public's initial shock about killers like Ed Gein and John Wayne Gacy had changed from repulsion to fascination. It got to the point where a police artist's sketch of the Unabomber became an iconic T-shirt. It was disturbing. Because despite how obviously horrible these killers were, despite their utter brutality and the pain they inflicted upon their victims, they'd somehow become romanti-cized. They were a new type of celebrity. And all the inconvenient details that interfered with this narrative—the loss of life, issues of mental health, and the victims themselves—were simply ignored. That wasn't something I was willing to accept.

CHAPTER 16

Gazing into the Abyss

You never get comfortable with the idea of serial killers. You never feel complacent. Or at least I didn't. But it is possible to get desensitized. I'd seen this happen with agents who no longer winced at particularly gruesome crime scenes—the type where a victim's blood smeared across the floors and lower third of the walls like paint—or found it easier to clock out and look away instead of putting in long hours. At that point, they were no longer compartmentalizing the grislier elements of the job. They'd simply accepted them. Ressler, who was something of a philosopher at times, chalked it up to a quote by Nietzsche: "Beware that, when fighting monsters, you yourself do not become a monster . . . for when you gaze long into the abyss, the abyss gazes also into you."

By 1995, I knew the truth of this quote for myself. I'd stared deep enough and long enough into the minds of serial killers to understand them as wholly as I could. And as I did so, they'd studied and analyzed me in return. Several knew the names of my children, others read all my publications, and one sent me an annual Christmas card, year after year after year. The borders between us had grown thin. It was time to move on.

So, in the summer of that same year, I stepped away from my role at the FBI to focus on the legal side of criminal psychology and to continue my teaching and research as a university professor. To be clear, I never officially ended my work with the Bureau—to this day, I still consult on cases when I'm asked. I simply made the decision to take my expertise in a new direction. I'd been thinking about next steps ever since that conversation in the library with Douglas in the mid-eighties when we'd talked about feeling trapped within the system we were trying to fix. I knew then that a change was coming. I just wasn't sure when or what that change would be. But when it did, it was like a revelation.

One morning in the summer of 1995, as I was engaged in my daily pacing of the halls at Quantico, I overheard two young agents talking about the paths that led them to the FBI. The first one's story was fairly common. He came from a military background and was recruited after a four-year tour of service abroad. But the second one's road to the Bureau caught my attention. I slowed down my pace to listen more carefully. He was talking specifically about the BSU and about the articles he'd read describing our successful cases when he said something that made me pause.

"The Kemper case, though. I don't know if you've heard about him. He's sometimes called the Co-ed Killer. He did some pretty crazy stuff and didn't get caught for years. He's my favorite serial killer."

That last line rang in my head. It was so strange. What did it even mean to have a favorite serial killer? Then, suddenly and with great clarity, I was struck by the significance of the remark. Serial killers were gaining notoriety for their crimes. As public fascination with these offenders grew, so too did their mythology. Their stories were becoming familiar, compelling, even entertaining—offering a never-before-seen glimpse into the darkest corners of human nature. The killers were becoming distanced from the heinous carnage they'd left behind and transcending into the status of cultural icons. And that made them powerfully attractive. People were drawn to the disturbing reality of how dark humanity could really get, the seemingly infinite blackness of what humans *could* become if social norms were stripped away or entirely disregarded. They could relate to the emotions of anger or even violent thoughts toward a fellow human being, just not quite to the degree of ever acting upon those urges. In serial killers, the public saw themselves—demasked and unbound— but still entirely possible.

That was the moment I realized the responsibility I had to share my insight with the public at large. I couldn't continue isolating myself, burying my research six flights belowground in a government office. It wasn't enough to refine the data anymore. I needed to make it public. Just like I'd worked to dispel public misperceptions of rape in the late seventies, it was time to do the same thing for the growing misconceptions surrounding serial killers. I had a chance to set the record straight, but the window was closing quickly. I knew I had to figure out a way to do this before the mythology of these offenders became too big to control.

At that time, I could already see the boundary between reality and fiction bleeding from one side to the other. Popular movies like *Silence of the Lambs*, *The Texas Chainsaw Massacre*, and *Natural Born Killers* were borrowing from real-world serial killers to create storybook villains that fit an entertainment mold. But they did so by oversimplifying. They took the nuance and reality of deeply disturbing criminal psychology and reduced it to a familiar narrative of good versus evil. They created characters that were easy for an audience to understand, consume, and empathize with. And the technique worked. The success of these films led to a surge in true crime TV, which led to prisons being inundated with fan mail as the public clamored to learn more about the criminals locked within them. There were even serial killer "groupies," of a sort, who professed their love through marriage proposals.

Surprisingly, the whole thing made sense. This morbid curiosity with serial killers was a logical consequence of Hoover's perpetual public relations campaign. The heroic acts of G-men could only capture the public's imagination for so long. It was just a matter of time before interest shifted to the antiheroes instead. Of course, this attention wasn't without consequence. In its usual way, the spotlight of entertainment glossed over reality and focused on serial killers only in their most appealing forms. Like Hannibal Lecter in *Silence of the Lambs*, killers were often portrayed as charismatic, even likable. They were given qualities of empathy and charm that made it easier to separate them from the unimaginable malice of their actions. They were made human. But that was just a useful reduction. What I'd learned was that serial killers had emotions, yes, but these emotions lacked depth. They didn't care about others. They didn't want to make friends. They didn't have empathy. They only wanted victims. Connection—through charm, flattery, or humor—was part of their act. It was simply a means to an end. And with this egocentric underpinning as the framework through which they navigated the world, they were free. They did as they pleased. And that made them dangerous.

The irony of what I saw unfolding in pop culture wasn't lost on me. In fact, part of me even wanted to laugh. I'd spent years at the BSU trying to analyze the minds of serial killers so that investigators could better understand who they were. Now, the media was taking a similar approach. But their end goal served entertainment rather than truth, and the implications of this were profound. Entertainment doesn't simply exist in a bubble; it has a conditioning effect. The public was becoming sympathetic to serial killers to the detriment of their victims. I already knew how this would play out in real-world trials with a real-world jury informed by fictionalized beliefs. They'd get caught up in the myth. The truth is, just like I'd seen happen with rape cases all those years ago, history was repeating itself. But this time I'd be ready.

From my years of experience with the BSU, I had already gained a reputation in the professional sphere as one of the leading experts on victimology, trauma, and the serial killer phenomenon. I'd also spent the last several years steadily giving more and more courtroom testimony on the types of bizarre cases where no one else could. I might not have had the resources to go toe to toe with the media's portrayal of serial killers, but I could still make a difference where it mattered most: their court cases. I could speak to a jury and cut through all the misperceptions, oversimplifications, and convenient reductions. I could speak a truth that few others knew—and in doing so, I found myself in a position where I could finally use that truth to help victims and their families receive the justice they so desperately deserved.

⸻ ◈ ⸻

My opportunity came in the summer of 1996, when Ressler and I got a call to see if we were interested in giving expert testimony at the trial of serial killer Henry Louis Wallace. The case checked all the boxes. It was high profile, captivating, and already a major focus of national media attention. It was also remarkably singular. Wallace— who had already confessed to raping and murdering nine women between 1992 and 1994 and who later volunteered that he murdered two additional women—was the first Black serial killer we'd ever come across. And on top of that, Wallace knew each and every one of his female victims before he took their lives. The majority of the previous murderers we'd cataloged were white males whose victims were mostly strangers. Wallace represented the possibility of an entirely new criminal profile—as much for the BSU as for the media.

But there was a catch.

It wasn't the prosecutor reaching out to us.

It was the defense.

The novelty of the case was proving to be a challenge for them. And they wanted to know what motivated Wallace's crimes, how deliberate they were, and the nature of his mental health. In other words, they needed someone with our level of expertise to give Wallace a formal evaluation ahead of his trial.

This request caught me off guard. I'd always considered a serial killer's defense team to be an adversary of justice. But Ressler, who had recently retired from the Bureau and was now interested in learning how the legal system worked, saw things differently.

"We're not here to pick sides, Ann. That was never the job anyway. It's always been about taking something complicated and trying to make sense of it. It's about finding the truth."

Ressler was right. Condemning serial killers wasn't the goal. We were after something bigger. We intended to cut through the pervasive myths surrounding serial killers to show a jury how the minds of these criminals really worked. Whether the defense or the prosecution used our insights, it didn't matter. What mattered was that we were revealing the truth. It was as simple as that.

The following week, in June 1996, Ressler and I entered the Mecklenburg County Jail in Charlotte, North Carolina, where Wallace was being held. But things had changed since our early days of interviewing for the BSU. When Ressler was an active agent, his badge gained us immediate access to any prison in the country, without question or hassle. Retirement lost him that privilege. We were at the mercy of the same bureaucratic process as everyone else. We couldn't even step foot through the front gate without signed letters from Wallace's co-counsel, Isabel Day and James P. Cooney III, a court document approving the interview, and our state-issued driver's licenses. It was a whole different process.

More than half an hour passed before we were finally escorted through three security stations and a series of metal detectors, then asked to wait near two locked doors for a second guard to arrive. Another five minutes passed before the doors slowly glided open and we were waved inside. In silence, we followed the guard down a long corridor, its edges framed by inmates staring out from behind the bars of their cells. I kept my eyes forward. Being a female visitor in an all-male prison isn't anything like in the movies. There's no caterwauling, no suggestive comments, no banging plates against a cell's bars. That behavior would be easy to dismiss—childish and naive. But it's the silence that's daunting. It's weighted and absolute. It's attentive. And I'd done enough research to hear through the silence. I knew what the inmates were thinking.

Our guard led us to a small room with a table, three chairs, and a staff kitchenette. He told us to "make yourselves at home," then left to get Wallace. Ressler got right to work setting up the video recording equipment.

We needed a quiet room to help create the ideal mood for the interview, and this space seemed about right. I looked around at the caged fluorescent lights, the bare walls, and then gasped. A towel was hanging in the kitchenette. I was shocked. This man had killed most of his victims by strangling them with a towel. I ran over and stuffed the towel in a drawer just as the door was opening. There, standing six-foot-four, three hundred pounds, Wallace blocked out the light as he ducked his head slightly to come inside the room. He was hand-cuffed and leg-chained, forced to walk with awkwardly restricted steps, the thick metal rattling and echoing off the concrete floor. Our guard looked kid-like in comparison.

This was prime time.

Henry Louis Wallace was more commonly known as the Charlotte Strangler or the Taco Bell Strangler—the latter because he worked as a manager of a Taco Bell. Nearly all of his victims were either his coworkers or friends and coworkers of his girlfriend, who worked at a local Bojangles restaurant.

Ressler extended his hand in introduction. "I'm Bob Ressler, retired FBI agent."

"And I'm Ann Burgess from the University of Pennsylvania," I added, offering my hand as well and awkwardly shaking Wallace's hand despite the impediment of his handcuffs. "We're part of your defense team. We look forward to talking with you today."

"I've been waiting to see you," Wallace said. He was polite, smiling widely as he looked us each in the eyes. "I haven't had—" A voice boomed over speakers in the hallway. A muffle of static called the inmates to gather for a meeting.

"We'll be hearing messages like that all day," Wallace apologized. "They never stop."

Ressler invited Wallace to sit down. The large man shuffled over to the far side of the table and took the single chair that faced opposite the camera and our two seats. To obtain his consent, I pulled a piece of paper from my notebook and asked Wallace to sign it if he was okay with us recording the interview for trial and teaching purposes.

"I hope you learn something about me," he said, slowly signing his name on the sheet in front of him. "Because I don't know why I did what I did."

There was a pause. His very presence suddenly made the room feel claustrophobic. Ressler then reached into his briefcase and pulled out a stack of *True Detective* magazines.

Wallace straightened in his chair. He tilted his head and watched closely as Ressler placed the magazines on the table.

"We've read all your records," Ressler said, patting the stack of magazines in a way that teased Wallace's view of the top magazine's cover. "We know that as a young boy you liked to read your mother's soap opera stories and also crime magazines."

Wallace nodded in agreement as Ressler pulled a magazine from the stack and laid it down near the center of the table. Its cover showed a picture of a woman whose clothes were mostly torn off. She was bound—her hands tied over her head—with a gag stuffed in her mouth, and she was cowering from a man holding a hunting knife against her large breasts.

"What's going on here?" Ressler asked.

Wallace peered down at the cover. "He looks like he's enjoying it."

Ressler pulled out another magazine and placed it on top of the first. "And this one? What's this picture leading to? What's your fantasy here?"

"I see a porn star, a woman becoming aggressive with the man. They're changing roles."

This back and forth went on for nearly an hour—long enough to discuss fifteen different magazines—with Wallace becoming more and more visibly animated throughout. He started pointing to the photographs he liked most, nearly bouncing up and down in his chair as he did so.

Ressler held up a bondage cover. "Does this match your fantasies?"

There was no hesitation. "It's the control," Wallace said. "I prefer forced relationships. I had girlfriends and 'dates'"—his word for prostitutes—"but it's the force that gives me the power I want."

Wallace then admitted that the magazines took him back to his adolescence. He distinctly remembered spreading the magazines across the floor of his childhood bedroom and savoring his pornographic collection, sometimes jerking off and sometimes just standing there, naked and aroused. At this point, Ressler returned the magazines to his briefcase. Wallace's hands disappeared beneath the table and he shifted slightly in his seat, admitting that the pictures were very arousing.

I scribbled an observation in my notebook: *Bondage is his pornography.*

The magazines, of course, were just an initial test. Other violent offenders had reacted the same way. For example, BTK Killer Dennis Rader told the investigators that he "was getting a hard-on" when they showed him his own drawings and photos of his dead victims. But with Wallace, it was important to see his reaction within a structured setting so that we could establish a baseline. We were trying to learn what, if anything, set him apart from his peers. And the influence of and connection between graphic detective magazines and certain violent sexual criminals was something well understood. So far, anyway, Wallace was just your average serial killer. We needed to find out more about his rape and murder fantasies—when they started, how they developed, and what triggered them to become sadistic.

Next, we asked Wallace to describe his upbringing and each of his murders. He'd already done this with detectives and investigators in Charlotte, but that process mostly served to fill out institutional forms. We were interested in something deeper. Wallace's unguarded responses would give us the answers we were really looking for—they would reveal how he saw himself. But to reach the innermost part of his psyche, we needed him to trust us. Offering up the magazines was one way of establishing our intent for good-faith communication. We needed him to feel like he was back in control.

Control is the core element of everything serial killers do. It's a symptom of their highly patterned way of thinking. It is the very framework of their fantasies and their interactions with victims. And it has always been their framework for interacting with us. That's why, despite already knowing much of Wallace's background prior to the interview, we still asked him about his upbringing to see whether he'd embellish or offer up false narrative. We wouldn't challenge him if he did alter the truth—we wanted Wallace to feel relaxed and open—but it was important to understand how he might manipulate the facts we already knew. Understanding this would also help us better anticipate how he might manipulate lesser-known details about his cases.

Our awareness of the dynamics of control also factored in to how we structured the interview in the first place. In the early days of our FBI interviews, we'd learned that it was most effective for one person to ask the majority of questions about a specific subject or event or theme. This way, if the offender got upset, the other interviewer could take over and quickly change the subject and leave behind the negative association with the questions that had come before.

It was my turn to go first. I knew Wallace would be less paranoid with me, less guarded. He'd still test me for reactions. He'd still try different angles to find out what I represented. But that process of testing boundaries would go more quickly with me. It always did. In the minds of offenders, I was simply a woman, and a woman could never be a threat. That's just how sexual killers thought. It was part of their predictable arrogance, which I'd learned to use to my advantage.

I invited Wallace to start off by talking about his childhood, and he answered in the monotonous cadence of someone uninterested in recapping a familiar story. He described growing up without plumbing or electricity. The family's water came from an outdoor well, and their bathroom was a set of chamber pots he had to empty as part of his chores. He also mentioned that the house was full of conflict. He loved his great-grandmother and she had even stepped in to help raise him, but she didn't get along well with his mother. The two of them would argue frequently, often late at night after his mother got back from long shifts working in a textile factory where she sewed socks. Wallace characterized his mother as a strict disciplinarian with a short fuse and a violent temper. She started beating him at a young age, before he was even two years old, often for normal childhood behaviors like soiling himself or crying when he was upset. On top of this, she often yelled at Wallace and told him she wished she'd never had him. And on days when she was too tired from work, she ordered Wallace's sister, Yvonne, who was three years older than Wallace and who tried to be as protective as she could, to go outside their cinderblock house to find a switch, which she then had to use to beat her brother as their mother watched. This upbringing instilled a deep sense of fear that continued even long after Wallace towered over his mother as a six-foot-four adult.

"I was terrified of her from junior high school through high school—that she'd try to kill me."

"Why would she kill you?"

"The beatings were brutal. She'd say she'd kill me. She stabbed at me with a butcher knife one time. I ducked and she took a big chunk out of the wall. My mother was not an expressive, love-giving person. In fact, there was very little expression of love from her. It was inferred."

"Tell me about your sister." I switched the topic.

"I've always cared a great deal for Yvonne and I mirrored a lot from her. We lived in a small house with no bathroom." Throughout their childhood, his sister had looked after him and guided him as best she could. His voice became noticeably softer when talking about Yvonne, completely unlike the sharply detached tone he'd used to depict his mother.

Wallace continued, "I always wondered what my father looked like—who he was and what he was like. I saw a picture of him once, and when I asked my mother about him, she said he was one of the teachers from her high school. There was one time he called the house and was supposed to come to see me. I stayed home from school to see him. I waited and waited, watched every car that drove by, but he never came."

I asked Wallace if there were any role models in his life. If there were any men he looked up to.

"My mother had a boyfriend that I liked a lot," Wallace said. "But I knew he wasn't my father and he wasn't a role model. He was married and was just fooling around with my mother."

Wallace's description of his upbringing was unsurprising. It fit the common mold the serial killer study established of single mothers, a violent childhood, and no male role models. In his case, at least, he was fortunate to have an attachment to his sister and his great-grandmother. But that connection still wasn't enough. He had a dominant fantasy life that started in grade school when he witnessed a gang rape in the neighborhood.

"Was that your first sexual experience?" I asked. "What do you remember about it?"

"No . . ." Wallace hesitated. He leaned forward on the table and looked at me without showing much expression. He then described growing up around a "small army of kids" and said that there was always something going on, "could be fights, shootings, or stabbings." He remembered being only eight or nine years old when he first had sex; the girl, on the other hand, was a teenager.

"I thought I was in trouble," Wallace admitted. "I saw her mother beating her and the mother came over to tell my mother what she'd seen between me and the girl. I was scared I'd get a beating, too. Instead, my sister and mother started laughing and teasing me, saying why didn't I pick a prettier girl. It was the teasing that bothered me the most."

Wallace then witnessed the gang rape just a short while afterward. "We had all gone to the high school football game. The Bush girl was led out of the game by some guys, and my friend and I followed. We saw her suspended in air and the guys raping her. She kept saying, 'Wait a minute, wait a minute.'"

"Did you think about that often? Did that ever come to mind during your own crimes?"

"Oh yes. I thought that'd be the perfect way." He smiled.

I made a note about Wallace's use of the word *perfect* to describe how the Bush girl was humiliated and controlled. The memory clearly pleased him. And he likely used it as raw fuel for his fantasies.

"The next day," he continued, "I learned two neighbors were being charged with rape. Since they got in trouble with the law, it was more exciting for me. I began to want someone strapped down and it came from seeing the boys doing it."

I added to my original note that witnessing the Bush girl's attack had opened up new possibilities in Wallace. He saw violence as a tool to re-create the trauma of his childhood. Only, this time, he'd be in the driver's seat. He was drawn to experiences of control.

Throughout this part of the conversation, Wallace's confidence noticeably swelled. He wasn't aggressive or anything like that, but he was displaying hints of something similar to pride—as if he'd settled into his memories and found a world of familiar comforts. In a way, he was sharing something very personal with us. It was only a subtle shift in behavior, but for Wallace, who had a very strong visual memory, the carefulness with which he began describing past events, the attention to detail—it came across like an offering. It felt like he was letting us in.

From there, Wallace took charge over the conversation without any prompting. He was self-reporting. He knew that we'd studied his crimes and had genuine interest in what he'd done. So he talked. He described starting high school in 1979, that his classmates liked him and teachers found him cooperative and polite. When his mother would not allow him to join the football team, he joined the cheerleading squad as the only man. He towered over the female cheerleaders, but no one feared him. His classmates considered him upbeat, enthusiastic, and creative. Wallace took pride in these friendships at school. He felt accepted by his peers, whereas at home he was often made to feel like an outsider, a freak—teased for being taller, darker, and slower than the rest of them.

In May 1983, Wallace graduated from high school and tried following in his sister's footprints by attending college. But he failed out of two schools in two semesters from lack of motivation and a tendency to drift into fantasizing about women rather than focusing on his work. Wallace looked notably dejected while discussing these failures, so I asked him if anything from those years made him feel successful. He perked up at the question and thought about it for a second. "I really liked my evening job as a disc jockey at the local radio station, WBAW." He was known as the Midnight Rider because of his smooth, deep voice. And he fashioned himself after the legendary rock and roll DJ Wolfman Jack, who broadcasted nightly and was known for playing great music on the airwaves, especially Black music that wasn't getting a lot of exposure. But the job was short-lived. Wallace was fired after several months when he was caught in the act of stealing the radio station's CDs.

With college a bust and his potential career in radio upended, Wallace decided to switch course and join the US Naval Reserve. This marked the most stable period in his life. Starting in December of 1984 and lasting eight years, Wallace kept his nose clean and built a reputation as a successful seaman, rising up the ranks to third class petty officer. It was also during this period that Wallace married his longtime on-and-off girlfriend, Marietta Brabham, becoming both a husband and a stepfather to Brabham's daughter. But the honeymoon phase didn't last long. Tension was building in the background. Wallace desperately wanted to have a child of his own, while Marietta refused to even consider it. The disappointment was too much to bear. Wallace found escape in crack cocaine and other drugs, which eventually led to his arrest and a two-year sentence for second-degree burglary. Marietta left him, and Wallace had no choice but to move back home with his mom and sister, who now lived near Charlotte, North Carolina.

"Did you ever think of killing Marietta?" I asked.

Wallace looked down at the table. "Yes, I did," he mumbled. "I even went to her house and stood outside for a long time. But then just left. I couldn't do it."

"Because you knew you'd have to go back and clean up?" Ressler asked.

"I was most concerned about blood and fingerprints," Wallace said softly. But his remorseful tone didn't last long.

Wallace quickly switched the subject and talked about how moving to Charlotte gave him a chance to start over, to meet new girls. He was thrilled when he managed to get one of his girlfriends pregnant— even though the relationship didn't last—because he'd finally become a father. The baby was born in September 1993. He named her Kendra, and he treasured her more than anything else in the world.

"What led up to the murders?" I asked, pulling Wallace away from a topic that I worried might make him sentimental and less talkative.

"Well, it wasn't money. I had no financial problems. My job was great. I was working at Walmart in loss prevention. I liked the job but was caught shoplifting. I was stealing equipment, mostly cameras, and using my position to exploit the situation. If I wasn't caught, I could have cleaned them out. I had a room in storage that had one lock and I used a lock cutter to open it.

"But when I was separated from my wife, Marietta, I started feeling anger towards her. She claimed she was raped in college and that it led to a child. I asked if she ever thought of that rape while we were having sex, and she said yes. That made me feel like I was raping her when we had sex. That's when the memories from my childhood reoccurred and I started acting out. The whole thing put me in a totally different frame of mind and the cocaine habit increased and the murders started."

Wallace committed his first murder in early 1990, two years after his release from the Navy, in his hometown of Barnwell, South Carolina. Using a gun, he forced Tashonda Bethea, an acquaintance of his, into his car. But even with the gun, she resisted. Wallace then drove to a wooded area, forced oral sex, raped her, and told her no one would ever find her. After he was done, he slashed her throat and threw her body in a pond.

"The next morning after the murder," Wallace recounted, "I felt paranoid and wasn't sure she was dead. I went back and looked in the pond. It wasn't that deep, but I couldn't find the body. I took my gun and shot into the pond. Then went across the street to see if her body drifted down. I was sure the cops would come. I was so paranoid, so for a couple of days I was really stressed. I kept going back to the scene, a total of three or four more times, and never saw her."

Bethea's body washed up several weeks later. With little evidence to go on, police questioned many of Bethea's acquaintances about her disappearance. This included Wallace, whose criminal record made him something of a red flag, but he was never considered a serious suspect.

Wallace's second murder took place in May 1992, while he was on a self-described "date" with Sharon Nance, a known prostitute and convicted drug dealer.

"I told her I wanted anal sex, and she said, 'Is that the way you like it?' That question just set me off. Then after having sex, she demanded money and I didn't have any money, and we got into a scuffle, and I beat her to death. I drove her in my car to a deserted area near some railroad tracks and dumped her out."

Her body was found a few days after that.

Little by little, Wallace's confidence grew with each of his crimes. He'd managed to dodge serious inquiry by police without much thought or effort. He felt like he could get away with anything he wanted. He felt untouchable.

"The only problem," Wallace added, tensing up as he spoke, "was living with my mother. It got so bad that I had to get separate phone lines. She treated me like I was fifteen when I was twenty-five. She didn't like some of the women I brought home. She had keys made for my car. She called me stupid."

"At what point did you lose control?" Ressler asked.

"Each victim varied," Wallace replied. "Shawna and I sat for an hour and just talked. I got up—like we always did—and embraced and kissed. Then the monster came out. The attack on Jumper was as soon as I came in the house. Bang, I was on it. I never thought it would happen with Jumper. Baucom was home at the time—an accident—just home at the wrong time. Slaughter, it could have been anybody."

"What about rage, anger, hostility? You stabbed your last victim thirty-eight times."

"That didn't come until later. But in between the rape and murder there were a multitude of rapes of prostitutes and I had multiple sex partners leading up to the murder. That's when I found out I preferred forced sex."

"Let me ask you this: one point that's very important to me is that you knew all your victims except for one. Why was that?"

"It was the nature of my personality to get them to trust me."

"Okay. But why not strangers?" Ressler persisted.

"As I met people, there were things about their personality that connected to my past—my mother, sister, and wife," Wallace explained. "With a stranger, I couldn't pull it off."

After a short break in the afternoon, I decided to take a different approach. I took out a stack of blank paper and colored pencils and asked Wallace if he wanted to draw his murders. He nodded yes. It didn't take much prompting from there. Wallace immediately concentrated on drawing stick figures that represented the pattern of his preferred chokehold, then used the same simple imagery to sketch out his rapes and strangulations. He also drew basic outlines that depicted the various houses he'd entered and the rooms as he saw them. Everything was clean lines and basic shapes, a simplicity that indicated feelings of aloofness in Wallace. His expression, too, reflected feelings of aloofness—a look of content concentration as he carefully transferred memories from his head to the blank page. All of this suggested that, for Wallace, the act of violence itself wasn't the point. What really thrilled him was playing out these crimes over and over again in his head, refining each recollection until he could vividly recall every last horrific detail. He'd committed his crimes to have memories of them. This was his means of finding and maintaining the emotional connections he'd failed to create with others.

Ressler took a second look at one of Wallace's drawings and commented, "This looks like you're up above and looking down."

"That's the way I felt." Wallace nodded. "Like I was watching it. I hovered over the scene observing. I wasn't connected. Sometimes it took hours to come back down after the murder. That's why I went back to the crime scenes."

"Could you have stopped yourself if you'd wanted to?" I asked.

"No." Wallace shook his head. "Once I touched them, it was over. I could think about it, but it was out of my control."

"How do you understand what you did?" I could sense that we weren't picking up on all of what he was trying to tell us.

"It's . . ." Wallace hesitated. "I feel within this shell are two people. One is an evil person and will adapt to any situation. With the other, it's a trusted person. A good person. He almost lures the other person, taking whatever measures to conceal the second identity, a mad, angry, explosive, destructive person."

This particular explanation, two people in the same body, really caught my attention. It broke trend with other serial killers in a way that was uniquely insightful. First, it illustrated how duality can develop in response to complex stressful environments early in life. And second, Wallace's evolution of two parallel identities demonstrated a fundamental lack of integration, both within himself and within society. This caused him to feel disconnected from the world around him. We'd seen other examples of duality in previous interviews, such as with Kemper, who described having a good and bad side. But the important distinction in Wallace's case was that this dissociation was something he was fully aware of. Many serial killers are not so self-observant.

"What would you think about? When you went out at night, what was your plan?"

"That's not me," Wallace said defensively. "That's the other person on the prowl. He's more comfortable when he's concealed. He'd stalk them.

"With Vanessa Mack, I stalked her for several months. I had fantasies of having rough sex with her. She was a very attractive woman. We went out a few times. But then rejection came. She didn't like the dinners. She led me to believe we'd be more than friends. Then she got pregnant by someone else.

"The night she was murdered, I knew she was home. I wore a black tucked-in jumper. I knew she was there. I hadn't seen her since she had the baby. But I knew she was upset with me because I'd dropped out of the picture. I was heavy into cocaine. I wanted to see if she had money. I tried to hug her. She pushed me away. I asked her for a drink. She wouldn't give me anything. So I tried again—I had to get behind her to choke her. I finally got her to make me a drink and then got behind her. She froze. I told her to cooperate with me. We went into the bedroom. I had her undress, and I got undressed with one hand. Had oral sex and then raped her. As she was putting on her clothes, I tied a pillow case on her neck and she passed out. Then I put the baby blanket around her neck. Her baby was in the room sleeping."

"Did you do anything to the baby?"

"No. I was concerned about the child. I had a child and a mother and sister. I was numb to what was going on as I think of it now. I thank God her oldest daughter wasn't there or I would have done it to her."

"Why's that?"

"I just would've. It went back to my being molested and molesting a female as a teenager. I needed someone else to make it to stop."

For the last part of our interview, Ressler and I asked Wallace to recount each individual murder. He went through the list mechanically, outlining his thought processes, remembering his victims' final words, and detailing with chilling specificity the agony in their eyes when he applied his signature choke hold, rendering them powerless before he raped them.

He explained that he'd fantasized about raping Caroline Love, who was a friend of his girlfriend, Sadie McKnight, for weeks leading up to the crime. He just couldn't stop thinking about her. He knew he could only regain control by acting on his fantasies. So, he broke into her apartment, snuck up behind her while she was watching TV, wrapped his hands around her neck, choked her, and then moved her to her bedroom, where he undressed her, tied her up, and raped her while she was semiconscious. When he was done, Wallace strangled her to death and threw her body into a shallow ravine at the edge of town.

"About two days after that I went back, and the body had almost decayed to the point where she looked like leather, an ET doll or something. Her body had decayed so badly. I went back about a week later and the only thing left was bones."

In contrast, Wallace described his murder of Shawna Hawk, whom he worked with at Taco Bell, as unexpected. The two had become friends and sometimes hung out after work. Wallace stopped by her house after a shift one night, but when Shawna started teasing him about a recent fight he'd had with his girlfriend, his temper took over.[*] He shoved her into her bedroom, forced her to take off her clothes, and commanded her to give him oral sex. She was afraid and cried the whole time, which Wallace liked—it made him even angrier when women fought back. Wallace then instructed her to put her clothes back on, led her into the bathroom, positioned her in a choke hold, and squeezed her neck until she passed out. Before he left, he drew water for a bath and staged her body within it, grabbing fifty dollars from her purse as he walked away from the scene.

Audrey Spain was another coworker of Wallace whose friendship cost her her life. She became a victim after the two smoked pot together at her apartment. His MO followed a now familiar pattern: after putting her in a chokehold, he dragged her into her own

---

[*] Teasing was a surefire way of triggering Wallace. It dredged up a flood of painful memories from his childhood—a period when neighborhood kids constantly picked on him and he felt no sense of control.

bedroom, then raped and strangled her. Afterward, he stole her credit card to fill his car with gas, then returned to Spain's apartment later that evening to use her phone, which he hoped would confuse police as they tried to nail down Spain's time of death.

Unlike some of the other women, many of whom he knew only briefly, Wallace admitted that Valencia Jumper was like a little sister to him. He never planned on killing her. It just happened. He had stopped by her apartment twice on the evening of August 10, 1993. The first time was just to talk. The second time, his intentions were to kill her. Wallace put Jumper in his usual chokehold but loosened his grip as she begged him not to hurt her, promising that they could have sex if he would just let her go. Wallace agreed, but he strangled her after they had sex regardless. He knew that she'd tell and that he wouldn't get away with the murder. He then took the batteries out of the apartment's smoke detector, staged the kitchen stove to start a fire, covered Jumper's body in rum, and set fire to her lifeless corpse with a match. He stole jewelry on the way out and sold it at a local pawnshop.

"I only had a strong connection to Jumper. The others were casual or no connection for weeks or months."

The stories continued like this for a while, with Wallace coolly recollecting how he preyed on women he knew: choking them, forcing oral sex, then raping and killing them. And although the pattern of his crimes stayed the same, the nature of his attacks grew more and more vicious over time. It took greater violence and a greater risk of being caught to satisfy his needs. Wallace was chasing a fading high. There was less rationale behind each of his murders, more desperation. He couldn't satisfy his fantasies any longer. He'd lost control. This was especially evident in the encounter with his second-to-last victim, Brandi June Henderson.

Wallace knew Henderson through her boyfriend, Berness Woods, whom he was friends with and had known for several years. Wallace described planning the murder for the evening of March 9, 1994, knowing Woods would be at work and that Henderson would stay home to watch after T.W., their ten-month-old son. At about five p.m., Wallace stopped by her apartment to say he was leaving something for his friend. Henderson invited him in, and when she turned to get Wallace a drink, he strangled her from behind and instructed her to go into the bedroom.

Wallace told her this was a robbery and demanded money. Henderson gave him a Pringles can filled with approximately twenty dollars' worth of coins and said there was no other money in the house. After ordering Henderson to undress, Wallace then grabbed her son, T.W., and laid him across her chest. Wallace raped Henderson while the baby laid pressed between them. I found this last detail particularly disturbing, noting to myself that it might represent a symbolic killing of the child Wallace saw inside himself or perhaps the baby he'd so desperately wanted but never had been able to have with Marietta.

When he finished, Wallace told Henderson to get dressed while he got a towel from the bathroom, which he then used to suffocate her to death, placing her lifeless body across T.W.'s bed. T.W. started crying, so Wallace gave him a pacifier and scoured the fridge for something T.W. could drink, to no avail. Frustrated, Wallace grabbed another towel from the bathroom and tied it tightly around T.W.'s neck, pulling until the child stopped fussing. On his way out, he stole a stereo and television, some food that had been delivered, and the container of coins. He sold the electronics for $175, which he used to purchase crack cocaine.

Even for us, Wallace was a very rare case. He was a confessed serial rapist and murderer who did not fit previously established criminal profiles. Yet, it may have been these very differences that helped him evade detection for so long. "He's all over the spectrum," Ressler noted. "I never got a good statement from him about why he did this."

Ressler was right that Wallace was difficult to understand. Part of this was because of victimology and the relationships Wallace had with his victims. And part of this was because Wallace was one of the first nonwhite serial killers that we'd ever encountered.

He also held beliefs and an overall attitude that were fairly unique and that did not follow the established patterns of others, even if he did share some characteristics of the outsider mentality that was prevalent among his peers. Unlike the lone wolf predator we'd come to expect, Wallace prided himself on being a good friend—an odd assertion considering the connection he had with his victims prior to taking their lives. He didn't struggle to find his place, and he didn't view the world as unjust. He did show traces of paranoia at times, but this could also be attributed to his drug use. He did not view authority and life as inconsistent, unpredictable, or unstable. Rather, he knew from the beginning that his crime spree would one day come to an end. He trusted in authority and believed that the law would find him and bring him to justice eventually.

The true distinction was Wallace's heightened obsession with control. Even more than the other serial killers we'd interviewed, Wallace was dominated by his own obsession with dominance. This is why he chose victims he knew—to more fully dominate his space in the immediacy of the world around him. Unlike other serial killers, who used violence and control to fix what they saw as flaws in the world around them, Wallace wasn't interested in fixing the world. He was interested in creating and maintaining a complete reality. He saw himself as godlike, floating above his crimes as he watched "Bad Henry," his name for the monster within him, commit horrific acts of violence below. And his meticulously crafted fantasy world helped pad the distance between how he viewed himself and how he viewed his crimes.

But Wallace's obsession with control went even deeper than that. While the act of rape satisfied his need to be *seen* as dominant, it wasn't enough to satisfy his primary need of wanting to *feel* dominant. This could only be achieved through an absolute disregard for the lives of others. For Wallace, the transition from rape to murder was the ultimate expression of his sovereignty. It allowed him to be creator and destroyer in one complete act. It was total dominance, a way of not just reshaping the world, but of reshaping the past, present, and future as well. Like a cassette being re-recorded over and over again until none of its original contents remained, Wallace used his victims to re-record his own history, smothering his past in the sounds of violence and terror, until only the faintest echoes of his own childhood trauma could be heard.

CHAPTER 17

The Monster Within

In his two years of terror, during which the Midnight Rider, Henry Louis Wallace, robbed the lives of nine young Black women across the city of Charlotte, the case remained largely ignored—by police, media, and the public in general. It was odd. The sheer number of victims should have drawn attention to the case on its own. Add that to the horrific nature of the crimes, and I couldn't help but wonder why the response hadn't been stronger. The Charlotte Police Department claimed that they'd tried, that they'd reached out to the FBI for help early in 1994, but that the Bureau didn't believe the murders fit the profile of a serial killer. And on the basis of how each of the murders was treated separately—several of the victims were filed as "missing persons," others weren't noticed at all, and in general the local medical examiners failed to consistently identify strangulation as the cause of death—there was likely some truth to the FBI's rationale. But it was clear to me that issues of race played a role too.

Wallace's victims weren't white women. They were Black. And just like I'd seen early on in my career while studying victims of rape, this was simply another example of how stigma could be a powerful enemy of justice. If something about a victim didn't fit a mold, if it seemed somehow threatening or made investigators uncomfortable, there were plenty of ways the case could be ignored. That was one of the biggest reasons that Wallace's spree lasted as long as it did. As Dee Sumpter, the mother of Wallace's fourth victim, Shawna Hawk, said: "The victims weren't prominent people with social-economic status. They weren't special. And they were Black."

And yet, as soon as investigators identified the physically imposing, six-foot-four, 180-pound Wallace as the culprit, the feeding frenzy ensued. His size and method of murder—slowly strangling the life out of women who were helpless to escape the power of his grasp—fit the bill of what the public considered to be a perfect monster. And the color of his skin made his story all the more compelling, adding a new twist to the public archetype of a serial murderer. The *Charlotte Observer* dubbed him "a calculated, cold blooded killer." The *New York Times* quoted a deputy chief in the investigation, saying, "The females in this community can feel safer when they go to bed." And *Time* magazine—quick to play up the monster trope with no subtlety at all—wrote an article about the investigation entitled "Dances with Werewolves."

At the same time, the coverage also noted that Wallace broke down in prayer, crying and asking for forgiveness after his arrest. It quoted friends who characterized him as intelligent, gentle, attractive. And even the over-the-top *Time* magazine article made a point of describing how "women, taken with his sweet smile, solicitous attitude and pleasant looks, trusted him."

The media strategy was a familiar one. Wallace was being painted with the same broad brush used on all serial killers—a balance of horror and entertainment. He was shown as a tormented individual whose extreme acts of violence crashed and collided against a humanity that still existed within him, buried somewhere way deep down inside. It was reductive—this technique of reducing Wallace to a two-dimensional caricature of who he actually was—but it made him more accessible, more reassuring. And by oversimplifying him this way, Wallace became one more iteration in the convenient narrative of good versus evil. There was nothing more to him than that.

This modern myth of the American serial killer was being codified in the minds of millions through familiarity and repetition. It didn't matter whether or not the jury saw a specific case's news articles. It didn't matter that Wallace was inherently different from every killer who'd come before him. The pattern had been established, reaffirmed, solidified.

And that was exactly what I was up against.

———◆———

Wallace's trial began in September of 1996 at the Mecklenburg County Superior Courthouse. It was a familiar setup: worn floorboards near the judge's bench, a court stenographer's tiny desk, and the tiered seats of the jury box, where twelve individuals would silently listen to the evidence so they could render a verdict in the case. Still, I was nervous. I saw Wallace as a culmination of everything I'd learned over the years—about rape, serial killers, and criminal psychology. And on top of that, the case was being closely watched by not only the legal community but also the public. The way Wallace was portrayed, how his crimes were characterized, and the integrity with which his victims were remembered: it all mattered. This was my chance to cut through the growing myths surrounding serial killers. This was my chance to expose the raw, deep truths at the core of who a serial killer was. I needed to get every detail right.

For the defense, the plan was simple. Because this was a death penalty case, and because Wallace had already confessed to his crimes—his confession had formally been admitted to the court record—the only available option was to convince the jury that he wasn't fully sane. This narrowed the trial's scope to a matter of sentencing: execution or life behind bars. And it put the burden of the case squarely on Ressler's and my shoulders. In our capacity as subject matter experts—specializing in serial offenders, crime classification, psychosocial development, and mental illness—we were responsible for shaping the jury's understanding of aggravating versus mitigating factors.* The aggravating factors in Wallace's case were severe, including murder during a rape, murder in front of a child, and multiple murders. But there were numerous mitigating factors that the jury needed to consider as well. Ressler and I could provide rare insight into Wallace's psychology at the time of his murders by contextualizing them in behavioral antecedents. We could explain the science of a serial killer's actions as we'd come to understand it over years in the field.

Of course, this was no small task. The jury's inherent bias against Wallace presented an almost impossible challenge. After all, he was a self-confessed serial killer. And the prosecutors had already made an emotional case by repeatedly—dramatically—standing in front of the jurors' box and asking them to "look at the victims' families. Put yourself in their shoes." Still, Ressler and I wouldn't play that game. We'd come to know Wallace. We'd interviewed him, his mother, his sister, and even his prison nurse fiancée. And although we could make emotional appeals of our own, we wouldn't. We'd stick to the facts. It was harder that way, but it was how we'd always operated. Our time

---

* Aggravating factors are a way of providing context for a criminal act so that the severity of one offender's crimes can be measured against similar crimes by similar offenders. Mitigating factors provide context for the lived experience of a specific offender. They often focus on physical, psychological, or intellectual handicaps and are intended to show why a defendant can't be held fully responsible for their own development and behaviors.

at the BSU had taught us to believe in the soundness of our methods, regardless of external pressures or doubts. There was no point in compromising that approach now. All we could do was testify to the best of our knowledge about the behavioral and psychological science of Wallace's state of mind at the time of his murders, as well as provide the historical aspect of his childhood. We'd tell the impartial truth. It would be in the jury's hands after that.

Ressler was up first and testified that Wallace exhibited signs of psychological instability. "Wallace always seemed to take one step forward and two steps back. He would take items and put them in the stove to destroy them by burning them, and then forget to turn the stove on."

Ressler proceeded to explain that Wallace's crimes displayed both organized and disorganized characteristics. He gave direct examples of how Wallace's behaviors corresponded to diminished mental capacity or mental illness. He pointed specifically to Wallace's reasoning for killing his second victim, Sharon Nance, citing Wallace's own explanation as he'd laid it out during our interview session.

"His reason was that she asked him a question that 'set him off.' And so then, after sex, when she asked for her money, he beat her to death." Ressler paused before adding: "He's all over the spectrum. I never got a good statement from him about why he did this. . . . If he elected to become a serial killer, he was going about it in the wrong way."

The conclusion was simple: these types of unplanned murders could only be attributed to the influence of mental or emotional disturbance. Wallace was particularly disturbed. And when these disturbances affected him, they controlled him.

It was my turn next. I took a seat on the witness stand, collected my thoughts, and then, through direct examination, testified my honest understanding of who Wallace was and how his mind worked.

"The defendant displays enough elements of mental illness that

I can confidently say he is incapable of forming specific intent or enacting a premeditated motive. He creates elaborate fantasies, acts upon them, and cannot differentiate between the world in his head and the world around him. This is evident in the defendant's pattern of targeting known victims. My professional opinion is that Wallace suffers from mental illness, which negates his ability to form specific intent."

I went on to explain my reasoning, starting with the fact that Wallace was in many ways an unlikely candidate to become a serial killer. He was well liked in school, could be charming and engaging, and was successful in the Navy. But in the same way all criminal behavior takes its cue from the culture at large, the nature of serial killers was always evolving, testing our preconceptions about what could or couldn't happen. Violence was a fluid expression of certain personalities. It responded to its environment and manifested in deeply personal ways.

For Wallace, everything stemmed from his struggle to have an authentic emotional life. That was the catalyst. It started with his family—especially his mother and wife—who were his aggressors as well as his only true positive emotional attachments. By choosing victims he had a connection to, Wallace was attempting to resolve the failed emotional links of his past. It was a confused understanding of connection that was further disoriented by Wallace's dualistic nature. But regardless of his internal chaos, his external methods of violence remained calm and composed. He used hate, sex, and murder to realize his ideals of power and control.

Wallace's modus operandi was similarly rare. He was, for the most part, an organized killer. But he stalked people he knew, exploited friendships, and used drugs to intensify his grandiosity and loosen his inhibitions. Few other offenders shared Wallace's level of social competence. It didn't matter that *he* felt disconnected from people.

What mattered was his ability to make people feel connected *to him*. This became an important weapon in Wallace's arsenal, one that enabled him to get away with multiple murders.

I also made a point of stressing the importance of fantasy in Wallace's development as a child and adolescent. He felt incredibly disconnected from the world around him through the repetitive abuses of his own mom and the abandonment of his father, and in turn, he became obsessed with creating and controlling a world of his own. This absence of connection, of meaningful relationships with other people, became the framework of his fantasy as well as the context through which he chose his victims. But the way it expressed itself was counterintuitive and uniquely cruel. Wallace was unable to externalize his feelings of hate, aggression, revenge, and fear onto strangers. He lashed out against people he knew by betraying their trust. After years of living in a fantasy world structured around the tremendous emptiness of a troubled childhood, this was his response. He was seeking affirmation. And he found release in the ritualistic killing of those who had shown him love. It was Wallace's way of seeing himself as whole. It's how he felt most connected.

At the end of my testimony, I reiterated Wallace's inability to separate reality from fantasy. I explained that he had a dualistic personality and that he was unable to differentiate or maintain control over the two. I cited this and other factors as suggestive of an unbalanced mental state. "Wallace, in my opinion—regardless of the horrible nature of his crimes—cannot be held fully accountable for his actions. His crimes were inevitable. They're part of his design, his psychology, a combination of inherited traits and environmental exposures that shaped him into a killer. But none of that means there's a monster within him, as Wallace himself believes. It means he's a complex and deeply flawed human being who's unable to function in society without posing a dangerous threat."

———•◆•———

On January 7, 1997, after a four-month trial that included over a hundred witnesses and four hundred exhibits, twelve jurors found the defendant guilty of nine counts of first-degree murder. According to the Appellate Report, "Each count was on the basis of malice, premeditation, and deliberation." Three weeks later, on January 29, the same jury ruled that Wallace should pay for his crimes with his life. Presiding judge Robert Johnston's declaration of punishment with nine death sentences included the penalties for rape and the multiplicity of other charges for which Wallace was convicted.

I understood the decision, even though I didn't agree with it. But I was encouraged that the jury had considered forty mitigating factors and found more than half of them to be relevant to sentencing. After all, that was the whole point of testifying for Wallace in the first place—to show that serial killers were more complex than the familiar trope of violent monsters. We'd asked the jury to consider psychological factors, upbringing, and the whole multifaceted reality of how individuals develop and all the ways that process can get derailed. And at the very least, we'd been heard.

After his sentencing, Wallace was given a chance to speak. He used the opportunity to make a statement to his victims' families, surprising me by showing a level of empathy and understanding I never expected from him. "None of these women, none of your daughters, mothers, sisters, or family members, in any way deserved what they got," he said. "They did nothing to me that warranted their death."

———•◆•———

In those days, I rarely had a moment to catch my breath, let alone time to wonder about a case. It was a constant rush of new trials to prepare for, university classes to teach, and lingering obligations to the BSU that never fully seemed to go away. Even so, I couldn't help thinking about Wallace from time to time. His case had been a turning point for me. It set in motion a wave of requests for my expert testimony at high-profile hearings, including for the Menendez brothers, the Bill Cosby case, and the Duke Lacrosse case. Still, I made time to check in on Wallace's appeals and read the occasional article that tried to make sense of his crimes.

But it wasn't just Wallace I was interested in. Through those early interviews as part of his defense, I'd gotten to know the women in Wallace's life too. They were victims in their own way. And through my interviews with them, we'd become connected. His mother, Lottie Mae, his sister, Yvonne, and his prison nurse fiancée, Becky, all shared invaluable insights about Wallace. And by listening to them, by applying the lessons I'd learned from providing specialized counseling to victims of rape early on, I offered something of value to them as well.

I learned from Lottie Mae that her own mother died at a young age and that her father then deserted the family. When I asked her about Wallace's father, she described being exploited by one of her teachers, a married man, who had sex with her in the school's auditorium during lunch breaks. He got her pregnant twice. The first time was written off as an accident, but when Lottie got pregnant again, the teacher got angry and said he could understand one mistake but not two. He walked out on Lottie, quit his job, and returned to his family. Lottie dropped out of school shortly afterward. It was traumatizing, and, looking back on it, she wondered if she took out her anger on Wallace.

Wallace's sister, Yvonne, told me how close she was with her brother. She'd always tried to protect him, but their childhood wasn't easy. She felt that Wallace had it particularly hard because he was a boy growing up without a father. And because of his size and soft-spoken nature, he was often picked on by his peers. Yvonne thought it might be specifically significant that some of the neighborhood girls taunted Wallace in a sexual manner because of how much bigger he was than the other boys.

Rebecca Torrijas was a petite blonde prison nurse who met and fell in love with Wallace while he awaited trial at the county jail. She resigned her job because of the relationship, telling me: "I knew I'd crossed a line." And though she was fully aware of Wallace's history, she felt that he was misunderstood and she supported him all throughout his trial—attending court every day and bringing Wallace freshly cleaned sets of clothes. She married Wallace in a brief, fifteen-minute ceremony with Wallace's public defender Isabel Day serving as an official witness and photographer. The wedding was held next to the execution chamber where he was sentenced to die. "You don't know the softer side of Henry," she told me over the phone.

She was right, of course. Although I received an occasional letter from Wallace to update me on his case, I certainly didn't know his softer side. What I knew were his complexities—the overwhelming tensions in his head that splintered into a chaos of real-world violence. It's what kept me thinking about Wallace. And the more I thought about who he was, the more I came to realize something new about the serial killer phenomenon. Up until Wallace, I'd always looked at the phenomenon through a clinical lens—as if serial killers represented a disease that I could somehow trace, pathologize, and learn to predict. But Wallace's description of the monster within helped widen my perspective. He truly saw himself as two distinct individuals, to the point of distinguishing his past behaviors as either the acts of "Good Henry" or "Bad Henry," but never a cohesion of both. It was a fractured way of understanding himself, and it reflected the fractured sum of his life's experiences. Like most serial killers, the pain Wallace inflicted on others was defensive in nature, a corrective response to the pain he'd incurred. Or at least it started that way. But once the switch flipped, all bets were off. Violence is permanent.

What drives a human being to kill? What separates those individuals from the rest of us as a whole? I've spent my career trying to figure it out. But the answer isn't so simple.

To rape, torture, or kill another human being is to shatter the most fundamental expectations of the human condition. These acts breach the unspoken social contract that binds humanity together. They're profane. They corrupt. And yet, in the eyes of a killer—an individual who exists on the outer fringes of humanity—these acts of complete and utter disregard for human life are a way to create meaning. They're a sense of purpose. A way of finding balance. To a killer, violence is an expression of something sacred.

What's fascinating about the criminal mind is how simultaneously foreign it is while being so disturbingly close to our own. And yet, the fixation on "figuring it out"—on solving the puzzle—often overshadows the reason this work is so important in the first place.

My decades studying serial killers weren't for the game of cat and mouse, nor because I found these killers entertaining. And I didn't do it because I empathized with their plight or because I was trying to rehabilitate and reform them.

For me, it's always been about the victims.

They are the reason I persist. They are the reason I stared down the darkness, time and time again. They are the tragic human cost of a serial killer's self-discovery, the helpless victims of chance and circumstance. They are living, breathing bodies of boundless possibility reduced to headlines and statistics. And although many of their names have been lost to history or relegated to footnotes in the retellings of serial killers and their crimes, I will never forget a single one.

It's the victims who matter. This story is as much theirs as it is mine.

ACKNOWLEDGMENTS

We dedicate this book to:

Lynda Lytle Holmstrom (1939–2021)

A visionary scholar and a trailblazer for interdisciplinary collaboration. Lynda and I met as new professors at Boston College, where we cotaught a course in health care. Even all these years later, I still remember the bright New England afternoon when Lynda talked to me about wanting to develop a new research topic, one that would impact women's lives and the relationship between the sexes.

Lynda had become interested in the topic of sexual assault after reading accounts within feminist literature and the reports from women in consciousness-raising groups in the late 1960s. But she noted that researchers seldom picked up on assaultive behavior as a research topic. That caught my attention. It made me wonder what we could learn by taking an academic approach to the topic. What insights could we gain by following victims of rape through the institutional processing—their interactions with the police, hospital, and court systems?

When I suggested adding a counseling aspect to the study, Lynda asked, "Can a sociologist and a psychiatric nurse work together?" We decided to find out for ourselves. And it was this willingness to pursue a novel form of collaboration that led to a new conceptualization of sexual victimization.

Lynda was very disciplined in her research. Nothing escaped her eagle eye, and everything was written down. No detail or data point escaped her. Her imprint on the rape movement left an enduring legacy for future generations of women and scholars.

Robert Roy Hazelwood (1938–2016)

It's rare that an individual has a significant impact on both investigative practice and research. And rarer still is an individual who leaves as indelible a mark on the scale of Roy Hazelwood, who impacted law enforcement, investigative science, and profiling. Roy had great energy, compassion, and dedication to anything he put his mind to. He was relentless in his pursuit of justice. But perhaps his greatest legacy is the example he set in fostering collaborative interactions and intellectual exchange among academics, forensic scientists, and practitioners, bridging different fields of study.

Robert Kenneth Ressler (1937–2013)

Bob was a legend in the FBI's Behavioral Science Unit. His vision and courage to "fight the monsters" as part of his quest to try to understand violent criminals was remarkable. He is credited with coining the term *serial killer* and worked tirelessly to push the boundaries of investigative science. But more importantly, Bob understood the traumatic impact on victims, and he always organized his investigations around the victimology. He was compassionate, had a big heart, and always made time to be available to family, colleagues, and friends. He was a powerful leader among the agents, an inspirational teacher to his students, and a hero to his readers. His legacy expands beyond the United States to international shores.

Acknowledgments

We also owe a great deal of thanks to the many individuals who have helped shape this book along the way.

To our agent, Alice Martell, who was quick to believe in this work and has been a fierce advocate from day one. To our editor, Carrie Napolitano, whose excitement and dedication has been more of an inspiration than she'll ever know. And to everyone at Hachette Books who has helped see this project through: Michelle Aielli, Michael Clark, Christina Palaia, Ashley Kiedrowski, Lauren Rosenthal, Lindsay Ricketts, Jeff Stiefel, Amanda Kain, Mary Ann Naples, Michael Barrs, Monica Oluwek, Julie Ford, and the entire HBG sales team.

Our profound gratitude to John Douglas, who was Bob Ressler's original partner in the serial killer study, and to Ken Lanning, both of whom were stars at Quantico and who have kept the momentum going.

We are most grateful to the FBI hierarchy who believed in the research and supported us: Director William Webster; Assistant Directors James McKenzie, Larry Monroe, and Dr. Ken Joseph; and Unit Chiefs Alan E. Burgess (Smokey), John Henry Campbell, and Roger Depue. Special thanks to friends and colleagues in the FBI Behavioral Science Unit who were supportive of the project and coauthors on some papers: Dick Ault, Al Brantley, Greg Cooper, Bill Haigmeier, Joe Harpold, Jim Horn, Dave Icove, Cindy Lent, Judd Ray, Jim Reese, Ron Walker, Art Westveer, and Jim Wright.

Other Department of Justice colleagues who supported the project: Candice DeLong—Chicago FBI, Bob Heck—US Department of Justice, and John Rabun—National Center for Missing and Exploited Children, and the Criminal Personality Advisory Board: James L. Cavanaugh Jr., MD; Herman Chernoff, MD; Charles R. Figley, PhD; Thomas Goldman, MD; William Heiman, JD; Marvin J. Homzie, PhD; Joyce Kemp Laber, RN, JD; Vallory G. Lathrop, RN, DNSc; Richard Ratner, MD; Kenneth Rickler, MD; and George M. Saiger, MD.

Acknowledgments

A very special thanks to the Boston City Hospital group, who spent long hours deciphering handwriting, entering and analyzing data, and writing reports for the study: Al Belanger, programmer; Allen G. Burgess, DBA, survey design; Holly-Jean Chaplick, administrative assistant; Marieanne L. Clark, editor for our papers and book; Ralph B. D'Agostino, Boston University statistician; Renee Gould, research assistant; Carol R. Hartman, DNSc, data interpretation of psychodynamics; Deborah Lerner, administrator; Arlene McCormack, PhD, data interpretation; Caroline Montane, transcriber; and Karen Woelfel, transcriber.

There were wonderful colleagues who each tutored us and believed in this futuristic concept of criminal investigation: A. Nicholas Groth, Carol Hartman, Susan J. Kelley, Anna Laszlo, Maureen P. McCausland, Arlene McCormack, Robert Prentky, and Wendy Wolbert Weiland.

We would be remiss not to thank our Boston College colleagues and leadership who have been supportive of our work: Connell School of Nursing Dean Susan Gennaro; President William P. Leahy, SJ; Provost David Quigley; Christopher Grillo; Tracy Bienen; and Mary Katherine Hart.

Thanks to colleagues from the University of Pennsylvania and the Williams House: Dean Claire Fagin, Ellen Baer, Jacqueline Fawcett, and Neville Strumpf, and research associate Christine Grant.

And last but not least, we want to express our heartfelt appreciation and gratitude to our families—Allen, Elizabeth, Benton, Clayton, and Sarah Burgess; and Monica and Milo Constantine—who showed a great deal of grace and patience in putting up with countless dinnertime conversations about the not-so-dinnertime-friendly material populating these pages. Thanks for being there.

SOURCES

Burgess, Ann Wolbert, and Lynda Lytle Holmstrom. "Rape Trauma Syndrome." *American Journal of Psychiatry* 131 (1974): 981–986.

———. "The Rape Victim in the Emergency Ward." *American Journal of Nursing* 73 (October 1973): 1741–1745.

Lanning, K. V., and A. W. Burgess. "Child Pornography and Sex Rings." *FBI Law Enforcement Bulletin* 53, no. 1 (January 1984): 10–16. NCJ Number 93131.

Ressler, R. K., and A. W. Burgess, eds. "Violent Crimes." *FBI Law Enforcement Bulletin* 54, no. 8 (1985): 1–31.

Ressler, R. K., A. W. Burgess, and J. E. Douglas. *Sexual Homicide: Patterns and Motivation.* New York: Free Press, 1988.

INDEX

Index

bondage, Wallace and, 261–262
Boston City Hospital, 12–13, 51
Boy Scouts, Joubert and, 41–42
Brabham, Marietta, 267–268, 276
brain, effect of trauma on, 134
Brown, Frances, 220
Brussel, James, 68–70, 161
BTK (Bind them, Torture them, Kill them) killer, 227–240
   advice on how to engage him, 233
   BSU profile of, 231–235
   communications from, 227–228, 235–236, 237
   confession and talk about murders, 239–240
   craving recognition through media, 229–230
   first involvement of BSU, 228–230
   "Ghostbusters" task force and, 231–232
   identifying with police, 235, 237–238
   inactivity between crimes, 232–233
   mimicking elements of other serial killers, 235–236
   photographing victims post-mortem, 233
   proactive media strategy to bait him into exposing self, 230
   psychiatric diagnoses of, 232
   Rader identified as, 238–240
   second involvement of BSU, 231–238
   sexual arousal from seeing drawings/photos of dead victims, 262
   as sexual sadist with vivid fantasy life, 233–234
   Son of Sam and, 230, 235–236
   stages of his murders, 239
   "super-cop" strategy, 233, 237–238
   symbol used in communication, 235–236
   Unabomber and, 241
   victimology, 234
Bundy, Ted, 201, 226
Bureau of Alcohol, Tobacco, and Firearms, Unabomber case and, 243
bystander effect, 132, 135

Calabro, Carmine, 205–207

Cantella, Dan, 111, 115, 116
case reports, Teten and Mullany's focus on, 63
Chang, Pete, 195
Charlotte Observer (newspaper), 280
Charlotte Police Department, 279
Charlotte Strangler. *See* Wallace, Henry Louis (Charlotte Strangler)
check attention–type polygraph, 105
Chicago Tribune (newspaper), 215
child abduction cases, BSU profiling for, 71–75. *See also* Illinois child abduction case
childhood sexual abuse, sexual murderers and history of, 198–199
childhood trauma, killers' reenactment of, 203
child molesters, 59
   signs and behaviors of, 60
child pornography article by author and Lanning, 60
child predators, behavioral analysis of, 59–60
child sex rings, 60
"Co-ed Killer." *See* Kemper, Edmund, III (Co-ed Killer)
cognitive technique of interviewing, 150
collaboration
   among profilers, agents, and local investigators, 107
   as BSU's greatest advantage, 106
   importance of interagency, 46
collaborative nature of profiling process, 164
common denominators among crime scenes and criminals, 84–85
conditioning effect, 252, 256–257
confidence-style rapist, 156–157
connection with victim, Kemper *vs.* Rissell and, 186
Consolidated Edison, 244n, 245
Consolidated Rail Corporation, 138, 139
control
   for agent in interviews with serial killers, 22–23
   male perpetrators of violence and obsession with, 10

Index

Index

Index

Index

Index